T0290592

CONTENT MARKETING LIKE A PRO

Clo Willaerts

With foreword by Guido Everaert

The All-In-One Guide to Digital Content Marketing:
From Planning to Promoting

Lannoo
Campus

D/2023/45/258 – ISBN 978 94 014 9547 9 – NUR 802
COVER DESIGN   Ines Cox en Wendy De Haes
INTERIOR DESIGN   Banananas

© Clo Willaerts & Lannoo Publishers nv, Tielt, 2023.

LannooCampus Publishers is a subsidiary of Lannoo Publishers,
the book and multimedia division of Lannoo Publishers nv.

All rights reserved.
No part of this publication may be reproduced and/or made public,
by means of printing, photocopying, microfilm or any other means,
without the prior written permission of the publisher.

LannooCampus Publishers
Vaartkom 41 box 01.02   P.O. Box 23202
3000 Leuven   1100 DS Amsterdam
Belgium   The Netherlands
www.lannoocampus.com

TABLE OF CONTENTS

PART III: OPTIMIZE

OPTIMISING FOR SEARCH AND SOCIAL

FOREWORD BY GUIDO EVERAERT

I was honoured when Clo asked me to write the introduction to her book. I am both the most and least qualified one to do so. Most qualified because my whole existence in the digital (and the real) world is centred and focused on content and storytelling. Writing, blogging, vlogging, podcasting, I've embraced it all with enthusiasm and the curiosity of a sixteen-year-old.

At the same time, I'm your worst possible example as a content marketeer, because I have made and still make all possible mistakes. I haven't got the discipline for content calendars, and I hate personas. I don't do keyword research, and sometimes publish at midnight, just because that's when I've finished writing. Heck, I don't even have a strategy, a reason why I do things. It's just the urge to voice opinions and add value to ongoing discussions, reach out and create 'stuff'.

Clo once called me 'the poet of the digital media'. I always considered that a sweet compliment, coming from 'la grande dame'. Now I am not even sure that it was meant as a compliment.

I honestly think this is the book we've all been waiting for. The reason is simple. Google 'content marketing books', and you get an overwhelming response. There's just this one caveat. We all think, describe, and write about content marketing from our own perspective. The growth hacker, the business owner, the blogger and copywriter or the digital marketer all have their own perspective, their own emphasis on certain aspects of this discipline. This book stands out because of the all-encompassing view on content marketing.

It's no small feat to produce insightful, meaningful and readable books on this subject. Yet Clo has succeeded once again to do so, as she has in her previous books. *Content Marketing like a Pro* will help management at small and large businesses to become and remain meaningful in their content marketing.

The book gives you clear direction on what to do, how to start and how to maintain your content marketing efforts. Because it is, as Clo so rightfully points out, 'a long-term effort' from the start. You might recognise some of the concepts, but the way and the structure in which they are presented allow for a step-by-step approach, suited to the size of your ambitions. Do not underestimate the power of her real-life examples. Not only are they original and within reach of all of us, but they also demonstrate her skills in analytical content marketing.

We all need to realise that a fragmented and haphazard approach towards content might have worked in the past, but the ever-increasing pressure on content creators from the tsunami of mediocre, self-centred content make for a situation where relevance and know-how become increasingly important.

Do not just read this book, but study it, dissect it, use it, and see it as the basis of how you want to build your own strategy. Your reward will come in the long term.

Guido Everaert

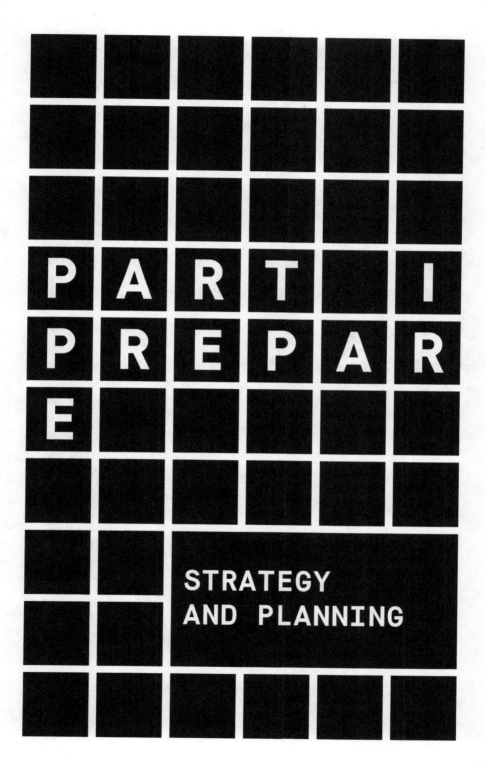

PART I PREPARE

STRATEGY AND PLANNING

Ø1

INTRODUCTION

WHAT IS DIGITAL CONTENT MARKETING?

Content marketing has been around for centuries, but it was in the digital age that it came into its own. The earliest forms of content marketing can be traced back to the late 19th century when John Deere began publishing *The Furrow* magazine. It provided farmers with information on new farming techniques, equipment, and best practices while promoting John Deere's products and services. The magazine was distributed to farmers free of charge. It was a great way for John Deere to connect with its target audience and establish itself as a trusted authority in the farming industry.

Fast forward to the present day and content marketing has become vital to any business's marketing strategy. It is a way to connect with customers, build trust and credibility, and ultimately drive sales. This handbook will explore the various tactics and techniques you can use to execute a successful content marketing campaign.

Content is the information and experiences that are created and shared with an audience. It can take many forms, including text, images, videos, audio, and interactive elements, and can be delivered through a variety of channels, such as websites, social media, email, and mobile apps.

In the context of content marketing, content refers to the information and experiences that are specifically created and shared with the goal of attracting, engaging, and retaining customers.

This handbook is an introduction to the concept of **content marketing**, which involves using content to achieve business and marketing goals. It will provide guidance on how to create and distribute effective content, as well as how to measure and improve your content marketing efforts.

Digital content marketing is a type of marketing that involves creating and sharing online content to attract, engage, and retain customers. This content can take many forms, including blog posts, articles, videos, social media posts, infographics, etc. The goal of digital content marketing is to provide valuable, relevant, and consistent information to customers, build trust and establish a long-term relationship with them.

Unlike traditional marketing, which often relies on interruptive advertising, digital content marketing focuses on providing valuable information and resources to customers, who can then engage with it on their own terms. This approach is designed to be more authentic and transparent and build customer trust and credibility.

Digital content marketing can effectively reach and engage with customers, especially in today's digital world, where people are constantly connected to the internet and are exposed to a vast amount of information. By creating high-quality, relevant, and engaging content, businesses can attract and retain customers and establish themselves as trusted sources of knowledge and expertise in their industry.

> Executing a great content marketing strategy demands creation of engaging content—content that they crave, content that they can't wait to eat up, content that they love sharing with their friends, relatives, and colleagues.
>
> The Stripped-Down Guide to Content ...
> John Egan

This handbook is a guide to creating and using **digital content marketing** to attract, engage and retain customers to achieve marketing and business goals. Tools to measure and improve content marketing are included. **Content** refers to text, images, videos, audio, blog posts, articles, social media posts, infographics and interactive elements that are developed for specific audiences and delivered to them in a targeted way via websites, social media, email and mobile phone apps.

Unlike traditional marketing, which often relies on interruptive advertising, digital content marketing focuses on providing high-quality, engaging, and relevant information and resources to customers that they value and can engage with on their own terms. This more authentic and transparent approach establishes businesses as credible sources of knowledge and expertise and builds more durable customer trust and loyalty.

WHY IS DIGITAL CONTENT MARKETING IMPORTANT?

Digital content marketing is essential for several reasons:

- Digital content marketing effectively reaches and engages with **customers in today's digital world**. With the proliferation of the internet and social media, people are constantly connected and exposed to vast amounts of information. By creating high-quality, relevant, and engaging content, businesses can attract the attention of their target audience and stand out from the competition.

- It allows businesses to attract and engage with their target audience **more authentically and transparently**. By providing valuable and relevant information, companies can establish themselves as trusted sources of knowledge and expertise, which can help to build trust and credibility with their customers.
- Digital content marketing can help businesses to retain their customers. By regularly providing valuable and engaging content, companies can keep their customers interested and engaged, which can help foster **long-term customer loyalty**.

> Content may rule, but your online content must be the right sort of content: Customer-focused. Compelling. Entertaining. Surprising. Interesting. In other words, you must earn the attention of people.
>
> Content Rules
> Ann Handley, C.C. Chapman, and Davi...

HOW DOES DIGITAL CONTENT MARKETING DIFFER FROM OTHER MARKETING TACTICS?

Digital content marketing differs from other marketing tactics in several important ways:

1. Digital content marketing focuses on **providing valuable and relevant information to customers rather than interrupting them with advertising messages**. This approach is designed to be more authentic and transparent and build customer trust and credibility.
2. Digital content marketing is **more adaptable and flexible** than other marketing tactics. Because it is digital, it can be easily updated and changed,

allowing businesses to quickly respond to changes in their industry and the needs of their customers.

3. Digital content marketing can be **more cost-effective** than other marketing tactics. Unlike traditional marketing, which often involves expensive advertising campaigns, digital content marketing is relatively low cost, making it accessible to businesses of all sizes.

> You must adopt the mindset that no matter how big or small your organization is and no matter how few tools you have, you can succeed at content marketing.
>
> The Stripped-Down Guide to Content ...
> John Egan

By leveraging these differences, businesses can effectively use digital content marketing to attract, engage, and retain customers.

02

DEVELOPING A DIGITAL CONTENT MARKETING STRATEGY

CONTENT MARKETING STRATEGY PLAN

> Strategy is about focus: making the right choices about what to do, and what to ignore.
>
> Digital Marketing Like a PRO
> Clo Willaerts

A **content marketing strategic plan** typically includes the following elements and steps:

1. Identify the specific **goals and objectives** of the plan. This could include objectives such as increasing website traffic, generating leads, or improving customer engagement.

2. Identify the **target audience**, including its demographics, interests, and behaviours, and the channels and platforms where they are most likely to be found.

3. List the **themes and topics** that will be covered in the content. This could include topics such as the business's products, services, industry, or other areas of expertise.

4. Specify the **types of content** that will be created, such as blog posts, videos, infographics, or podcasts to insure that the content is diverse and engaging, and will attract different audience segments.

5. Devise a strategy for **distributing and promoting** the content, such as through social media, email marketing, or paid advertising. This will make sure the content reaches the intended audience and drives the desired results.

6. Create a **content calendar** showing the day or week when each piece of content will be published.

7. **Metrics and analysis**: Finally, the plan should include a system for tracking and measuring the performance of the content marketing efforts. This could include metrics such as website traffic, engagement, and conversions, and should be used to continually optimize and improve the content marketing strategy.

> A content marketing plan is the summary of your strategies – everything you plan to do in content marketing and hope to achieve for your company using the available marketing channels.
>
> Digital Marketing Like a PRO
> Clo Willaerts

FROM BUSINESS GOALS TO CONTENT MARKETING OBJECTIVES

As you create a content marketing strategic plan, identify the specific goals and objectives the plan will aim to achieve. They will serve as the foundation of your content marketing efforts and guide the creation and distribution of your content.

> Specifically, creating content as a cornerstone of your marketing can: Attract customers. Educate your buyers about a purchase they are considering. Overcome resistance or address objections. Establish your credibility, trust, and authority in your industry. Tell your story. Build buzz via social networks. Build a base of fans and inspire customers to love you. Inspire impulse buys.

Content Rules
Ann Handley, C.C. Chapman, and Davi...

Content marketing objectives are the specific goals a business aims to achieve through its content marketing efforts. Content marketing objectives might include:

- generating demand or leads for the business
- enhancing brand recognition and awareness
- building up trust and credibility with customers
- informing and educating target groups about the business and its products or services
- boosting brand loyalty and customer retention
- acquiring prospective customers or e-mail subscribers
- positioning the business as an opinion leader or thought leader in its industry
- supporting product launches and promoting new products or services
- generating event participants or attendees
- recruiting and retaining employees
- boosting sales and revenue

By setting specific content marketing objectives, businesses can better align their content marketing efforts with their overall goals and measure the success of their efforts. In addition, by regularly reviewing and adjusting their content marketing objectives, businesses can make sure that their content marketing efforts are effective and help them achieve their desired results.

> "To gain followers" is not a viable reason in and of itself, but "to gain followers on Facebook to drive traffic back to our website to enlist subscribers" is.
>
> Content Inc.
> Joe Pulizzi

When setting marketing objectives, aligning them with your overall business goals is essential.

For example: your business goal is to increase sales. In that case, your digital content marketing goal might be to generate leads and conversions through your content. In this case, your objectives include increasing the number of email subscribers, increasing the number of blog post views, and increasing the number of conversions from your content.

Applied to content marketing, the objectives could be, for example, to create and distribute:

- Engaging and informative content that can showcase the new product or service and its benefits and encourages the audience to purchase it.
- Persuasive and compelling content that can explain the new pricing strategy and its advantages that can convince the audience to switch to it.
- Personalized and targeted content that can attract and retain high-value customers and build their trust and loyalty.

> Your goal is to drive subscriptions from every page of content. Treat every page like a landing page, and monitor top pages for ways to increase traffic to a specific page, as well as increase the conversion of readers to subscribers.

Content Inc.
Joe Pulizzi

Different types of content are well-suited to different goals, and choosing the right content format can help you effectively reach your desired outcome. Here are a few examples of how different content formats can be used to achieve different goals:

- Your goal is to generate leads – a blog post or article might be suitable, as it provides in-depth information that can persuade potential customers to take action.
- Your goal is to engage with your audience on social media – a video or infographic might be the best choice, as these formats are well-suited to capturing attention and driving engagement.

> The customer journey (sometimes also called consumer decision journey) is the imaginary trajectory that a customer travels from first contact with a product or service to final purchase, and includes the period after the purchase. During this journey, the consumer passes a variety of touch points (sometimes also called MoT, or Moments of Truth), moving from awareness to engagement, to purchase and repurchase.

Digital Marketing Like a PRO
Clo Willaerts

The phase of the **customer journey** you want to influence must also be considered, that is, the various stages a customer goes through when considering, purchasing and using your product or service. Each step presents different opportunities for engagement and influence.

Table 1. Customer vs. Marketing Objectives

CUSTOMER JOURNEY	MARKETING OBJECTIVES
SEE (Awareness)	Increase brand or product awareness
THINK (Consideration)	Increase brand engagement, Educate audience on benefits
BUY (Activation)	Increase traffic to website, Generate sales leads, Influence buyers with videos
USE (Loyalty)	Improve customer experience, Increase sales volume, Recruit new users, Improve conversions
LOVE (Advocacy)	Foster customer loyalty, Incentivize referrals, Boost shares on social media

For example, if your goal is to generate leads, your objectives might focus on the awareness and consideration phases of the customer journey, where you want to attract and engage potential customers. Your content marketing objectives include increasing:

- the visibility of your content;
- the number of social media followers; and
- the number of website visits.

Or, if your goal is to increase conversion, your objectives focus on the decision and action phases of the customer journey, where you want to persuade potential customers to make a purchase. In this case, your objectives include increasing the number of:

- email subscribers;
- blog post views; and
- conversions from your content.

> You want your videos to convert.
> Conversion is any action that follows
> from the video but isn't about the video
> (or the video channel) itself. So not just
> watching or engaging, but clicking
> buttons, visiting websites, downloading
> white papers, or buying products.

Video Marketing Like a PRO
Clo Willaerts

By aligning your goals and objectives with the different phases of the customer journey, you can create a more effective digital content marketing strategy tailored to your target audience's specific needs and behaviours at each stage of the journey.

CASE: MOONLIT APPAREL AND THE S.M.A.R.T. FRAMEWORK

As an example, we will use an imaginary company called Moonlit Apparel to illustrate various concepts and strategies. Here is what their Wikipedia entry could look like:

> *Moonlit Apparel is a streetwear clothing brand founded in the early 2010s by friends passionate about skateboarding culture and streetwear fashion. The brand was founded to create high-quality, stylish clothing that reflected the founders' love for these subcultures.*
>
> *Based in the United States, Moonlit Apparel has gained a dedicated following of customers who appreciate the brand's commitment to authenticity and quality. In addition, the brand is known for its unique, edgy designs and commitment to sustainability and social responsibility.*
>
> *As the brand has grown, Moonlit Apparel has continued to tell its story through its content, sharing its history, mission, and values and highlighting customer stories and successes. Today, Moonlit Apparel offers a range*

of clothing and accessories for men and women, including hoodies, t-shirts, hats, and sneakers.

In addition to its online store, Moonlit Apparel has a strong presence on social media. It works with influencers and celebrities to promote its products. The brand has also been recognized for its impact on the fashion industry, having won several awards and accolades for its commitment to sustainability and social responsibility.

Business goals:

1. As a business, Moonlit Apparel will likely aim to **drive sales** of its clothing and other products to its target audience. This could involve creating and promoting campaigns and sales promotions and offering high-quality, stylish products that appeal to customers.
2. Ultimately, all businesses aim to achieve **financial success**. Moonlit Apparel may strive to achieve this by driving sales, expanding into new markets, and managing its expenses and resources effectively.

Marketing objectives:

1. Moonlit Apparel may aim to **increase its brand awareness** among its target audience of streetwear and skateboarding enthusiasts. This could involve creating and distributing engaging content that showcases the brand's unique style and values and promoting the brand through various channels such as social media, email marketing, and paid advertising.
2. Moonlit Apparel may also aim to expand its reach beyond its current customer base and **expand into new markets**. This could involve exploring new distribution channels, targeting new demographics, and adapting the brand's marketing and content strategy to appeal to these new audiences.
3. **Fostering customer loyalty** is essential for any business. Moonlit Apparel may aim to do this by consistently delivering high-quality products and providing excellent customer service. The brand may also seek to engage with its customers through content and social media and encourage customer loyalty through loyalty programs or other incentives.

S.M.A.R.T. Content marketing objectives

For Moonlit Apparel these content marketing objectives could include creating high quality, informative and engaging content by:

- increasing website traffic; and/or
- generating leads and improving customer engagement.

The **S.M.A.R.T. Framework** is a valuable tool for defining and setting goals in a content marketing strategy context. It ensures that your goals are Specific, Measurable, Attainable, Relevant, and Time-bound, helping to make them more focused and effective, impactful and, thus, more likely to achieve the desired results.

Following are rephrased content marketing objectives for Moonlit Apparel using the S.M.A.R.T. Framework

1. **Increase website traffic** by 10% in the next quarter by creating at least one high-quality blog post per week and promoting the content through social media and email marketing.
2. Generate at least 50 leads in the next quarter by creating and promoting a landing page with a **lead generation** form and offering a valuable resource such as an e-book or webinar in exchange for contact information.
3. Improve **customer engagement** by 15% in the next quarter by creating and distributing engaging content that resonates with the target audience and responding to customer comments and inquiries on social media within 24 hours.

SMART is a mnemonic acronym (Specific, Measurable, Achievable, Relevant and Time-Bound) that outlines criteria for setting strong and realistic objectives, and can be applied to a range of fields (e.g. project management, employee-performance management or personal development).

Digital Marketing Like a PRO
Clo Willaerts

DEFINE YOUR TARGET AUDIENCE THROUGH BUYER PERSONAS

Identifying your target audience is essential in developing a successful digital content marketing strategy. Your target audience is the subset of people who are most likely to be interested in your products or services and who are most likely to engage with your content.

It is essential for a content marketing professional to represent their target audience with **buyer personas** because it helps to guide the creation of content tailored to the specific needs, desires, and behaviours of the target audience.

> Buyer personas (sometimes referred to as marketing personas) are semi-fictional, generalized representations of your ideal customers. Whenever possible, they should be based on market research and actual data about your existing customers.
>
> Digital Marketing Like a PRO
> Clo Willaerts

A **buyer persona** describes the character aspects of a fictional individual that represents the ideal customer for a business or product. It is based on market research and accurate data about the target audience. It helps to provide a detailed understanding of the target audience's characteristics, goals, and motivations. Buyer personas:

- Guide content creation to ensure it resonates with the target audience and effectively addresses their needs and pain points. This can increase the content's effectiveness.
- Ensure the authenticity and relatability of content, as it is based on a realistic representation of the target audience. This can build trust and credibility with the target audience and increase the chances of engagement.

- These points, independently and together, increase the chances of converting the target audience into customers.

TEENAGER NOAH

Target audience: male teenagers who are interested in skateboarding and streetwear fashion. Let us call this persona Noah. When he is not in school, you can find him at the skatepark perfecting his tricks or browsing the latest streetwear trends online. Noah is always up for trying new skate spots and loves to show off his style through his clothing and skateboard setup. He is always looking for new brands and designers to follow and is excited to see where his interests take him in the future.

ACTIVE SENIORS IRIS AND JOHN

Target audience: retired seniors who are interested in staying active and healthy through fitness and nutrition. Meet Iris and John, who fit this profile. In their younger years, they were avid runners and gym-goers, and they have carried that love of physical activity into their retirement. They enjoy hiking, biking, and yoga, and always make sure to fuel their bodies with nourishing, whole foods. In their free time, Iris and John also love to travel and explore new destinations, always looking for new opportunities to stay active and healthy while they are on the go.

BUSY MOM EMILY

Target audience: working mothers in their 30s who live in urban areas and have a household income of over $75,000 per year. Buyer persona: Emily. As a busy mom, Emily values efficiency and organisation in her daily life. She relies on technology to help her manage her busy schedule and keep her family on track. In her free time, Emily enjoys spending quality time with her family, trying new restaurants and coffee shops in the city, and practicing yoga and meditation to stay healthy and balanced.

Note: These are just examples and are not meant to be definitive or exhaustive. The specific characteristics of a well-defined target audience will vary depending on the business and its goals.

To identify *your* target audience, you need to gather as much information as possible about them, including their demographics, interests, needs, and behaviours. This information can come from various sources, including market research, customer surveys, social media, and web analytics. Once you have gathered this information, you can start to create detailed profiles of your target audience.

> To create a buyer persona based on your actual customers, interview or analyze your best customers, talk to your sales or customer care colleagues, and/or dig into your customers' data.
>
> Digital Marketing Like a PRO
> Clo Willaerts

FROM BUYER PERSONA CANVAS TO CONTENT CHANNELS, FORMATS AND TACTICS

A **Buyer Persona Canvas** is a tool used by businesses to create a detailed and comprehensive profile of their target audience, allowing for more effective marketing and sales strategies that align with their audience's needs, preferences and behaviours.

The elements of a Buyer Persona Canvas typically include the following information about the target audience:

- Basic demographic information like the age, gender, location, and income level.
- The specific **behaviours, habits, and motivations** that drive their decisions and actions.
- **Jobs to be done**, meaning the specific goals, challenges, and needs that they are trying to address or solve using the business's product or service.
- The **media and platforms** that they use to consume information and make purchasing decisions.
- **Influencers and advocates**, the people and organisations they trust and look to for advice and recommendations.
- Channels used during their **customer journey,** the steps and stages that they traverse when making a purchasing decision.

DEMOGRAPHICS VS DEVICE AND MEDIA USE

Don't target demographic: this is rarely an indicator of buying intent or interest in a particular topic.

Video Marketing Like a PRO
Clo Willaerts

It is unwise to assume buying behaviour or content needs from demographics alone because demographic information, such as age, gender, and income level, is not always a reliable indicator of an individual's interests, preferences, and needs.

For example, the causality between life stage and content needs means that an individual's life stage can influence the type of content they are interested in and find valuable. Examples:

- Traditionalists and Baby Boomers, for example, may be interested in content related to retirement, health and wellness, and their experiences during historical events such as World War II and the Civil Rights Movement.
- Generation X may be interested in content related to career development, parenting, and personal finance.
- Millennials and Gen Z may be interested in content related to entrepreneurship, social and environmental issues, and technology and innovation.
- A teenager going through the process of applying to college may be interested in content related to higher education and career planning.
- A new parent may be interested in content related to parenting and child development.

Again, these are generalisations, and the content needs of any given individual may vary depending on their personal interests and experiences.

Consider a range of factors beyond demographics, such as their interests, preferences and behaviours target and engage with customers most effectively. As individuals move through different life stages, their priorities and interests can change, leading to shifts in the content they find valuable and engaging.

There are, however, a few general conclusions that can be drawn about media and device use based on global demographics.

- Younger age groups tend to have higher levels of media and device use, with teenagers and young adults often being the heaviest users. This is likely due to the increasing role of technology in education and socialisation for younger generations.
- Developed countries tend to have higher levels of media and device use compared to developing countries, likely due to higher levels of internet access and infrastructure.
- There are often significant differences in media and device use within and between countries, depending on factors such as income level, education, and urban vs. rural location.

Some sources for device and media used linked to demographics include:

- Statista.com – some of its data is accessible for free statista.com/markets/424/internet/
- The *Digital Around the World* reports by Datareportal datareportal.com/global-digital-overview
- PEW Research Center – U.S. market only pewresearch.org/topic/internet-technology/

PSYCHOGRAPHICS VS CONTENT TYPES

Another way to create detailed profiles of your target audience is by using **psychographics**.

Psychographics studies delve past demographics to assess people's attitudes, values, interests, and lifestyles, their motivations, preferences and behaviours to better define your content marketing strategy and messaging.

> Begin by choosing people based on what they dream of, believe, and want, not based on what they look like. In other words, use psychographics instead of demographics.
>
> This Is Marketing
> Seth Godin

There are various ways to conduct psychographic research:

- **Surveys** and **questionnaires** can be used to gather information about attitudes, beliefs, values, interests, and lifestyles. Surveys can be conducted online, in person, or over the phone, depending on the preferences of your audience and the goals of your research.

- **Focus groups** are small, moderated groups of individuals who are representative of your target audience. Focus groups allow you to gather in-depth information about your attitudes, beliefs, and behaviours through open-ended discussions and feedback.
- **Social media** and **online communities** can be used to gather information about your interests, opinions, and behaviours through posts, comments, and discussions on social media platforms and online communities relevant to your business or industry.
- One-on-one **customer interviews** and conversations with individual customers or groups in person or using video calls can help you better understand the specific needs and preferences of your audience.

Your content should answer some unmet desire or question for your audience.

Content Inc.
Joe Pulizzi

Psychographic profile for people like Emily:

- Busy and time-conscious, always looking for ways to save time and simplify their lives.
- Health-conscious and focused on maintaining a healthy lifestyle for themselves and their families.
- Interested in staying connected with friends and family and maintaining a strong support network.
- Value education and personal development, willing to invest in themselves and their children's future.
- Technology-savvy and comfortable using digital tools and platforms to manage their daily lives and stay organised.
- Financially stable and able to afford higher-end products and services that align with their values and lifestyles.

People with a persona like Emily's that are time-conscious and seek to simplify their lives may prefer content that is concise, to the point, and easy to digest. This could include content that is well-organised and structured, with clear headlines, bullet points, or numbered lists, and that provides practical, actionable tips and advice that can be easily implemented.

In addition, this type of person may appreciate content that is visually appealing and easy on the eyes, such as images, videos, or infographics, that help to break up the text and make the information more engaging and memorable.

Psychographic profile for people like Noah:

- Independent and self-directed, with a strong sense of personal style and individuality.
- Interested in pursuing their passions and interests, and willing to take risks to achieve their goals.
- Confident and self-assured, with a rebellious streak and a desire to challenge the status quo.
- Active and energetic, with a love for physical activity and outdoor sports.
- Social and outgoing, with a strong network of friends and peers who share their interests and passions.
- Trend-conscious and up to date on the latest fashion and style trends.

Someone like Noah may prefer content that is original, authentic, and reflective of their personal values and beliefs. This could include content that is thought-provoking, insightful, or provocative, and that challenges conventional wisdom or encourages independent thinking.

In addition, this type of person may appreciate content that is personalised and tailored to their interests and preferences, such as articles, videos, or podcasts that are related to their specific passions or hobbies.

Overall, content that is focused on providing inspiration and empowerment, and that helps independent and self-directed individuals to pursue their passions and interests may be most appealing to this audience.

Psychographic profile for people like Iris and John:

- Active and energetic, with a strong desire to maintain their physical health and fitness as they age.
- Health-conscious and focused on maintaining a balanced and nutritious diet.
- Independent and self-directed, with a strong sense of personal responsibility and self-care.
- Interested in staying mentally sharp and engaged and seeking opportunities for learning and personal growth.
- Social and outgoing, with a strong network of friends and peers who share their interests and passions.
- Value-conscious and careful with their spending, seeking affordable and high-quality products and services to support their health and well-being.

People like Iris and John may prefer content that is informative, transparent, and trustworthy while providing value and quality, helping value-conscious couples to find affordable and high-quality products and services to support their health and well-being. Some examples:

- Content that is well-researched and fact-based, with clear and objective information about the quality, price, and benefits of different products and services, and that provides honest and unbiased reviews and ratings from other customers or experts.
- Content that is practical and relevant, such as guides, how-tos, or FAQs, that provide step-by-step instructions or advice on how to make the most of their purchases and get the best value for their money.

JOBS TO BE DONE VS CONTENT TOPICS

Defining the Jobs to be Done for your target audience involves identifying the specific tasks, problems, or goals they wish to accomplish or address through your product or service. This can help you better understand your audience's needs and motivations and develop solutions tailored to their specific needs and preferences.

Job-to-be-done, developed by Harvard Business School's Clayton Christensen, is a theory of consumer action. It describes the mechanisms that cause a consumer to adopt an innovation. The theory states that markets grow, evolve and renew whenever customers have a Job to be Done, and then buy a product to complete it (get the Job Done).

Digital Marketing Like a PRO
Clo Willaerts

One example is the buyer persona Emily, whose Job to be Done is 'planning and preparing healthy and convenient meals for her family on a busy weekday evening'. This Job involves several key elements:

- The need to save time and effort.
- The desire to provide healthy and nutritious meals.
- The requirement to satisfy the tastes and preferences of multiple family members.

Products that win in the market help customers get a job done: - It saves them money - It saves them time - It improves their life somehow

Digital Marketing Like a PRO
Clo Willaerts

A brand could create digital content to help working mothers plan and prepare meals, such as:

- A meal planning app with features like meal prep ideas, grocery lists, and recipes.
- A meal delivery service with options for healthy, convenient meals for busy families.
- A cookbook with quick and easy recipes that can be prepared in under 30 minutes.
- Blog posts or articles with tips and strategies for meal planning and preparation, like batch cooking and using leftovers.
- Infographics or videos with step-by-step instructions for preparing meals, like chopping vegetables, cooking rice, or seasoning meat.
- Personal stories or testimonials from other working mothers who have successfully used meal planning strategies to save time and improve their family's health and well-being.

Another example is Noah, whose Job to be Done is 'finding and purchasing the latest streetwear clothing and accessories to show off his personal style and impress his friends'. This Job involves:

- The need to stay up to date on the latest trends and styles.
- The desire to express his individual identity and personality.
- The requirement to fit in with his peer group and social circle.

A brand could create digital content to help male teenagers find and purchase streetwear, such as:

- online fashion retailers;
- clothing subscription services;
- streetwear magazines or blogs;
- online look books or style guides;
- videos or podcasts featuring interviews with streetwear designers, influencers, or tastemakers;
- online or virtual events offering special discounts, promotions, or exclusive access to new collections or limited-edition products;
- personal stories or testimonials from other male teenagers who have successfully used the brand's product or service to find and purchase streetwear.

Finally, Iris and John's Job to be Done is 'finding and joining a fitness and wellness program tailored to their individual needs and goals and offering support and motivation to help them stay on track'. This Job involves:

- The need to find a program tailored to their individual needs.
- The desire to achieve specific fitness and wellness goals.
- The requirement for support and motivation to stay on track.

For example, a brand could develop content to help them find and join a fitness and wellness program, such as:

- Online platforms or apps that offer personalized fitness and wellness plans and track progress.
- Personalised training programs or one-on-one sessions with a digital personal trainer
- Webinars or virtual workshops that provide support and motivation to help individuals stay on track.
- Virtual wellness retreats or challenges that offer a holistic approach to wellness, including nutrition, exercise, and mindfulness.
- Blog posts or articles that provide tips, strategies, and inspiration for finding and joining a fitness and wellness program that is right for them.
- Videos or infographics that showcase the benefits and features of different fitness and wellness programs and how to choose the best one for their needs and goals.

INFLUENCERS AND ADVOCATES YOUR TARGET AUDIENCE LOVES

To find the types of influencers or brand advocates that are most relevant and effective for your target audience, you can follow these steps:

1. Research the **social media** platforms, forums, or blogs that your target audience is most active on and use these platforms to search for influencers or brand advocates who match your buyer persona.
2. Look for influencers or brand advocates who have a **large, engaged, and authentic following**, and who consistently produce high-quality and relevant content that aligns with your brand's values and messaging.

3. Identify the influencers or brand advocates who are the **best fit for your brand**, and who can help to reach, engage, and convert your target audience in an authentic and credible way.

Some examples:

- Noah, a male teenager, may be drawn to influencers or brand advocates who are fashionable and trendy. These influencers may be professional skateboarders or streetwear designers, and brand advocates may be customers or employees knowledgeable about the products or services Noah is considering.
  At the time of writing, the list might look a little like this:
  - A$AP Rocky: An American rapper, songwriter, and record producer known for his style and fashion sense.
  - Noah, the Creator: An American rapper, singer, songwriter, record producer, and fashion designer.
  - Offset: An American rapper and member of the hip-hop group Migos, known for his style and fashion collaborations.
  - Kid Cudi: An American singer, songwriter, and actor known for his unique fashion sense and collaborations with brands such as Fear of God and Supreme.
  - Post Malone: An American singer, songwriter, and rapper known for his eclectic fashion style and collaborations with designers such as Crocs and Supreme.

- Emily, a working mother might: look up to influencers or brand advocates who are relatable and offer genuine, inspiring content whereby influencers may be other working mothers who share their daily experiences and offer practical advice on topics like parenting and careers.
  - Some popular influencers in these fields may include Chrissy Teigen, Giovanna Fletcher, and Rosie Huntington-Whiteley for parenting and family content and Sheryl Sandberg and Lean In for career and professional development content.
  - Brand advocates may be customers or employees who provide honest and unbiased reviews.

- Iris and John, retired seniors, may be interested in influencers or brand advocates who are knowledgeable and experienced and offer motivating content. Influencers may be health and wellness experts or personal trainers, and brand advocates may be satisfied customers or employees:
  - Some popular influencers may include Dr. Sanjay Gupta or Dr. Ruth for health and wellness content, and Suze Orman, Dave Ramsey, and John Bogle for financial planning and investment content.

TOOL: TRAACKR

Traackr.com is a tool that helps users to identify, manage, and track influencers in their field. As an 'Influencer Management Platform', it offers a range of features designed to help content marketers find, engage, and measure the impact of influencers on their business.

Some of the key features of Traackr include:

- **identifying influencers** based on criteria like location, industry, audience size, and engagement rate;
- **management of relationships with influencers**, including tracking interactions and collaboration efforts; and
- **Analysing and reporting** the impact of influencers marketing campaigns.

In addition to Traackr, there are several other tools available for finding and managing influencers, including:

- BrandSnob.com
- BuzzSumo.com
- Klear.com
- Mention.com
- Neoreach.com

CHANNELS USED DURING THE CUSTOMER JOURNEY

Table 2. Customer Journey vs. Channels, Touchpoints & Listening Posts

CUSTOMER JOURNEY	CHANNELS, TOUCHPOINTS, LISTENING POSTS
SEE (Awareness)	PR, Radio, TV, Print, Billboards, Events, Product Placement, Social Media, Web Video, Banners
THINK (Consideration)	Search Engines, Social Media, Customer Review platforms
BUY (Activation)	Store, Web Shop, Website
USE (Loyalty)	Email, Website, Social Media
LOVE (Advocacy)	Social Media, Word-Of-Mouth, Personalized Email

During the **Awareness phase** of the Customer Journey, individuals learn about a product or service and consider whether it might meet their needs or solve their problems, the most used digital channels are typically advertising and social media.

> SEE (awareness phase) Latent need: the product is not yet in view of the buyer.

Digital Marketing Like a PRO
Clo Willaerts

- In the case of advertising, individuals may encounter ads for a product or service on websites, apps, or social media platforms, and the ads may include links or calls to action that encourage them to learn more or take a specific action.
- In the case of social media, individuals may use platforms such as Facebook, Instagram, or TikTok to discover and learn about products or services through the posts, stories, or ads that are shared by their friends, peers, or influencers.

By using these digital channels, individuals can easily and quickly access a wide range of information and perspectives and make informed decisions about whether a product or service is right for them.

During the **Consideration phase** of the Customer Journey, when individuals are actively comparing and evaluating different options and solutions to meet their needs or solve their problems, the most used digital channels are search engines.

> THINK (consideration)
> Different products and suppliers
> are compared with each other;
> buyer asks for
> recommendations.
>
> Digital Marketing Like a PRO
> Clo Willaerts

- In this phase, individuals may use more specific and advanced search queries to find better understand the features, benefits, or drawbacks of different products or services, found on websites, blogs, forums, or reviews that provide detailed and comparative information.
- In addition, individuals may use search engines to find information about the prices, availability, or reputation of different products or services, and to identify the businesses or vendors that offer the best value or customer experience.

By creating and publishing content that is optimised for Search Engines, brands can help their target audience access a wealth of information to make more informed and confident decisions about the products or services that are best suited to their needs and preferences.

During the **Conversion phase** of the Customer Journey, when individuals are ready to make a purchasing decision and select a product or service to meet their needs or solve their problems, the most used digital channel for converting customers is typically the brand's own website.

> BUY (activation) The hard conversion – the buyer becomes a paying customer.
>
> Digital Marketing Like a PRO
> Clo Willaerts

- In this phase, individuals may visit the brand's website to view and compare the specific products or services that they are interested in purchasing, such as the available options, colours, or sizes, and to read customer reviews or ratings.
- In addition, the brand's website may include a shopping cart or checkout process that allows individuals to complete their purchase easily and securely and choose their preferred payment, shipping, or delivery options.

Brands can use a variety of content to effectively convert website visitors into customers. Information that can help drive a purchase decision includes:

- Product or service descriptions that clearly and concisely explain the features, benefits, or specifications of the product or service, and that highlight its unique selling points or advantages over competitors.
- Customer reviews or ratings that provide honest and unbiased feedback from other customers who have used the product or service.
- Product demonstrations or videos that show the product or service in action, and that provide an engaging and interactive experience for visitors.

- Personalised recommendations or suggestions that are based on the visitor's interests, preferences, or behaviour, that can help to identify the most relevant or suitable products or services for them.
- Clear and compelling calls to action that encourage visitors to take a specific action, such as adding a product to their shopping cart, completing a form, or subscribing to a newsletter.

Identify the most appropriate social media channels for each of your buyer personas and optimize your social profiles and the content you publish there accordingly.

Digital Marketing Like a PRO
Clo Willaerts

Following are examples of the digital channels our three persona groups might be active on. Businesses can gather information on a personas specific interests, habits and preferences to define this and then tailor their product or service information for the relevant sites.

Emily's preferred Digital Channels

Some potential digital channels that working mothers like Emily might be active on include:

- social media platforms (such as Facebook, Instagram, and Pinterest);
- online forums and discussion boards related to parenting and motherhood; and
- blogs and websites focused on parenting, family, and lifestyle.

Noah's preferred Digital Channels

Some potential digital channels that people like Noah might be most active on include:

- social media platforms (such as Instagram and TikTok);
- online forums and discussion boards related to skateboarding and streetwear; and
- blogs and websites focused on skateboarding, fashion, and street culture.

Iris and John's preferred Digital Channels

Some potential digital channels that this personas like Iris and John might be active on include:

- social media platforms (such as Facebook and LinkedIn);
- online forums and discussion boards related to fitness and health; and
- blogs and websites focused on fitness, nutrition, and wellness.

Identifying your target audience is crucial in developing a successful digital content marketing strategy. By gathering as much information as possible about your target audience and creating detailed Buyer Persona for them, you can make content that is relevant, engaging, and effective at reaching and engaging with your target audience.

FRAMEWORK: TOFU-MOFU-BOFU

The TOFU-MOFU-BOFU Framework is a useful tool for creating a content marketing strategy that aligns with the different stages of the customer journey. The framework suggests that different types of content and messaging will be most effective at various stages of the customer journey.

The three components of the TOFU-MOFU-BOFU Framework are:

- TOFU (**Top of the Funnel**) represents the "**Awareness**" stage where potential customers become aware of a business and its products/services. They seek information and solutions to their problems and are not yet ready to purchase. TOFU content aims to attract and engage potential customers by providing educational and informative content to build awareness and interest.

- MOFU **(Middle of the Funnel)** represents the "**Consideration**" stage where potential customers evaluate if a business's products/services fit their needs. At this stage, they have a basic understanding of the business and its offerings and seek more detailed information to make a decision. MOFU content aims to nurture leads by providing specific information about the benefits of the business's products/services and how they can solve their problem.

- BOFU **(Bottom of the Funnel)** represents the "**Conversion**" stage where potential customers are ready to purchase. At this stage, they understand the business and its products/services and are looking for a final push to make a purchase. BOFU content aims to convert leads into customers by providing highly persuasive content to overcome objections and encourage a purchase.

Table 3. TOFU MOFU BOFU vs. Customer Journey

TOFU	Awareness	Blog posts, infographics, social media posts
MOFU	Consideration	Product demos, case studies, webinars
BOFU	Conversion	Product comparisons, testimonials, special offers

By understanding the different stages of the customer journey and aligning content and messaging accordingly, businesses can create a more effective marketing strategy that meee needs of their potential customers at each stage.

CONTENT THEMES AND TOPICS

A key component of any content marketing strategic plan is the list of themes and topics covered in the content. These themes and topics should be carefully selected to align with the goals and objectives of the content marketing plan and the interests and needs of the target audience.

CONTENT FOCUS, TILT AND NICHE

To identify your brand's unique content offer, start by considering your brand's values and goals. What makes your business unique, and what do you want to achieve with your digital content marketing?

> Always start with the focus, and then determine which format is best suited to the story that you want to tell.

The Content Fuel Framework
Melanie Deziel

Content focus refers to the specific topics or themes that a brand chooses to focus on in its content marketing efforts. This could include:

- topics related to the brand's products or services;
- industry trends, customer interests; or
- other areas that are relevant to the brand and its target audience.

> The inherent tension in marketing is that companies always want to talk about themselves and what their products or services can do. Everyone else, meanwhile, only wants to know what those products or services can do for them.

Content Rules
Ann Handley, C.C. Chapman, and Davi...

Content focus is an important aspect of content marketing strategy, as it helps to ensure that the brand's content is **relevant,** engaging, and aligned with its overall business objectives.

> Your value proposition answers a fundamental question: Why should I buy from you rather than your competitor? To answer this question, your value proposition should state the specific benefits a person will get from your product or service.
>
> Digital Marketing Like a PRO
> Clo Willaerts

A brand can define a clear content focus in several ways, including:

- Identifying and identifying the brand's unique **value proposition,** the key benefit or advantage that it offers to its customers, allows brands to create a clear and compelling content focus that is aligned with its unique selling points.
- A brand's competitors are the other companies that offer similar products or services in the same market. By **analysing its competitors**, a brand can

> Avoid "sales speak." Sometimes there are business reasons to do this, but the more you talk about yourself, the less people will pay attention or value your content.
>
> Content Inc.
> Joe Pulizzi

identify gaps and opportunities in the market and define a content focus that differentiates the brand from its competitors and addresses the unique needs and concerns of its target audience.

- Finding your brand's **content tilt**.

Joe Pulizzi, an entrepreneur best known for his work in content marketing, developed the concept of **content tilt**. This concept, like the similar concept of **concept niche**, refers to the idea that a brand should focus on a specific topic or niche to differentiate itself from its competitors and create a unique and compelling content marketing strategy. According to Pulizzi, content tilt is the point at which a brand's content becomes so focused and specialised that it can attract a loyal and passionate audience that is interested in the specific topic or niche that the brand is covering. By focusing on a specific topic or niche, a brand can create a consistent and cohesive content marketing strategy that resonates with its target audience and drives business results.

The content tilt. Finding an area of little to no competition so that our content can break through the clutter

Content Inc.
Joe Pulizzi

Have the confidence to find your niche, define who you are, then declare it again and again and again and again. If you do it persistently enough, you will own that niche. People will not be able to imagine that niche without you.

Video Marketing like a PRO
Clo Willaerts

The main difference between the content tilt and content niche is that:

- content niche is broader and refers to the general topic or area that a brand is focusing on; while
- content tilt is more specific and refers to the point at which a brand's content becomes so focused and specialized that it can attract a loyal and passionate audience.

CONTENT THAT IS TAILORED TO YOUR AUDIENCE'S NEEDS

Next, consider your target audience. What are their needs, preferences, and behaviours, and how can your brand's voice and tone resonate with them?

> Figuring out what your prospective customers are interested in, creating stuff that meets those needs, and delivering it to them is what you need to do. And that, by the way, is exactly what publishers do.
>
> Content Rules
> Ann Handley, C.C. Chapman, and Davi...

Now match these values and personality with the psychographics of your target audience. What are they looking for?

- Trustworthy and reliable might work for our working mom Emily as she carries a lot of responsibility and may be seeking products and services that they can rely on.
- This type of content is also a safe bet for our retired couple Iris and John, as they may be looking for products and services that are safe, effective, and backed by expert knowledge and research.
- Fun and playful might work for our skater boy Noah, as he may be looking for products and services that are engaging and exciting.

> Good writing serves the reader, not the writer. It isn't self-indulgent. Good writing anticipates the questions that readers might have as they're reading a piece, and it answers them.

Everybody <mark>Writes</mark>: Your...
Ann Handley

> Keep it simple. Stick to an approach of being simple, but not simplistic, with your brand's storytelling. Don't talk above or below your audience.

The Stripped-Down Guide to Content ...
John Egan

THE IMPORTANCE OF UP-TO-DATE CONTENT

In today's fast-paced digital landscape, ensuring that your content is up to date is more important than ever. Here are a few reasons why:

1. **Relevance**: Your audience expects your content to be receive relevant and timely info. that addresses their current needs and interests.
2. **Trust**: Outdated or incorrect information can erode trust with your audience. Regularly refreshing and **updating** your content can demonstrate your commitment to providing accurate and reliable information.

3. **Search engine optimisation**: Search engines prioritise fresh and relevant content in their search results, so content that is updated will reach a larger audience.
4. By staying current on trends and events in your industry or niche, you can stay ahead of your competitors and maintain a **competitive advantage**.

CONTENT CHANNEL MIX

A content **channel** is a platform or medium through which you deliver your content. Some common content channels include:

- your website or blog
- social media platforms (e.g., Facebook, Instagram, TikTok)
- Email newsletters
- online publications or industry blogs
- video-sharing platforms (e.g., YouTube, Vimeo)
- podcasts

Use the Paid Owned Earned model to define a mix of: - Maximum 3 paid channels, e.g. Facebook and Instagram Advertising, Google Ads. - Maximum 3 owned channels, e.g. Website, Newsletter, Podcast series. - Maximum 3 earned channels, e.g. Facebook Company Page, LinkedIn Company Page, and Twitter account.

Digital Marketing Like a PRO
Clo Willaerts

It's essential to determine which channels are most appropriate for your content and target audience. For example, social media platforms may be more effective than email newsletters if you target younger audiences while the opposite may be true if you are targeting professionals.

YOUR CONTENT NEEDS A HOME

It is important to choose wisely when choosing where to publish your content. After all, **your content needs a home, and you don't want to build it on rented land**. Third-party sites and popular social media platforms can be tempting choices for publishing your content. But it is important to remember that these platforms are not your own. Your content could be taken down or altered at any time and your level of visibility and reach may be limited compared to that published on your own website.

Additionally, investing in 'rented land' (i.e., social media) means risking your entire investment in content on a platform whose management may make changes to it that don not benefit you. Although it is important to use social media platforms, podcasting networks, and other rented territory to reach some audiences, but do not build a strategy designed to keep them there, as that approach ultimately benefits the platform's business objectives, not yours.

Instead, **use social media platforms as rivers** to carry users to your own home – your website, resource centre, or email newsletter. Encourage visitors on rented platforms to visit your own home and think about how to tailor content for rented land that makes it easily transferable to sites you control. Or take advantage of the reach and engagement offered by social media platforms by only posting content there that you are willing to lose.

> Consider your website or e-commerce site a mobile-first conversion machine. Within your digital assets ecosystem, this site functions like a hub, with traffic building tactics as its spokes.
>
> Digital Marketing Like a PRO
> Clo Willaerts

In essence, your website can play a central role in the management of your digital content strategy by acting as your **content hub,** the home of your **owned**

media. It is from there that you can direct selective publication of it on social media sites relevant to your targeted audience. This ensures your complete control over what is published and how long it remains visible, while exploiting the power of social media sites to drive traffic back to your website, benefiting your search engine rankings and overall online visibility.

> Your website is the ultimate 'owned media' that is openly accessible by anyone on the web, the only place on the internet you do have full control over.
>
> Digital Marketing Like a PRO
> Clo Willaerts

An essential element of any content marketing plan is the strategy for distributing and promoting the content to the intended audience. Three main categories of channels and tactics can be used for content distribution and promotion:

- **Paid media** channels are those you pay to use, such as advertising on television or social media.
- **Owned media** channels, such as your website or blog, are your own or you control.
- **Earned media** channels are those that you do not pay for and do not directly control, such as when your content is shared by others on social media or mentioned in the press.

Each media channel has its advantages and disadvantages, and the right mix of channels will depend on your specific goals and audience:

- Paid media channels can effectively reach a large audience quickly, but they can be expensive.
- Owned media channels can be more cost-effective but may reach fewer people.

- Earned media channels can be powerful because they come from trusted sources (such as friends or influencers). Still, they can be difficult to predict and control.

By considering these different channels, you can choose the right mix for your content and audience. Further considerations on these three media channels follows.

PAID MEDIA

Paid channels and tactics refer to those that require an investment, such as paid advertising or sponsored content. These channels can effectively reach new audiences or promote specific campaigns or products. Still, it is essential to carefully consider the budget and targeting options and ensure that the content is relevant and engaging for the intended audience.

> Paid media is where you pay for your target audience's attention. In the context of your digital points of presence audit, these could be Google Ads, Facebook Ads, banner campaigns,
>
> Digital Marketing Like a PRO
> Clo Willaerts

Here are some examples of paid channels and tactics:

- **Paid advertising** includes platforms such as Google AdWords, Facebook Ads, and Instagram Ads, which allow brands to pay to place their ads in front of specific audiences based on demographics, interests, and behaviours.
- **Sponsored content** is created and paid for by a brand but published on a third-party platform such as a blog or news website. Sponsored content is typically marked as such and is designed to appeal to the audience of the platform on which it is published.

- **Influencer marketing** refers to paying influencers, or individuals with a large following on social media or other platforms, to promote the brand's products or services to their audience. Influencer marketing can be an effective way to reach a targeted audience and build trust and credibility.
- **Display advertising** includes banner ads or other ads displayed on websites or other online platforms. Display advertising can target specific audiences based on demographics, interests, and behaviours. It can be an effective way to reach new audiences or promote specific campaigns or products.
- **Native advertising** is content created and paid for by a brand but designed to blend in with the editorial content of a platform. Native advertising is typically marked as sponsored content. It is designed to appeal to the audience of the platform on which it is published.

OWNED MEDIA

Owned media are owned and controlled by the brand, such as the company's website, blog, or newsletters. These channels can effectively reach the brand's existing audience and engage with them directly. Therefore, creating high-quality, relevant, and engaging content for these channels and optimizing them for search and social media is essential.

> Owned media are your company's proprietary digital assets, such as its websites and apps. Their most significant advantage is that it is easier to access essential data-gathering tools like Google Analytics.
>
> Digital Marketing Like a PRO
> Clo Willaerts

Here are some examples of owned channels and tactics:

- The brand's **website** is a critical owned channel that can showcase the brand's products, services, and values and provide information and resources to customers and potential customers. Create high-quality, informative, and engaging content for the website and to optimize it for search engines and user experience.
- A company **blog** is a valuable tool for sharing insights, news, and stories about the brand, industry, and products. It can effectively engage with the brand's existing audience and attract new visitors through search and social media.
- An **email newsletter or marketing campaign** can effectively reach the brand's existing audience directly through their inbox. Create targeted, relevant, and timely email campaigns and consider the impact of email frequency and subject line on the campaign's success.
- A **mobile app** can be a valuable tool for engaging customers and providing them with personalised content and experiences. Create a high-quality, user-friendly app and regularly update it with new features and content.

> If you are in doubt about what you do or don't own a particular media, ask yourself: Is there someone we can call when something goes wrong? If the answer is 'no', then you do not own these media.

Digital Marketing Like a PRO
Clo Willaerts

EARNED MEDIA

Earned media refer to those that are not directly controlled by the brand but are generated through the actions and interactions of others, such as media coverage, word-of-mouth referrals, or customer reviews.

> Earned media is what used to be called
> 'word of mouth' or 'free media'. It still
> involves what print, broadcast or online
> channels publish about your company,
> but today includes what is said about you
> by others (including angry customers
> and industry journalists) on social media
> platforms,
>
> Digital Marketing Like a PRO
> Clo Willaerts

These channels can be highly effective for building trust and credibility with the target audience. Therefore, fostering and encouraging earned media opportunities is essential for creating high-quality, valuable content and engaging with customers and industry influencers.

> Ours is a world where technology and
> social media have given us access and
> power: every one of us now has the
> awesome opportunity to own our own
> online publishing platforms—websites,
> blogs, email newsletters, Facebook pages,
> Twitter streams, and so on.
>
> Everybody Writes
> Ann Handley

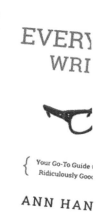

Here are some examples of earned channels and tactics:

- **Social media accounts** on platforms such as Facebook, Instagram, and TikTok can be effective earned channels for reaching and engaging with the brand's existing audience. Creating high-quality, relevant, and engaging content for these platforms, regularly interacting with followers, and responding to comments and inquiries are essential.

- **Social media mentions** of the brand or its products or services on social media by industry influencers or other individuals can be an effective way to reach a large audience and build credibility and trust. Engaging with these mentions and encouraging influencers to share content about the brand is essential.
- **Customer reviews** can be valuable for building trust and credibility with potential customers. When customers leave reviews about a brand's products or services, they provide an independent perspective that can be very influential for other consumers considering making a purchase. Therefore, brands need to encourage customers to leave reviews and respond to any negative reviews constructively and professionally. For example, suppose a consumer has had an unsatisfactory shopping experience. In that case, they may contact the retailer to share their experience, stop shopping at the retailer, or share their experience on social media. A brand can improve its reputation and attract more business by effectively managing customer reviews.
- **Media coverage** of the brand or its products or services by news or media outlets, such as newspapers, magazines, television, or radio programs can be an effective way to reach a broad audience and build credibility and trust.
- **Word-of-mouth referrals** made by customers or other individuals to their friends, family, or colleagues can be highly effective for building trust and credibility with the target audience and are often more reliable than other forms of marketing.

A CONTENT CALENDAR FOR THE COMING YEAR: HERO, HUB, HELP

A **content calendar** is a tool that helps businesses to plan, organise, and schedule their digital content marketing efforts. It provides a clear overview of what content will be created and published and when, and it can help businesses stay on track and meet deadlines.

> The editorial calendar is essential in ensuring that activity aligns with goals and strategy and that you are adequately serving the needs of both the company and your target audiences. It should ideally be a structured, centrally accessible calendar that accounts for all elements of the creation process.
>
> Digital Marketing Like a PRO
> Clo Willaerts

Google's **Hero, Hub, Help (HHH) framework** is a content strategy framework that can help you to organise your content calendar and create a cohesive and effective content marketing plan. The framework is based on creating a hierarchy of content organized around three main categories: Hero, Hub, and Help.

> Formerly named Hero, Hub, Hygiene, the Hero, Hub, Help was primarily used as a content classification for YouTube, but is now frequently used for all types of content marketing. This 3H model can also help you map out all of your content throughout the year.
>
> Digital Marketing Like a PRO
> Clo Willaerts

Here is how the HHH framework can help you to organise your content calendar:

1. **Hero content** is the most important and impactful content you create. This might include long-form content such as blog posts, eBooks, and whitepapers or high-impact visual content such as videos or infographics. Hero content should be focused on your key messages and objectives. It should be designed to attract and engage your target audience.

2. **Hub content** is the core of your content marketing strategy and should focus on building your brand and establishing your expertise. This might include content such as case studies, product demos, or how-to guides. Hub content should be designed to support and amplify your hero content. It should be focused on delivering value to your audience.

3. **Help content** is designed to support and assist your audience and might include content such as FAQs, customer service resources, or troubleshooting guides. Help content should be focused on solving problems and answering questions. It should be designed to make it easy for your audience to find the information they need.

Start with putting your Hero moments in a calendar, e.g. an advertising campaign in May and another one in October. Then, schedule your Help content on regular intervals throughout the year. Finally, fill in the content gaps with Hub content.

Digital Marketing Like a PRO
Clo Willaerts

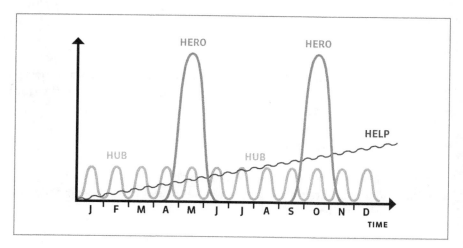

By organising your content calendar around the HHH framework, you can create a cohesive and effective content marketing plan focused on delivering value and engaging your audience. You can use the framework to plan out your content calendar and ensure that you are creating a range of high-quality content that meets the needs of your audience and supports your business goals.

CONTENT FORMATS AND TOPICS

To create a content calendar, start by identifying the goals and objectives of your digital content marketing and the formats and topics you will focus on. This will help you plan the types of content you will create and the topics you will cover.

> For our purposes as content creators and brand storytellers, the format is the way that a piece of content is brought to life: the form it takes when it leaves your brain and enters the world, and the means by which our audience can engage with or consume it.
>
> The Content Fuel Framework
> Melanie Deziel

The **content format** refers to the type of content you create, such as articles, videos, podcasts, infographics, etc. Different formats can be more effective for different types of content and goals. For example, an infographic may be more effective for explaining complex concepts. At the same time, a video may be more engaging for demonstrating a product.

As you develop your content strategy, it's essential to consider the strengths and limitations of different formats to choose the most effective ones for your goals and target audience.

Table 4. Strengths and Limitations of Content Formats

CONTENT FORMAT	STRENGTHS	LIMITATIONS
Blog Posts	Flexible and cost-effective for sharing information and engaging with audiences. Can be valuable for explaining complex topics, sharing stories, or providing updates and news.	Can be time-consuming to create and may require more in-depth research and writing. May have a shorter lifespan than other formats as they can be quickly replaced by newer content.
Video Content	Highly engaging and effective for demonstrating products or showcasing customer stories. Can be valuable for explaining complex concepts or showcasing events.	Time-consuming and costly, especially if creating high-quality videos with professional equipment and editing. Can be more challenging to optimise for search engines.
Infographics	Helpful for visualising and explaining complex data or concepts in an easy-to-understand way. Highly shareable and effective for driving traffic and engagement.	Time-consuming, especially when working with complex data or visualising complex concepts. May require specialised design skills or software to create high-quality infographics.
Podcasts	Useful for providing long-form content that can be consumed on the go. Valuable for interviews, discussions, or storytelling.	Time-consuming to produce, especially if creating long-form content or conducting interviews. May require specialised equipment and software to record and edit high-quality podcasts. Can be crowded and competitive, making it more challenging to stand out and reach a large audience.

By considering the strengths and limitations of different content formats, you can choose the most effective ones for your goals and target audience. This can help you create more targeted and compelling content that resonates with your audience and helps achieve your marketing objectives.

FREQUENCY AND CONSISTENCY

Next, decide on the frequency with which you will publish your content. This could be daily, weekly, or monthly, depending on your goals and objectives and the resources and capacity of your business.

> Consistency is the great hallmark of a successful publisher. Whether you publish an Instagram channel or daily email newsletter, the content needs to be delivered on time and as expected.

Content Inc.
Joe Pulizzi

CREATING A CONTENT CALENDAR

Then, create a calendar that shows the dates and times your content will be published and the formats and topics of each piece of content. Depending on your preferences and needs, you can use a physical calendar, a digital calendar, or a spreadsheet to create your content calendar.

> Use daysoftheyear.com, a curated overview of the world's weird, funny, wonderful, unknown and bizarre national days, to fill in the gaps in your social media content planning.

Digital Marketing Like a PRO
Clo Willaerts

A content calendar is a tool that helps you plan and schedule your content in advance. It can be a valuable resource for content marketers, as it allows you to ensure that you are consistently publishing new material and staying on top of your content marketing efforts.

Here are a few ideas for content that you can include in your content calendar:

Moonlit Apparel, as you may remember, is a fashion company specialising in trendy streetwear and skater apparel for teenagers.

Here are some ideas for content that the company can include in its content calendar throughout the year:

Table 5. Example of Content Calendar

MONTH	BLOG POST	INSTAGRAM POSTS	EMAIL NEWSLETTER
January	'New Year, New You' style resolutions blog post	Instagram posts featuring winter streetwear trends	Email newsletter with a round-up of the best deals and new arrivals for the month
February	'Valentine's Day Outfit Ideas"' blog post	Instagram posts featuring date night streetwear outfits	Email newsletter with a special promotion for customers to celebrate the holiday
March	'Spring Cleaning Your Closet' blog post with tips for organising and refreshing your streetwear wardrobe	Instagram posts featuring spring streetwear trends	Email newsletter with a round-up of the best new arrivals for the season
April	'Earth Day' sustainability blog post	Instagram posts featuring eco-friendly streetwear options from Moonlit Apparel	Email newsletter with a special promotion for customers to celebrate the holiday
May	'Mother's Day Gift Guide' blog post	Instagram posts featuring gift ideas for moms	Email newsletter with a special promotion for customers to celebrate the holiday

June	'Summer Streetwear Essentials' blog post	Instagram posts featuring beach vacation streetwear outfit ideas	Email newsletter with a round-up of the best summer deals and new arrivals
July	'4th of July Streetwear' blog post with patriotic outfit ideas	Instagram posts featuring red, white, and blue streetwear options from Moonlit Apparel	Email newsletter with a special promotion for customers to celebrate the holiday
August	'Back to School Streetwear' blog post with tips for creating a stylish and functional wardrobe for the school year	Instagram posts featuring school streetwear outfit ideas	Email newsletter with a round-up of the best deals and new arrivals for the month
September	'Fall Streetwear Preview' blog post with a sneak peek at the latest trends for the season	Instagram posts featuring fall streetwear trends	Email newsletter with a round-up of the best new arrivals for the season
October	'Halloween Costume Ideas' blog post featuring streetwear-inspired costume ideas	Instagram posts featuring Halloween costume ideas and Moonlit Apparel clothing options	Email newsletter with a special promotion for customers to celebrate the holiday
November	'Thanksgiving Outfit Ideas' blog post featuring streetwear-inspired Thanksgiving outfits	Instagram posts featuring Thanksgiving streetwear outfit ideas	Email newsletter with a special promotion for customers to celebrate the holiday
December	'Holiday Gift Guide' blog post featuring gift ideas for teenagers	Instagram posts featuring gift ideas for the holidays	Email newsletter with a round-up of the best deals and new arrivals for the month

By including a mix of these types of content in their content calendar, Moonlit Apparel can make sure that they consistently provide value to their teenage audience and stay at the forefront of their minds throughout the year.

REVIEWING YOUR CONTENT CALENDAR

Finally, regularly review and update your content calendar to ensure it remains relevant and accurate. This will help you to stay on track, avoid missing deadlines and allow you to make changes to your digital content marketing strategy.

METRICS AND ANALYSIS

Tracking and measuring the performance of your content marketing efforts essential. A system to effectively system is required to collect and analyse relevant data. These data can then be used to optimise and improve the content marketing strategy over time.

EXAMPLE: MOONLIT APPAREL'S CONTENT MARKETING PLAN

A strategic content marketing plan includes several key components: goals and objectives, a target audience, content themes and topics, content formats, distribution and promotion strategies, and a content calendar. It also includes a system for tracking and measuring the performance of the content marketing efforts through metrics and analysis.

An essential starting point is to identify the specific goals and objectives of the plan and to align them with the overall business objectives. Next, define the target audience through the creation of buyer personas and select content themes and topics that will be of interest and value to this audience. Next, choose the appropriate content formats and distribution channels to effectively reach and engage the target audience, and create a content calendar to plan and schedule the production and distribution of content. Finally, put a system in place to track and measure the performance of the content marketing efforts and use data analysis to continually optimise and improve the strategy.

By following these steps, you can create a comprehensive and effective content marketing plan to help you achieve your business goals.

Here's what that could look like for Moonlit Apparel:

Moonlit Apparel is a new clothing brand focused on sustainable and ethical fashion. As part of its overall marketing strategy, Moonlit Apparel is looking to create a strategic digital content marketing plan to help increase brand awareness and drive sales.

To achieve these goals, the strategic digital content marketing plan for Moonlit Apparel will include the following elements:

- **Goals and objectives** *The plan will increase website traffic, generate leads, and improve customer engagement by creating high-quality, informative, and engaging content.*
- **Target audience** *The target audience for the content marketing efforts will be conscious consumers interested in sustainability and ethics. Buyer personas will be created to better understand this audience's demographics, interests, and behaviours and tailor the content to their needs.*
- **Content themes and topics** *The content will focus on topics related to sustainable and ethical fashion, including the environmental and social impact of the fashion industry, the benefits of choosing sustainable and ethical brands, and tips for building a more sustainable wardrobe.*
- **Content formats** *The content will be produced in various formats, including blog posts, videos, infographics, and podcasts, to reach different segments of the target audience and keep the content diverse and engaging.*
- **Distribution and promotion** *The content will be distributed and promoted through social media, email marketing, and paid advertising to reach as many potential customers as possible.*
- **Content calendar** *A content calendar will be created to plan and schedule the production and distribution of content regularly. The calendar will include a mix of hero, hub, and help content to ensure a balance of big campaigns, evergreen content, and tactical or educational content.*
- *Metrics and* **analysis** *The performance of the content marketing efforts will be tracked and measured through metrics such as website traffic, engagement, and conversions. Data analysis will be used to continually optimize and improve the content marketing strategy.*

By following this strategic digital content marketing plan, Moonlit Apparel can effectively increase brand awareness and drive sales by creating and distributing high-quality, informative, and engaging content.

CHOOSING THE RIGHT DIGITAL CONTENT FORMATS

Consider the preferences and behaviour of your target audience to determine which digital content format is best for your business.

Asking the right questions can help guide this process, such as:

- Is text or visual content more appropriate for my audience?
- Should I focus on long-form or short-form content?
- Should I use stock or flow content?
- Should my content be gated or ungated?
- Should I create permanent or temporary content?

AUDIENCE PREFERENCES

Your audience's content format preferences can vary greatly depending on in-dividual preferences and needs. However, here is a potential list of digital con-tent formats sorted by preference based on what customers might generally expect from each:

1. Customers prefer **videos** due to their visual appeal and the ability to convey information concisely and engagingly.
2. Customers might prefer **social images** and **infographics** due to their visual appeal and ability to present information clearly and concisely.
3. Customers appreciate **blog posts** and **short articles** due to their ability to provide in-depth information and analysis on a particular topic.
4. Customers like **emails** and **newsletters** due to their convenience and ability to deliver information directly to their inboxes.
5. Customers prefer **PDF form** due to the ability to save and read the content later.

CREATE FOR MOBILE FIRST

Never assume that your text, images or videos will be seen from a desktop computer with a large screen and a broadband internet connection. By creating content that is **optimised for smartphones**, you can reach a wider audience and engage with them more effectively.

> Mobile first: ensure website's compatibility with mobile (directly affects its search rankings).
>
> Digital marketing like a PRO
> Clo Willaerts

Creating content optimised for consumption on mobile devices is essential for several reasons:

- Mobile devices are increasingly becoming the primary way people access the internet. In fact, **'mobile first'** is becoming the norm, with more and more people using their smartphones and tablets to browse the web, check social media, and consume other digital content.
- People spend more and more time on the go and increasingly rely on their mobile devices to stay connected. This means that it's essential to create content that is easily accessible and consumable on mobile devices, as it is more likely to be consumed by your audience.
- People tend to have a more personal and authentic connection to their mobile devices. This means that content optimised for consumption on mobile devices is more likely to engage and connect with your audience on a deeper level.

As a result, it's important to consider the unique challenges and opportunities of creating content for mobile devices. For example, vertical videos of people talking straight into the camera and short videos that can be watched without sound are both well-suited formats for consumption on mobile devices.

TRANSACTIONAL OR RELATIONSHIP-BUILDING CONTENT?

Regarding content marketing, there are two main types of content: transactional and relationship-building. **Transactional content** encourages a specific action, such as making a purchase or signing up for a newsletter. It is focused on the audience's immediate needs and is typically more promotional in nature.

Examples of transactional content include:

- Emails promoting a sale or special offers
- landing pages encouraging a purchase
- social media posts, including a call-to-action to make a purchase
- pop-up ads offering a discount or promotion
- pay-per-click ads directing the user to a purchase page
- print advertisements with a coupon or special offer
- product review pages with a 'buy now' button
- E-commerce product pages with pricing and purchase options

Transactional content is effective at driving conversions and can be a powerful tool for businesses looking to sell.

On the other hand, **relationship-building content** is designed to establish and strengthen the relationship between a brand and its audience. Therefore, it is not focused on a specific action and is not as promotional. Instead, it aims to provide value to the audience and build trust and credibility over time.

Examples of relationship-building content include:

- educational articles
- blog posts
- social media posts that provide valuable information or insights
- podcasts discussing industry trends and best practices
- infographics that visualize data or statistics
- webinars that provide expert insights and knowledge
- newsletters that provide valuable information to subscribers
- video tutorials that teach a new skill or provide helpful tips

This type of content is designed to engage the audience and establish a connection with them over the long term.

Businesses need to use transactional and relationship-building content in their marketing efforts. Transactional content can be effective at driving conversions. In contrast, relationship-building content can help to establish trust and credibility with the audience. By finding the right balance between the two, businesses can create a strong and effective content marketing strategy that meets their goals and objectives.

TEXT OR VISUAL?

The choice between text or visual content can be difficult for content marketers, as both have unique strengths and benefits. However, there are a few key reasons why **focusing on visuals** can be particularly effective:

- Visuals are processed 60,000 times faster than text. This means that people are more likely to quickly understand and retain information presented visually.
- Visuals play a significant role in processing information. It's estimated that 90% of the data transmitted to the brain is visual. Visuals are an essential part of how we process and understand information.

Video is a visual medium. 90% of information transmitted to the brain is visual, and visuals are processed 60,000 times faster in the brain than text.

Video Marketing like a PRO
Clo Willaerts

- Visuals can help to trigger attention. The human brain is wired to pay attention to visual stimuli, which can be an effective way to grab someone's attention and get them to engage with your content.

- By using visuals to convey information, you can help to reduce the cognitive load on your audience, making it easier for them to understand and retain the information you are presenting.

Using visuals in your content can engage your audience, convey information quickly and effectively, and help reduce cognitive load. Whether you focus on text or visual content will depend on your goals and audience, but incorporating visuals into your content marketing strategy can be a powerful way to engage and connect with your audience.

AUDIO FORMATS?

Audio content has become increasingly popular as more people listen to audio while on the go or multitasking. However, it's important to note that there may be circumstances where your audience might be unable to turn on audio, such as being in a public space or at work or when they do not have their headphones on. As a result, consider the strategic use of **audio formats** in your content marketing strategy while keeping in mind alternative options for those instances where audio might not be possible.

Several types of audio content can be used in your strategy, including:

1. **Podcasts** are a great way to share in-depth information and insights on a particular topic. They can be produced in various formats, including interviews, roundtable discussions, and solo shows.
2. **Audiobooks** are a great way to reach a wider audience, especially those who prefer to listen to content rather than read it. They can be used to share information on a particular topic or to promote a written book.
3. **Music streaming** can be used to build brand awareness and engage with audiences in a fun and interactive way.

When deciding which audio format to use, consider your audience and what they might be doing when they are listening, as well as the potential limitations they may face in terms of listening to audio.

For example, suppose your audience is primarily commuters. In that case, a podcast might be a good option as they can listen to it during their commute.

On the other hand, an audiobook might be a better option if your audience is mostly busy professionals, as they can listen to it while working.

Additionally, consider providing a written transcript of your audio content for those who may not be able to listen at that time.

VERTICAL OR HORIZONTAL VIDEO?

When it comes to content marketing, the choice of video format can be a tactical decision that can significantly impact the effectiveness of your message. Vertical and horizontal videos are two common formats, each with strengths and weaknesses.

Vertical video is often used for up-close and personal content, such as vlogs, social media stories, and live streams. The subject of the video is typically the creator, and the content is short and fleeting, meant to be consumed in the moment. This format is well-suited for creating a sense of intimacy and immediacy with the audience.

> Vertical videos are the default for mobile-first video platforms and ephemeral media like Stories (that disappear 24 hours).

Video Marketing Like a PRO
Clo Willaerts

On the other hand, **horizontal video** is typically used for storytelling, and the subject of the video can be anything. The format can range from a quick 6-second clip to a longer 6-hour film. In addition, horizontal videos are often archived and can be used for long-term content marketing strategies.

> Horizontal is perfect for storytelling. In theater, new elements are most often introduced on the left side of the stage. As they push the story forward, they move from left to right. This left-to-right movement still feels natural for actions in storytelling.

Video Marketing Like a PRO
Clo Willaerts

Here is a comparison table of the two formats:

Table 6. Vertical vs. Horizontal Video

ARGUMENT	VERTICAL VIDEO	HORIZONTAL VIDEO
Up-close and personal	Yes	No
Subject	Creator	Anything
Length	Short	Can range from 6 seconds to 6 hours
Archived	No	Yes
Fleeting	Yes	No
Telling a story	No	Yes

Ultimately, the choice between vertical and horizontal video formats will depend on your content marketing strategy's specific goals and objectives. Both formats have their strengths and weaknesses, and the best choice will depend on the message you want to communicate and the audience you are trying to reach.

LONG-FORM OR SHORT-FORM?

Long-form content refers to longer and more in-depth content, such as long articles, eBooks, or videos. Short-form content, on the other hand, refers to shorter and more concise content, such as social media posts, infographics, or memes.

In general, **long-form** content:

- provides detailed information;
- covers complex topics; and
- builds thought leadership and credibility.

It is also well-suited for in-depth research and analysis and for providing valuable insights and solutions to your audience.

Short-form content is best for:

- providing quick, bite-sized information;
- engaging with your audience;
- promoting your brand or products;
- sharing updates, announcements, or news; and
- driving traffic to your website or other content.

> TikTok is the leading destination for short-form mobile video and is very popular with younger generations.
>
> Video Marketing like a PRO
> Clo Willaerts

The ideal length of your content depends on your goals and your audience's preferences. It's best to offer a mix of long-form and short-form content to provide value and engage your audience.

Here are a few general guidelines to consider:

Table 7. Type of Text vs. Ideal Length

TYPE OF TEXT	IDEAL LENGTH
Website text lines	12 words
Titles and headlines (social media)	70 characters or fewer
Titles and headlines (websites and blog posts)	60 characters or fewer
Paragraphs	3-4 lines, maximum
Email subject lines	50 characters or fewer
Social media posts (Twitter)	280 characters or fewer
Social media posts (Facebook)	100 characters or more
Instagram captions	125 characters or fewer
Blog posts (search-optimized)	1,500 words
eBooks	30,000-50,000 words

Keep in mind that there is no one-size-fits-all solution regarding the ideal length of a piece of content. Focus on being useful to your audience rather than reaching a specific word count.

Ultimately, the key is to create valuable content that resonates with your audience, regardless of length.

EXAMPLE: RICOLA'S *SHE'S (COUGH) JUST A FRIEND* CAMPAIGN (2014)

Ricola's *She's (cough) Just a Friend* campaign is an excellent example of how short-form copy can be powerful in advertising. The campaign, launched in 2014, featured a series of short and witty print and television ads that used the tagline 'She's Just a (cough) Friend' to promote Ricola's cough drops.

The campaign's short-form copy was clever and memorable, making it easy for people to remember the brand and its message. The word 'friend' in the tagline was also clever because it made people think of the product as a friend they can rely on when they need it, which helps to establish a positive emotional connection to the brand.

The campaign's visuals were also simple and striking, featuring a silhouette of a person with a speech bubble that reads 'She's (cough) just a friend' and Ricola's logo. This simple yet effective visual helped to make the message clear and memorable, and it was easy for people to understand the message even if they saw the ad for only a moment.

The campaign also used different media to reach a broad audience, from print ads to TV commercials. Using humour and relatable situations helped engage the audience and make the message stick in their minds.

CASE IN POINT: KFC'S TENDER WINGS OF DESIRE BOOK

KFC's *Tender Wings of Desire* book was a marketing campaign that was launched in 2017 in celebration of Mother's Day. The campaign involved the publication of a 100-page romance novella written by KFC's mascot, Harland Sanders. The book was offered as a free eBook. It was marketed as a way for mothers to 'escape from motherhood into the arms of your fantasy Colonel'.

The campaign was designed to be humorous and playful, and it successfully generated buzz and attention for KFC. It was also a unique and unexpected way for the fast-food chain to connect with its audience and promote its products. The campaign was widely shared on social media and received coverage in various media outlets, helping to further increase its reach and visibility. KFC's *Tender Wings of Desire* book was a successful example of content marketing that used a creative and unexpected approach to engage with its audience and promote its brand.

CASE IN POINT: YUME CAMPING YOUTUBE SHORTS AND TIKTOK VIDEOS

Yume Camping is a content marketing campaign that showcases the power of **short-form video content** and audience engagement on multiple platforms. The founder of Yume Camping has established a strong presence on TikTok (tiktok.com/@campingtips100), where they post short snippets of their life spent camping alone. In 2023 their YouTube channel (youtube.com/@yumecamping6841) became even more popular, with over 500 million lifetime views and one million subscribers.

The channel's success on YouTube can be attributed to several factors. Firstly, the creator is open and transparent about their dislike for rain, and viewers love to see how they cope with it when it pours down on their camper van. This relatability and authenticity help to build trust and engagement with the audience. Secondly, the creator's content is visually stunning, with high-quality video and photography showcasing beauty of the great outdoors. This evokes a sense of wanderlust and adventure, likely attracting viewers passionate about camping and the outdoors.

Yume camping's goal is to monetise its content by selling camping equipment and accessories. The channel's website (yumecamping.com) offers a wide range of outdoor gear. In addition, they can drive conversions and increase sales by showcasing the equipment in action in their videos. This is an excellent example of how content marketing can build an engaged audience and drive revenue through e-commerce.

STOCK OR FLOW?

In content marketing, it's essential to strike a balance between creating content that stays, also known as 'stock', and content for social media feeds, also known as 'flow'. These content types serve different purposes and can effectively achieve different goals.

Stock content, as described by American author Robin Sloan, is durable stuff. The content is as interesting in two months or two years as it is today. This type of content is often discovered through search engines. It spreads slowly but surely, building a loyal following over time. Examples of stock content include blog posts, eBooks, whitepapers, and infographics.

Flow content, on the other hand, is the stream of daily and sub-daily updates that remind people you exist. It's the content you create for social media feeds, such as posts and tweets. Flow content is meant to be consumed quickly and is often used to drive engagement and traffic in the short term.

The magic formula, as Sloan suggests, is to maintain your flow while working on your stock in the background. This means regularly posting on social media and creating engaging flow content while investing in creating high-quality stock content that can drive long-term results. It is essential to consider the purpose and goals of your content marketing efforts when deciding between creating stock or flow content. Flow content may be more effective if your goal is to drive short-term engagement and traffic. Instead, focus on creating high-quality stock content to build a loyal following and drive long-term results.

> You can turn your flow into stock.
> For example, a lot of the ideas in
> this book started out as tweets,
> which then became blog posts,
> which then became book chapters.
> Small things, over time, can get big.

Show Your Work!: 10 Ways to Share Y...
Austin Kleon

Ultimately, the choice between creating stock or flow content should be guided by your overall content marketing strategy and the specific goals you hope to achieve. You can effectively reach and engage your target audience by striking a balance between the two and maintaining a consistent flow of content.

GATED OR UNGATED?

Gated content is digital content that lies behind a paywall or requires users to provide certain information, such as their name and email address, to access it. Gated content is often used as a lead generation tool, or sales funnel. This allows businesses and organisations to collect valuable information about potential leads, such as their name and email address, from which they can build targeted lists of potential leads to nurture. The content accessed can be used to showcase the business's research and expertise in the field. It is, of course, crucial to be transparent about the information that is being collected and to comply with privacy regulations and best practices.

Gated content can take the form of:

- **eBooks**
- **Webinars** that provide opportunities to engage with the audience in real-time
- **White papers**

On the other hand, **Ungated content** is freely accessible to anyone without any requirements or barriers, so it is not, necessarily an effective lead-generation tool. Nonetheless, it is essential to ensure that ungated content is valuable and relevant to the target audience to maximize its effectiveness. It is often used to provide value to audiences and build trust and credibility over time. Examples of ungated content include blog posts, articles, and social media posts that provide valuable information or insights to the audience, to build brand awareness, showcase the business's expertise or position them as a thought leader in the field .

Ungated content can take the form of:

-   **blog posts**
-   published **articles**
-   **social sites** where their interactivity affords the possibility to build relationships and trust with the audience

Ultimately, the choice between gated and ungated content should be based on the business or organization's specific goals and objectives and the target audience's needs and preferences:

-   Gated content can be an effective lead-generation tool. It is critical that gated content is valuable and relevant to the target audience to maximize its effectiveness.
-   Ungated content can be a useful way to build relationships with the audience and provide value. However, it may not be as effective for lead generation.

PERMANENT OR TEMPORARY?

Social media platforms like Instagram and Facebook have two main types of content: permanent and temporary. **Permanent** content, also known as '**Feed**' content, remains on the platform indefinitely unless it is deleted by the user. This includes posts on the user's profile page and any comments and likes on other users' posts.

Temporary content, also known as '**Stories**', is a type of content that disappears after a certain amount of time. For example, on Instagram, Stories last for 24 hours before disappearing, while on Facebook, Stories last for only 24 hours on the user's profile but can be added to a highlight reel, which remains on the user's profile indefinitely.

Snapchat introduced the Stories format in 2013, allowing users to share photos and videos that disappear after 24 hours. You can change the privacy settings on your Stories just like you would for posts, and Stories do not use captions, but many watch them with the sound off. Consider using text and visual overlays to provide context.

Other social media platforms soon copied the Stories format:

- Instagram introduced the Stories feature in 2016, allowing users to share photos and videos that disappear after 24 hours. The feature works similarly to Snapchat.
- Facebook introduced the Stories feature on its main and Messenger apps in 2017. The feature works similarly to Instagram and Snapchat, with photos playing for 5 seconds each and videos up to 60 seconds. TikTok introduced the Stories feature in 2020. The feature works similarly to Instagram, with photos playing for 5 seconds each and videos up to 20 seconds.
- LinkedIn introduced the Stories feature, called LinkedIn Stories, in 2020, then deactivated it in the same year due to lack of uptake by members. The feature worked similarly to Instagram, with photos playing for 5 seconds each and videos up to 20 seconds.

There are several ways to create permanently accessible content for social media platforms such as Instagram and Facebook. Here are a few options:

- Instead of creating a Story, you can create a post on your Instagram or Facebook feed. These posts will remain visible on your profile until you choose to delete them. You can also highlight specific posts on your profile for a more permanent presence.
- On Instagram, you can save your Stories to a **"Highlights"** section on your profile. This allows you to curate a collection of your best Stories and make them permanently visible to your followers.
- Facebook Pages: If you have a Facebook Page for your business or personal brand, you can use it to publish and save content that will remain visible indefinitely. This can include posts, photos, videos, and other types of content.

There are several reasons why a content marketer might choose to create content that is permanently accessible or saved rather than disappearing after a certain amount of time. This includes:

- **Building a more permanent online presence** for their business or organisation. This can be particularly useful for building trust and credibility with the audience, as it shows that the company is committed to providing valuable content over the long term.
- **Engaging with their audience over the long term**. This can be useful for building relationships with the audience and encouraging them to continue visiting and interacting with the content.
- **Improving their search engine ranking** because search engines tend to favour websites with a high volume of high-quality, long-form content that is regularly updated.
- **repurpose or reuse the content** in different formats or channels. For example, a blog post could be repurposed into an infographic or a podcast episode.

Content marketers need to consider their goals and objectives when deciding between temporary and permanent content types.

For example, suppose the goal is to engage with the audience over the long term and create a more permanent online presence. In that case, permanent content may be a more suitable choice. If, instead, the goal is to create a sense of urgency or to highlight current events or trends, then temporary content may be a more appropriate choice.

INSOURCED OR OUTSOURCED?

When it comes to content marketing, one of the key decisions brands must make is whether to insource or outsource production. Each approach has its own set of advantages and disadvantages, and the choice ultimately depends on the specific needs and goals of the brand.

In-housing, or **insourcing**, refers to a company producing content marketing internally with their own employees and resources. Brands like Microsoft (Microsoft Stories Newsroom), Ikea (Ingka Content Factory), Sony Pictures Entertainment (Performance Media Group), Anheuser-Busch InBev (Corona Studios), and more have been building in-house capabilities since 2020.

The main driver for building in-house capabilities is to retain control of media spending, brand voice, and other aspects of content production. In addition, in the current economic climate, brands seek to find cost-cutting opportunities.

On the other hand, **outsourcing**, hiring an external agency or freelancer to handle content production, is an effective means to tap into specialised expertise and quickly manage a large volume of content production. But these benefits may come with some loss of control over the production process and the final product, and they may have less visibility into the day-to-day work of the agency or freelancer.

Ultimately, the decision to insource or outsource content marketing production will depend on the specific needs and goals of the brand. For example, brands that prioritise control and long-term cost savings may opt to insource. In contrast, those who prioritise speed and access to specialised expertise may outsource.

Table 8. In-House vs. External Content Production

ACTIVITY	IN-HOUSE	EXTERNAL
Content Strategy	X	
Copywriting	X	
Website Updates through CRM	X	
Content Creation (e.g. blog posts, videos, infographics)	X	
Social Media Management	X	
Influencer Marketing		X
Paid Advertising		X
SEO	X	
Analytics and Reporting	X	
Email Marketing	X	

Note: X indicates that the activity is typically done in-house or can be done in-house. While empty cells indicate that the activity is typically done externally or can be done externally. The table is not limited to the given rows and can be added more as per the requirement.

Evaluate each approach's pros and cons and carefully consider the brand's specific needs before deciding.

PART 2
RUN

CREATING AND
DISTRIBUTING

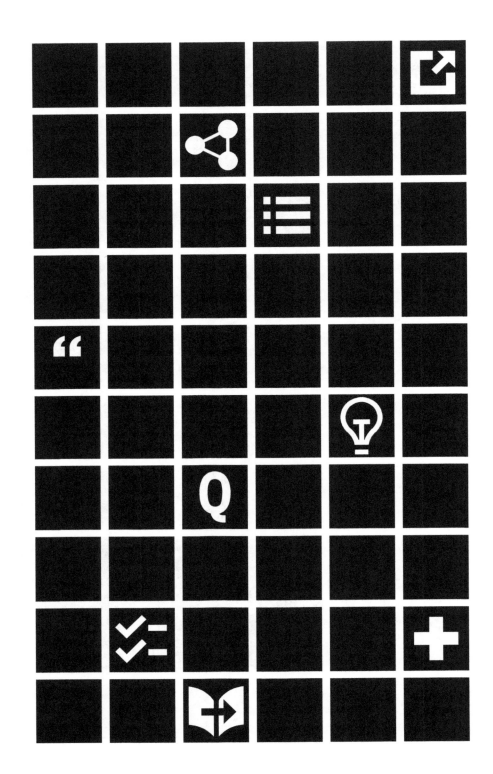

In the PREPARE section, we discussed the importance of creating a solid content marketing strategy and planning out your content. Now, it is time to put that plan into action and start executing on your chosen channels and tactics.

In this section, we will go over the different channels available for content marketing and the tactics you can use to engage with your audience and drive results. We will also discuss how to measure the success of your content marketing efforts and make any necessary adjustments along the way.

By the end of this chapter, you will have a deep understanding of the channels and tactics available to you, and you will be equipped with the knowledge and tools to effectively run your content marketing campaign.

03

CREATING EFFECTIVE DIGITAL CONTENT

IDENTIFYING YOUR BRAND'S VISUAL STYLE

Defining your brand's **visual style** is essential because it helps create a consistent and cohesive image for your company. By identifying the types of images representing your brand, you can make sure that all your marketing materials and products convey the same message and aesthetic. Some examples of images that can help define the visual style of your brand include:

- **Brand style guides** that outline the visual elements of a brand, including colours, fonts, and images.
- **Banners** are images, often large, commonly used as headers or backgrounds on websites or advertising.
- **Buttons** are small images representing actions, such as clicking to view more information or make a purchase.
- **Ads** are images to promote products or services, often in the form of banner ads or display ads.
- **Promo images** to promote a specific product or event, often in the form of a banner or poster.
- **Blog post images** to accompany blog posts or articles, often to illustrate a point or add visual interest.
- **Newsletter images** for email newsletters, often to promote products or events.

- **Social media images** for social media platforms, such as profile pictures or posts.
- **Physical product images** of the actual product that are often used in online stores or catalogues.
- **Lifestyle images** that depict a product used in a real-life setting are often used to show how the product fits into a person's lifestyle.
- **Stock-style images** that are pre-made images that can be purchased and used for various purposes, such as website backgrounds or blog post images.

IDENTIFYING YOUR BRAND'S CONTENT STYLE

Your brand's content style is the unique way your business communicates and interacts with your customers. It plays a crucial role in shaping how your customers perceive your brand.

> Words matter. Your words (what you say) and style (how you say it) are your most cherished (and, yet, undervalued) assets.
>
> Everybody Writes
> Ann Handley

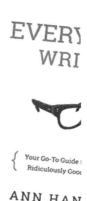

Identifying your brand's unique content style is essential for creating compelling digital content. It is a process of experimentation and iteration and will involve reviewing your existing content, considering your brand values and audience, and monitoring and tracking the performance of your content.

Start by reviewing the content that your brand has already produced, such as blog posts, videos, social media posts, and other materials. This will give you a sense of the tone, voice, and overall style of your brand's existing content.

Next, consider the **values** and **personality** of your brand. What makes your brand unique? What are the core values that you want to communicate through your content? This will help to guide the tone and voice of your content.

Values and personality are important aspects of a brand, as they help to differentiate the brand from its competitors and create a unique and consistent brand identity. Some examples of values and personality that a brand might have include:

TRUSTWORTHINESS AND RELIABILITY

A brand that positions itself as **trustworthy** and **reliable** might emphasise its commitment to customer satisfaction, its history of successful products or services, or its adherence to industry standards and regulations.

You'll find examples of this type of brands in the banking and health industry (**KBC, Johnson & Johnson**). In the car industry, **Toyota**'s personality is defined by its long-lasting and high-quality products.

Its content should emphasise a brand's:

- commitment to customer satisfaction;
- history of successful products or services; and
- its adherence to industry standards and regulations.

This could include content such as:

- case studies or customer testimonials that showcase how the brand has helped its customers to achieve their goals;
- detailed product or service descriptions that highlight the features and benefits of the brand's offerings;
- industry news and updates that demonstrate the brand's expertise and knowledge in its field; and
- FAQs or other resources that provide clear and accurate information about the brand's products or services.

FUN AND PLAYFUL

A brand that has a **fun** and **playful** personality might use humour, lighthearted language, or colourful and imaginative visuals in its content. This can help to create a sense of excitement and engagement with the audience.

> Humor is highly subjective, and there's no guarantee that you have what it takes to make someone else laugh. If you try to be funny and no one laughs, you end up with one terrible video.

Video Marketing Like a PRO
Clo Willaerts

A brand that has a fun and playful personality might create:

- content that uses humour, lighthearted language; or
- colourful and imaginative visuals.

This could include content such as:

- Quizzes or games that engage the audience and make the content more interactive and enjoyable.
- Humorous or whimsical blog posts or social media posts that use humour to convey a message or promote a product or service.
- Creative videos or infographics that use animation or other visual effects to bring the content to life in a fun and engaging way.
- Contests or promotions that use playful language and offer exciting prizes to engage the audience and drive action.

Many brands are known for creating funny and humorous content as part of their marketing and branding efforts to engage with their audience and build a strong brand identity. Here are a few examples of brands that are famous for making the most entertaining content:

- **Old Spice** is a personal care brand known for its humorous and memorable advertising campaigns. The company's *The Man, Your Man Could Smell Like* campaign, which featured actor Isaiah Mustafa, was a viral hit and helped to establish Old Spice as a fun and humorous brand.
- **Skittles** is a fruit-flavoured candy brand known for its humorous and offbeat advertising campaigns. The company's *Taste the Rainbow* slogan and tagline have become iconic. Its ads often feature bizarre and humorous scenarios and characters.
- **Snickers** is a chocolate bar brand known for its humorous advertising campaigns. The company's *You're Not You When You're Hungry* campaign, which features celebrities and other famous figures acting out of character when hungry, is a classic example of the brand's humorous approach.

BOLD AND INNOVATIVE

A brand that positions itself as **bold** and **innovative** might create content that focuses on its:

- cutting-edge products or services;
- its leadership in the industry; or
- its commitment to pushing the boundaries of what is possible.

For examples, look at the content marketing of companies like **Tesla**, **Apple**, **Google**, or **SpaceX**.

This could include content such as:

- **Product demonstrations** or previews that showcase the latest and greatest features of the brand's offerings.
- **Industry insights** or thought leadership articles that provide unique perspectives on the latest trends and developments in the industry.
- **News or announcements** about the brand's latest partnerships, collaborations, or initiatives that demonstrate its commitment to innovation and progress.
- **Case studies** or success stories that highlight the brand's impact and success in helping its customers to achieve their goals.

LUXURIOUS AND SOPHISTICATED

A brand that has a luxurious and sophisticated personality might use high-end visuals, elegant language, and exclusive offers in its content. This can help to create a sense of exclusivity and prestige for the brand.

Some examples of this type of brand personality are **Louis Vuitton**, **Rolex**, **Mercedes Benz** and **Tiffany & Co**.

A brand that has a luxurious and sophisticated personality might create content that uses:

-   high-end visuals;
-   elegant language; and
-   exclusive offers to create a sense of exclusivity and prestige.

This could include content such as:

-   Product or service demonstrations that showcase the luxury and sophistication of the brand's offerings.
-   High-quality images or videos that capture the luxurious feel of the brand's products or services.
-   Exclusive promotions or offers that are only available to a select group of customers, such as members of a loyalty program or VIP club.
-   Influencer partnerships or collaborations that help to elevate the brand's image and create a sense of luxury and sophistication.

> A critical step in developing great content is to develop your own distinct voice.

Content Rules
Ann Handley, C.C. Chapman, and Davi...

Your brand's personality defines the tone and voice of your content. Is it formal or informal, serious or humorous, direct or indirect?

The tone and style of your content should be appropriate for your brand and your target audience. They should be consistent across all your digital content.

ALIGNING YOUR BRAND'S VOICE AND TONE

Identifying your brand's unique content style, also known as tone and voice, is essential in creating compelling digital content. **Tone** refers to the attitude or mood conveyed in your content. In contrast, **voice** refers to your content's overall personality and style.

> No one likes phoniness. Try to be as authentic as you can in your storytelling. It'll make your brand more relatable.
>
> The Stripped-Down Guide to Content ...
> John Egan

> Your brand's voice is the consistent expression of your brand through words and writing styles that engage and motivate. Words have power! Your brand's tone adds a specific flavor to your voice based on the context: factors like audience, situation and channel.Think of it in terms of your own voice and tone: you have one voice, but you probably use a particular tone when you are talking to friends or family, and an entirely different one with your boss or customers.
>
> Digital Marketing Like a PRO
> Clo Willaerts

By aligning your brand's tone and voice with your values and goals and considering your target audience, you can create authentic, consistent, engaging content that resonates with your customers.

For the fictional brand Moonlit Apparel, defining the brand's values and goals might involve identifying the following:

- **Mission statement** Moonlit Apparel is dedicated to creating comfortable, stylish, and sustainable clothing that empowers people to embrace their unique identities.
- **Brand personality** Moonlit Apparel is a fun, adventurous, and inclusive brand that values creativity, individuality, and sustainability.
- **Target audience** Moonlit Apparel's target audience is young adults looking for stylish and comfortable clothing that reflects their values and identities. This includes people who are interested in sustainability, adventure, and self-expression.

By defining these values and goals, Moonlit Apparel can create content that is authentic, consistent, and aligned with the brand's mission and target audience. This can build a strong brand identity and connect with customers in a meaningful way.

Here's an example for the product page of Moonlit's signature hoodie:

> *Get ready to conquer any adventure in style with Moonlit Apparel's signature hoodie. Made from eco-friendly materials and featuring unique designs, this hoodie is perfect for you. Plus, with our commitment to sustainability, you can feel good about your purchase. Order your Moonlit Apparel signature hoodie now and let the adventures begin.*

WHERE TO FIND CONTENT INSPIRATION

Content marketing can effectively reach and engage your target audience, but finding ideas for your content can be a challenge. Here are some practical tips for finding inspiration for your content marketing efforts:

- **Keyword research tools** can help you identify the types of content that are likely to interest your target audience. Look for keywords and phrases with high search volume and consider creating content around those topics.
- **Social media and online forums** can be a great source of inspiration for content ideas. Keep an eye on what topics are being discussed and consider creating content that addresses those issues or questions.
- Pay attention to what your **competitors** are doing with their content marketing efforts. This can help you identify gaps in the market that you can fill with your own content.
- **Customer feedback** can be a valuable source of inspiration for your content marketing efforts. See surveys, social media comments, and reviews to see what topics your audience is interested in and create content addressing those issues.

By keeping these sources in mind, you should be able to find plenty of input and ideas for your content calendar. Just remember to keep your target audience in mind and create valuable and relevant content.

TOOL: FEEDLY

Feedly.com is a powerful tool for finding and organizing content to curate and share with your audience. By regularly using Feedly to discover and keep track of the latest developments in your industry, you can stay up-to-date and create a well-rounded content marketing strategy.

To use Feedly, create a free account and set up your interests and topics. Search for and follow websites, blogs, and other sources that cover your chosen topics. Feedly will then aggregate the latest articles and content from these sources into a single feed, making it easy to find and organize relevant content.

You can also use Feedly's advanced search functionality to find specific types of content, such as infographics or thought leadership articles. You can also use Feedly's categorization and tagging features to organize your content and make it easier to find later.

KEYWORD RESEARCH AS A SOURCE OF INSPIRATION

Keyword research is a valuable tool for content marketers, as it can help you identify the types of content that are likely to interest your target audience.

> Use answerthepublic.com to reveal the most popular questions being asked in web search. Using auto-suggest data from search engines like Google, you'll be able to discover what people really want to know about the world's biggest organisations.
>
> Digital Marketing Like a PRO
> Clo Willaerts

By looking for keywords and phrases with high search volume, you can create timely, relevant content that resonates with your audience. Below is an example of how keyword research can be used to inspire your content marketing efforts.

Table 9. Example of Keyword Research

TYPE OF CONTENT	HIGH VOLUME KEYWORD	CONTENT
Blog post	streetwear hoodies	'10 Streetwear Hoodies to Elevate Your Wardrobe' Streetwear fashion is all about making a statement, and what better way to do that than with a trendy hoodie? From oversized and slouchy to fitted and sleek, there's a streetwear hoodie out there for every style. In this post, we'll be showcasing 10 of the hottest streetwear hoodies on the market that are sure to elevate your wardrobe. [etc.]

Instagram post	skater sneakers	Are you a skater in need of a new pair of sneakers? We've rounded up the best sneakers for skaters, so you can shred in style and comfort. Whether you need a shoe that can withstand the wear and tear of the skatepark or something sleek for street skating, we've got you covered. Check out our top picks below and get ready to dominate the skate scene. #skatersneakers #skatepark #skatestyle
YouTube Video	streetwear brands	'Streetwear Brands to Know in 2022" Description: Stay ahead of the fashion game with our list of the top streetwear brands to know in 2022. From established names to up-and-coming labels, these brands are making waves in the streetwear scene and are worth keeping on your radar. Whether you're a streetwear fanatic or just looking to add some fresh brands to your wardrobe, this video has you covered. Tags: - streetwear brands - fashion - style - clothing - 2022 trends - street style - brand recommendations - streetwear fashion - trendy brands

PAY HEED TO SOCIAL MEDIA FOR CONTENT IDEAS

Social media and online forums can be valuable inspiration for content marketing. By keeping an eye on what topics are being discussed and what questions are being asked, you can create content that addresses the needs and interests of your target audience. Here are a few ways you can use social media and online forums to find content inspiration:

- Keep an eye on relevant **hashtags** on social media platforms like Twitter, Instagram, and TikTok. These hashtags give you a sense of what topics are trending and what issues are being discussed by your target audience.

- Follow **industry influencers** on social media to see what types of content they share and what topics they discuss. This can suggest content that is relevant and timely.
- Join **online forums** related to your industry and keep an eye on the discussed topics. These forums can be a great source of inspiration for content that addresses the needs and interests of your target audience.

WATCHING (BUT NEVER COPYING) YOUR COMPETITORS

Monitoring your competitors can be a valuable source of inspiration for your content marketing efforts. By paying attention to what your competitors are doing with their content marketing, you can get a sense of what is working for them and what gaps may exist in the market that you can fill with your own content. Here are a few tips for finding inspiration by watching your competitors:

- Sign up for your **competitors' newsletters** to see what content they are creating and how they position themselves in the market.
- **Follow them on social media** to see what types of content they are sharing and what topics they are discussing.
- Look at your competitors' **websites** to see what content they are creating and how they organise it. This can give you ideas for your own content and help you identify gaps in the market; let it inspire you to create unique and valuable material.

Just remember, it is important to never copy your competitors' content.

> Do a competitive analysis of other content creators in your space. Pay attention to what's out there so you can learn from other people's successes and failures.
>
> Hook Point
> Brendan Kane

> You should learn from your competitor but never copy. Copy, and you die. (Jack Ma, founder and CEO of the Alibaba Group)

Digital Marketing Like a PRO
Clo Willaerts

CUSTOMER FEEDBACK AS CONTENT INPUT

Customer feedback is a valuable source of inspiration for your content marketing efforts. By looking at surveys, social media comments, and reviews, you can get a sense of what topics your audience is interested in and what issues they are trying to solve.

> Collecting customer feedback used to be too time-consuming, not to mention expensive. Thanks to customers' extensive use of online and other digital channels, this type of market research has evolved from pen-and-paper surveys, one-on-one interviews and focus group discussions into something more instant and convenient for all parties involved.

Digital Marketing Like a PRO
Clo Willaerts

Here are a few tips for using customer feedback to stimulate your creation of relevant and timely content that addresses the needs of your audience:

- Look for **common themes** to develop ideas on content tactics.
- Pay attention to the **questions that your customers are asking**, whether it is through surveys, social media, or reviews to identify their needs and interests.
- Look for customer feedback that highlights **pain points** or challenges that your audience is facing to conceive of solutions you can offer to your audience.

DATA BASED STORYTELLING

Data-based storytelling is a way to present data to an audience through storytelling to engage and inform them. It involves using data insights from a company's data set to create a story that is informative and enjoyable for the audience.

> Inspiration means your content is inspired by data (more on this later) or it's creatively inspired (or both). It's fresh, different, well-written, well-produced, nicely designed—and it feels like it could come only from you.
>
> Everybody Writes
> Ann Handley

Content marketing professionals can use this technique to show a company's knowledge and leadership while providing valuable information to its audience. It can be presented in different formats, such as blog posts, videos, infographics, or interactive tools.

The effective use of this technique requires analytical skills to find and understand relevant trends in the data and the ability to craft a compelling narrative.

Here are some tips on how to unearth exciting insights and trends within a company's data set:

- Identify the fundamental **questions or problems you want to address** before diving into the data. Decide what you want to achieve or learn from it. Identifying key questions or problems upfront will help you find the most relevant insights.
- **Clean and organize the data** before analysing it to ensure it is organised in a usable format. This may involve remove errors or inconsistencies and rearranging it.
- **Visualise the data** to ease the identification of patterns and trends that may not be detectable in the raw data. Tools like charts, graphs, and maps can help you understand the data more intuitively and interactively.
- **Test and validate your findings** to ensure they are accurate and supported by the data. This may involve testing different hypotheses or using statistical techniques to confirm your results.
- Data can be dry and uninteresting. To make it more compelling, try to find **connections** between different data points, and put the data in **context**. For example, consider how the data relates to broader market trends or customer needs when analysing sales data.
- Once you have identified interesting insights and trends within the data, the next step is to craft a story around those insights to make the data more engaging and compelling. This may involve **storytelling techniques**, such as setting the scene, introducing characters, and providing a clear narrative arc.

EXAMPLE: OKCUPID

OkCupid.com , a dating website launched in 2001, could leverage its data to create engaging and shareable content that not only attracted millions of views and social media shares but also garnered significant press attention.

OkCupid had millions of data points on a universally appealing topic: dating and relationships. By analysing this data, the OkCupid team was able to uncover insights and trends that were not only interesting but also had the potential to challenge societal norms and spark conversations.

For example, OkCupid used its data to show that men, regardless of age, tend to prefer women in their 20s. In contrast, women tend to seek out similarly aged partners as they age. The team also analysed data on race and messaging and found that African American women sent the most messages but received the fewest responses. They also identified key features of a message that increase the likelihood of a response.

Creating compelling data-based stories requires a significant investment of time and resources. For example, the OkCupid team had two full-time bloggers working on its blog, which is a substantial commitment for a start-up. It also requires a keen eye for finding interesting insights and trends within the data and the ability to craft a story that engages and informs the audience.

However, the rewards of data-based storytelling can be significant. By using data to tell engaging and shareable stories, companies like OkCupid were able to attract a large and engaged audience, as well as considerable press attention.

TOOLS FOR CONTENT DISCOVERY

Many tools and resources are available to help content marketers discover new ideas and inspiration for their campaigns.

INSPIRING NEWSLETTERS

Newsletters are a valuable tool for content discovery. They allow users to receive regular updates on the latest news and trends in their chosen fields of interest. Subscribing to newsletters from industry leaders, thought leaders and other relevant information sources can help keep you informed and inspire new ideas for content marketing.

Here are some newsletters that might be relevant and useful for content marketers:

- The Content Marketing Institute's newsletter (contentmarketinginstitute. com/articles/tag/newsletter/) updates the latest trends, research, and best practices in content marketing.

- Joe Pulizzi's newsletter, The Tilt (thetilt.com/tilt-author/joe-pulizzi), covers content marketing and strategy topics.
- The MarketingProfs Today newsletter (marketingprofs.com/newsletters/marketing/) features articles, research, and insights on various marketing topics, including content marketing.
- HubSpot's Marketing Blog newsletter (blog.hubspot.com/marketing) provides updates on the latest marketing trends and strategies, including content marketing.
- The Moz Blog's newsletter (hsinfo.moz.com/moz_blog_subscribe) covers a wide range of topics related to search engine optimization (SEO) and online marketing, including content marketing.
- Social Media Examiner's newsletter (socialmediaexaminer.com/subscribe/) updates the latest social media marketing strategies, including content marketing.
- Copyblogger's newsletter (copyblogger.com/subscribe/) covers topics related to copywriting and content marketing, including tips, techniques, and case studies.
- Contently's newsletter (contently.com/topic/newsletter/) updates the latest trends and best practices in content marketing.

In addition to subscribing to newsletters from established sources, you can create your own newsletter to share your content and insights with your audience. This can help to build your brand and establish yourself as a thought leader in your industry.

REDDIT, ALLTOP, QUORA AND TRENDSPOTTR

Reddit.com is a popular social media platform that can be a valuable source of inspiration for content marketing. With more than 36 million user accounts and billions of comments, it is a vast repository of information and ideas on various topics.

To use Reddit for content marketing, start by identifying the relevant **subreddits** (forums dedicated to specific topics) that align with your brand and target audience. These subreddits can provide valuable insights into the interests and concerns of your audience, as well as ideas for content that may interest them.

Here are a few examples of subreddits:

- /r/videos: dedicated to sharing and discussing videos on a variety of topics
- /r/AskReddit: a forum for asking and answering questions on any topic
- /r/gifs: a collection of GIFs (short, looping video clips) on various topics
- /r/pics: a collection of images on various topics
- /r/funny: humorous content on various topics
- /r/news: a collection of news articles and discussions on current events
- /r/science: a forum for discussing scientific topics and news
- /r/technology: a forum for discussing technology and tech news
- /r/books: a forum for discussing books and literature
- /r/food: a forum for discussing food, cooking, and recipes

Once you have identified the relevant subreddits, engage with the community by participating in discussions and asking for feedback and ideas. This can help you better understand your audience's needs and preferences and generate ideas for content that will be valuable and resonant with them.

Remember that Reddit is a platform that allows for open and uncensored discussion, so you may encounter potentially **NSFW** (not safe for work) content while using it. So be prepared for this and use your discretion when browsing the platform.

With the right subject matter, a targeted strategy, and a bit of luck, your content marketing efforts on Reddit have the potential to go viral and reach a large audience. By engaging with the community and creating valuable and engaging content, you can leverage the power of Reddit to inspire and drive your content marketing efforts.

A few other places where you might find content ideas:

- AllTop.com is a news aggregator that collects and organises articles from various sources on various topics. It can be a helpful tool for finding relevant and timely content for your audience.
- TrendSpottr.com is a tool that helps users to identify and track emerging trends and topics in real-time. It can be a valuable source of inspiration for creating timely and relevant content that resonates with your audience.
- Quora.com is a question-and-answer platform where users can ask and answer various topics. It can be a valuable source of inspiration for content

marketing, as it provides insights into the questions and concerns of your target audience.

CONTENT TACTICS

Content tactics refer to the specific strategies and techniques used to execute a content marketing plan. These tactics can take many forms, such as creating blog posts, producing videos, designing infographics, or developing interactive tools.

The choice of tactics will depend on the content marketing campaign's goals and the target audience's preferences. Therefore, it is important to regularly assess the effectiveness of different content tactics and adjust as needed to achieve the desired results.

CONTENT TACTICS WITH A BRAND FOCUS

Content marketing is essential for building a solid brand and connecting with your target audience. One approach to content marketing is focusing on the brand rather than solely on the customer. By highlighting your brand's unique value proposition, mission, and personality, you can create a narrative that resonates with your audience and differentiates your brand from competitors.

A brand-focused content marketing strategy can help establish your brand as a thought leader in your industry, build trust and credibility with your audience, and ultimately drive conversions and sales.

MODEL: BRAND NARRATIVE FRAMEWORK

The following table presents a content framework for brand-focused content marketing. It outlines the key elements that should be included in your content to effectively connect with and engage your target audience. By focusing on how they live their lives, the problem they have, the final straw that drove them to taking action, who can help them (your brand), how they will change through success derived from your brand and how life will look without the problem that your brand solved for them, you can create a compelling narrative that resonates with your audience and positions your brand as a solution to their pain points and struggles.

Table 10. Brand Narrative Framework Examples

ELEMENTS	DESCRIPTION
How They Live Their Lives	Target audience's daily routines, habits, and struggles
The Problem They Have	Specific problem that the target audience is facing
The Final Straw Before Taking Action	Moment when the target audience realises that they need to take action
Who Will Help Them (Your Brand)	Introduction of your brand and how it can help solve their problem
How They will Change Through Success	Positive changes and benefits the target audience will experience
How Life Looks Without the Problem	The outcome and picture of how life will be different and better without the problem

COMPANY PAGES

Company pages are a great way to provide information about your business and build trust with your audience. These pages can include information about your company's history, mission, values, and team members. They can also have press releases, awards, accolades, and customer testimonials. In addition to providing valuable information, company pages can help improve your search engine optimisation and establish your brand as an authority in your industry.

Brand storytelling: Use your content to tell your brand's story and what makes it unique. This can involve sharing your brand's history, mission, and values and highlighting customer stories and successes.

Here is an example from Moonlit Apparel:

Moonlit Apparel was founded in the early 2010s by a group of friends who were passionate about streetwear fashion and skateboarding culture. The brand was born out of a desire to create high-quality, stylish clothing that reflected their love for these subcultures.

The founders of Moonlit Apparel were a close-knit group of friends who had been skateboarding and hanging out in the same circles for years. They had always dreamed of starting their own clothing brand and finally decided to turn their passion into a business. They started small, designing and producing their first collection in a shared workshop in their hometown.

As the brand grew, Moonlit Apparel gained a dedicated following of customers who appreciated their commitment to authenticity and quality. In addition, the brand became known for its unique, edgy designs and commitment to sustainability and social responsibility. Today, Moonlit Apparel continues to tell its story through its content, sharing its history, mission, and values and highlighting customer stories and successes.

PRODUCT AND SERVICE PAGES

By creating clear and compelling content that showcases the value of your products and services, you can effectively market and sell to your target audience.

Product pages are essential for showcasing and selling your products. A good product page should provide detailed information about the product, including features, benefits, specifications, and pricing. It should also include high-quality product images and customer reviews to help potential buyers make informed purchasing decisions.

Introducing the Moonlit Apparel Signature Hoodie!
Made from soft, high-quality fabric, this hoodie is the perfect combination of comfort and style. It features a sleek, modern design with the iconic Moonlit Apparel logo on the front. The hoodie also has a kangaroo pocket, ribbed cuffs and hem, and a drawstring hood.

Not only is this hoodie stylish, but it's also practical. It's made from a blend of cotton and polyester that is durable and easy to care for. It's also designed to keep you warm on cool evenings, making it the perfect addition to any streetwear wardrobe.

In addition to its features and benefits, the Moonlit Apparel Signature Hoodie is also affordable. Furthermore, it's available in a range of sizes from small to XL, making it suitable for many customers.

Check out our product images and customer reviews to see why the Moonlit Apparel Signature Hoodie is a must-have for any streetwear enthusiast. Order yours today and join the Moonlit Apparel community!

Service pages are an important way to showcase and sell your services to potential clients. These pages clearly outline the services you offer, the benefits of each service, and any relevant pricing information. It is an example for the imaginary Personalised Workout Plans for Seniors service, SeniorFit:

Welcome to SeniorFit!

Are you a senior looking to stay active and healthy through exercise but needing help sticking to a consistent workout routine? Our team at SeniorFit is here to help.

We offer personalised workout plans and coaching services for seniors. Our team of certified trainers will work with you to develop a program tailored to your fitness goals, needs, and abilities. We will also provide ongoing support and encouragement to help you stay motivated and on track.

With our services, you will receive the following:

- *__Customised workout plans__ We will develop a programme tailored to your specific goals, needs, and abilities.*
- *__One-on-one coaching__ Our trainers will provide ongoing support and encouragement to help you stay motivated and on track.*
- *__Flexible scheduling__ We offer a range of scheduling options to accommodate your busy schedule.*
- *__Affordable pricing__ We offer competitive pricing for our services, making it easy for seniors to stay active and healthy.*

Do not let age hold you back from living a healthy and active lifestyle. Contact us today to learn more about our services and how we can help you reach your fitness goals.

CASE STUDIES

Case studies, in the form of written narratives or video testimonials from satisfied customers,

are a powerful tool for demonstrating the value and effectiveness of your products or services to potential customers. By sharing real-life examples of how your business has helped others solve a problem or achieve a goal, you can showcase your offerings' results and benefits in a credible, compelling and persuasive way.

It is an example for SeniorFit:

> Hi, my name is Iris, and I'm a senior citizen. I've always been active and loved staying fit. Still, as I've gotten older, it's become harder and harder to stick to a consistent workout routine. That's where SeniorFit has been a game changer for me.
>
> I've been working with SeniorFit for the past few months, and I've seen such a difference in my health and well-being. The personalized workout plans and one-on-one coaching have been so helpful in keeping me motivated and on track. And the flexible scheduling has been perfect for my busy schedule.
>
> I can't recommend SeniorFit enough. If you are a senior looking to stay active and healthy, give them a try. You won't be disappointed. Thanks, SeniorFit!

PRODUCT DEMOS AND TUTORIALS

Product demos and tutorials are another effective way to showcase the features, benefits and problems your products solve to potential buyers.

Product demos can take many forms, such as videos, infographics, or written guides. They can be a potent tool for complex or technical products. In addition, they can help potential buyers visualise how the product works and how it can be used in their own lives or businesses.

On the other hand, **tutorials** can help demonstrate how to use your products or provide step-by-step instructions for specific tasks. These can be especially useful for software or online products. In addition, they can help users become more familiar with the product's features and functionality.

It is an example tutorial for our meal-planning app, PlatePlanner:

Welcome to PlatePlanner! This tutorial will walk you through how to create a personalised meal plan using our app.

1. *To get started, sign up for an account on our app.*
2. *Once you've signed up, you will be taken to the meal planning page. You can select your dietary preferences and restrictions by clicking on the 'Preferences' tab.*
3. *After you have set your preferences, you can generate a personalised meal plan by clicking the 'Generate Meal Plan' button.*
4. *Our app will create a customised meal plan based on your preferences and restrictions. You can view your meal plan by clicking on the 'Meal Plan' tab.*
5. *You can also use our shopping list feature to ensure you have all the ingredients you need for your meals. Simply click on the 'Shopping List' tab to view the ingredients for each meal.*
6. *That's it! With PlatePlanner, meal planning is easy and convenient. Start using our app today and take control of your health and wellness. We hope you enjoy using PlatePlanner and see a difference with it.*

These types of content can also help provide step-by-step instructions or demonstrate how to use your products. Creating and promoting product demos and tutorials can help potential customers make informed decisions about whether your products are right for them.

FAQS

Help potential buyers better understand your offerings and make informed purchasing decisions by providing clear and concise answers to common questions about your products or services. Here are some tips for writing practical **FAQs**:

- Start by **brainstorming** a list of questions your customers or clients might have about your products or services, such as pricing, features, compatibility, or anything else on their minds.
- Organise the questions into logical **categories or themes**. This will help make the FAQs easier to navigate and more user-friendly.
- Keep the answers **brief and to the point**. Use clear, concise language and avoid unnecessary jargon or technical terms.

- Use **bullet points or numbered lists** to break up long blocks of text and make the FAQs easier to scan.
- Consider using **images or videos** to illustrate your points and make the FAQs more engaging.

By following these tips, you can create FAQs that are helpful, informative, and easy to understand, which can ultimately lead to more informed and satisfied customers.

ADVERTISING IN 3 BEATS MODEL

Advertising with a strong brand focus is essential to any content marketing strategy. One of the most effective ways to do this is through ad campaigns. **Ad campaigns** allow brands to create consistent messages and images that resonate with the target audience.

Focusing on consumer gains in advertising is a best practice because it highlights the benefits that the customer will receive by choosing a particular product or service, so that the ad resonates with the target audience and creates a sense of value.

The *Advertising in 3 Beats* model is a framework that can be used to structure an ad campaign and ensure that it is focused on consumer gains. The model has three main elements: Customer Promise, Proof, and Price.

- The **customer promise** is the statement the brand makes about the benefits the customer will receive by choosing the product or service. It should be a clear and concise statement that communicates the product's or service's value to the customer.
- The **proof** is the evidence that supports the promise. It can be in the form of testimonials, statistics, or demonstrations that show how the product or service has delivered value to other customers. The proof serves to build trust and credibility with the target audience.
- The **Price** is the final call-to-action of the ad and is intended to drive the customer to take action. It should be presented in a clear and easy-to-understand format. It should include any discounts or promotions that are currently available.

By using the *Advertising in 3 Beats* model, brands can create ad campaigns that are focused on consumer gains and are more likely to resonate with the target audience. This approach can build trust and credibility with the target audience and drive conversions.

CASE: COCA-COLA ADVERTISING

Coca-Cola is a classic example of a brand that has used ad campaigns to build a strong brand identity. Throughout the years, Coca-Cola has used a variety of slogans and taglines to promote its brand. Some of the most iconic slogans include 'The Real Thing', 'Open Happiness', and 'Taste the Feeling'. Each slogan captures the essence of the Coca-Cola brand and evokes a sense of joy and happiness.

Coca-Cola's advertising strategy highlights the benefits that the customer will receive by choosing Coca-Cola.

- The **promise** is the brand's statement, such as 'You will be happy if you buy Coke!'
- The **proof** is the evidence that supports the promise, such as 'All of these people are happy, and they drink Coke!'
- The **price** is the final call-to-action of the ad, such as '$4.99 for a twelve-pack! Here's a coupon for $1 off'!

CAMPAIGN MATERIAL

When creating content for a specific campaign or offer, it is essential to focus on making the value of your offer clear and compelling to your target audience. Here are a few strategies you can use to create compelling content for a specific campaign or offer:

1. Creating dedicated **landing pages** for specific campaigns or offers can help you capture leads and drive conversions. These pages should be consistent with your brand's messaging and aesthetic. They should clearly communicate the value of your offer to the user.

2. Use targeted **email campaigns** to promote your offer to your email list. Make sure to clearly explain the value of your offer and provide a clear call to action.
3. Use **social media** to promote your offer and drive traffic to your landing page. Create engaging posts that showcase the value of your offer and include a clear call to action.
4. Partner with **influencers or industry experts** to promote your offer and reach a new audience. Collaborate on content showcasing your offer's value and including a call to action.
5. Use **paid advertising** channels such as Google AdWords or social media advertising to reach a targeted audience and drive traffic to your landing page.

An example of a launch campaign for a meal-planning app called PlatePlanner.

Objective: *To increase awareness and adoption of PlatePlanner by health-conscious individuals looking for a convenient and personalised solution for meal planning.*

Target Audience: *Health-conscious individuals looking for a convenient and personalized solution for meal planning, including working professionals, busy parents and seniors.*

Key Messages:

- *PlatePlanner makes it easy to plan healthy, delicious meals for the week.*
- *PlatePlanner offers personalised meal plans based on your dietary preferences and restrictions.*
- *PlatePlanner's shopping list feature helps ensure you have all the necessary ingredients.*

Social media post:

'Take control of your health and wellness with PlatePlanner! Our meal-planning app makes it easy to plan healthy, delicious meals for the week. Plus, our personalised meal plans and shopping list feature make it a breeze to stay on track with your health goals. So, sign up now and see the difference it can make in your daily routine!'

Email subject line:

'Revolutionise your meal planning with PlatePlanner.'

Influencer Instagram post:

> 'As a busy mom, finding time to plan healthy meals can be challenging. That's why I love PlatePlanner! It makes it easy to plan delicious and nutritious meals for the week. Plus, their personalized meal plans and shopping list feature are game changers. If you want to take control of your health and wellness, give PlatePlanner a try!'

By focusing on your brand and incorporating these strategies into your content marketing efforts, you can create a cohesive and memorable brand experience for your audience.

SHORT VIDEOS E.G. FOR TIKTOK

Companies can use storytelling frameworks to produce engaging content on TikTok that resonates with their audience and drives emotional value. The following storytelling frameworks from tiktok.com/business show how businesses can use brand storytelling to create compelling content on TikTok:

- **Share your story** of your product, service, or brand and how it connects to your audience. This can be done by leveraging user-generated content, introducing the product or service with clear messaging, connecting assets that directly involve the brand's users, and ending with a clear call to action. Tips:
  - Leverage user-generated content (UGC) or DIY-style assets that address the user directly.
  - Introduce your product or service with clear messaging.
  - Connect assets that directly involve your brand's users.
  - Connect imagery of the process, where it started, or its best-suited environment.
  - End with a clear call-to-action (CTA).

- **Results first & work backward** Show the audience the result first, then work backwards through editing techniques to create the story of how it was achieved. Tips:
  - Use assets that show the result of your brand, product, or service.
  - Break down the steps of how you got there through captioning.
  - Show a different version or shot of the result, tying to a clear CTA.

- **Elevator pitch** Convey the identity of your brand to the audience simply and concisely. Tips:
  - Use captions to introduce your message or tagline.
  - Use assets that showcase the experience of your product or service.
  - Filter through assets that show how it is used or accessed with fast-paced editing.
  - Source assets that showcase how a user of your product feels (e.g., surprise) tied with a clear CTA.

- **Step by step** Explain the easy steps for using or accessing your products or services through captions and key visuals that describe the process. Tips:
  - Set up the steps you will be taking the audience through by captioning, tied to a key visual of your product.
  - Source assets that show the process.
  - End with a UGC-style reaction or comment on the use and feeling it provides. tied to a clear CTA.

- **Adaptability** Showcase how easily your product or service and brand to integrate into users' lifestyles by highlighting its use through a 'Day in The Life' lens. Tips:
  - Introduce your product through UGC or a DIY-style asset that addresses users directly.
  - Demonstrate this in 3 or more types of environments or routine-based parts of life.
  - Use the reaction or comment from the creator to address the ease and accessibility.
  - Highlight your product or service with a clear CTA.

- **Easy, fast & reliable** Highlight the ease, speed and reliability of using your product. Tips:
  - Use UGC or DIY-style assets to introduce the product.
  - Demonstrate this in different environments.
  - Highlight the product or service with a clear call to action.

Note: 'Assets' in this context refers to the visual and audio elements used in TikTok videos, such as images, videos, music, and captions. These elements are used to create the overall look and feel of the video and convey the message or story being told. Examples of assets include photos, videos, screenshots, audio recordings, animations, and illustrations. These assets can be used to create a cohesive visual story that can help to communicate the brand's message, product, or service and how it connects to the audience.

These frameworks give companies a structure to tell their brand's story and connect with their audience in a meaningful way.

EXAMPLE: APPLE'S 'SHOT ON IPHONE' AND 'THINK DIFFERENT' CAMPAIGNS

Apple is a technology company known for its innovative and storytelling-driven marketing campaigns with compelling and engaging content that tells a story and showcases the features and benefits of its products.

One of the key ways that Apple uses storytelling in its marketing campaigns is by highlighting the real-life experiences and benefits of using its products. For example, the company's *Shot on iPhone* campaign showcases the impressive photography capabilities of its iPhone devices by featuring stunning photos taken by users around the world. This campaign showcases the features and benefits of the iPhone and tells the stories of the people who use the device and the impact it has had on their lives.

In addition to showcasing the features and benefits of its products, Apple also uses storytelling to convey its values and vision. For example, the company often highlights its commitment to innovation, design, and user experience in its marketing campaigns and tells stories about its history and culture.

For example, Apple's *Think Different* campaign, which ran in the late 1990s, was a prime example of how the company used storytelling to convey its values and vision. The campaign featured a series of television and print ads that showcased the stories of influential and innovative figures, such as Albert Einstein, Mahatma Gandhi, and Martin Luther King Jr. The campaign's 'Think Different' tagline encouraged people to embrace creativity, innovation, and individuality, which aligned with Apple's brand values and vision.

Apple's use of storytelling in its marketing campaigns has contributed to its success and helped establish it as a leading brand in the technology industry. By highlighting the real-life experiences and benefits of its products and conveying its values and vision, Apple has engaged and connected with its audience in a meaningful and authentic way.

CONTENT TACTICS WITH AN AUDIENCE FOCUS

When it comes to content marketing, it is crucial to focus not only on your brand but also on how it resonates with and engages your audience. Here are a few content tactics that focus on the needs and preferences of your target audience:

- **Storytelling** is a powerful content tactic that can help you engage and connect with your audience. This can involve telling personal stories, creating characters or plotlines, or using other techniques to bring your content to life. By using storytelling, you can create more relatable and memorable content that resonates with your audience.

> But telling stories about others—
> customers, community partners,
> neighbors, vendors—allows
> organizations to shine the spotlight on all
> of the people who impact the
> organization and demonstrate its values.

The Content Fuel Framework
Melanie Deziel

- Sharing **customer stories** or testimonials can effectively showcase the value of your products or services and build trust with your audience. This can be in the form of written testimonials, video testimonials, or case studies.
- Creating **interactive content** such as quizzes, polls, or surveys can effectively engage and involve your audience. This can help you understand your audience's needs and preferences and create more targeted content.

- **Personalising** your content for different audience segments can help you create more targeted and relevant content. This can involve personalisation tools or creating different versions of your content for different audience segments.

EXAMPLE: YAMASA'S 10,000 STEPS PER DAY

Yamasa, a Japanese brand, is credited with popularising the idea of taking 10,000 steps per day to maintain good health. In the 1960s, the company developed the first pedometer to measure steps taken and marketed it as a tool to help people track their progress toward taking 10,000 steps per day.

To promote the product, Yamasa used storytelling to create a narrative about taking 10,000 steps per day. They positioned the pedometer as a way for people to easily measure and track their progress toward this goal. They encouraged them to incorporate more physical activity into their daily routine by setting the goal of taking 10,000 steps per day.

By creating a simple and memorable message around the benefits of taking 10,000 steps per day, Yamasa effectively communicated the value of its product and persuaded people to buy it. This storytelling tactic helped the company differentiate its pedometer from other products on the market and establish it as a widespread and trusted tool for tracking physical activity. Storytelling is that powerful.

CASE IN POINT: SIGNIFICANT OBJECTS (2012)

The book 'Significant Objects' by Joshua Glenn and Rob Walker illustrates the power of stories to drive emotional value through an experiment they conducted. First, they purchased various thrift store items for a small amount, such as a ceramic ashtray, a plastic dinosaur toy, a vintage postcard etc. Then they commissioned writers to create fictional stories about each object. They then sold the objects on eBay and found that the objects that had stories written about them sold for significantly more than their original purchase price, demonstrating the power of stories to increase the subjective value of an object.

TACTIC: STORYTELLING

Storytelling is one of the most powerful tools in content marketing, as it allows brands to connect with their audience on an emotional level. There are two ways to get your brand message across: repeating it so often that people start believing it is true, known as the **illusory truth effect**, or wrapping it inside an emotion, which is the essence of storytelling.

> Storytelling as it applies to business isn't about spinning a yarn or a fairy tale. Rather, it's about how your business (or its products or services) exist in the real world: who you are and what you do for the benefit of others, and how you add value to people's lives, ease their troubles, help shoulder their burdens, and meet their needs.
>
> Everybody Writes
> Ann Handley

- By using storytelling in your content marketing, you can create a narrative that captures the **attention** of your audience and that resonates with their experiences, values, or aspirations.
- Through storytelling, you can create a **connection** with your audience that goes beyond the facts and figures about your product or service, and that can help to build trust, credibility, and loyalty with them.
- In addition, storytelling can help to **differentiate your brand from competitors** by highlighting your unique vision, mission, or culture, and by creating a distinct and memorable brand identity.

> When talented people write well, it is generally for this reason: They're moved by a desire to touch the audience.

Story
Robert McKee

According to Robert McKee, a renowned expert on storytelling, 'Structure is the soul of a story.' When it comes to content marketing, using a storytelling format can effectively engage and persuade your audience.

MODEL: THE STORY SPINE (KENN ADAMS)

The **Story Spine** is a storytelling framework created by Kenn Adams that provides a structure for creating compelling stories. The framework consists of six key elements: Once upon a time; And every day; But one day, Because of that; And because of that; The end.

The story's structure follows the emotional arc, which is the change in the emotional state of the characters and the audience throughout the story. The emotional arc can be broken down into three main stages: **Rising Action**; **Climax**; **Falling Action**.

Here is a table that compares the elements of The Story Spine with the structure and function of the emotional arc:

Table 11. The Story Spine vs. Emotional Arc

THE STORY SPINE	STRUCTURE	EMOTIONAL ARC	FUNCTION
Once upon a time	Beginning	Rising Action	Introduce the setting, characters, and conflict
And every day	Middle	Rising Action	Builds tension and sets up the problem
But one day	The Event	Climax	The turning point where the problem reaches a crisis
Because of that	Climax aftermath	Falling Action	The aftermath of the climax and the resolution of the problem
And because of that	Middle	Falling Action	The emotional fallout and learning of the characters
The end	End	Falling Action	The outcome of the story and the emotional resolution for the audience

The Story Spine provides a structure for creating a story that follows the emotional arc, which is the change in the emotional state of the characters and the audience throughout the story. The **emotional arc** is used to create tension and suspense and to guide the audience through the story.

Using The Story Spine framework, the storyteller can create a compelling story that resonates with the audience and leaves a lasting impression.

MODEL: KURT VONNEGUT'S SHAPE OF STORIES

The **Shape of Stories** model, created by Kurt Vonnegut, is a storytelling framework that describes the shape of a story in terms of its emotional arc. The model identifies six different shapes of stories, each with its own unique emotional trajectory: Rags to Riches, Riches to Rags, Man in a Hole, Icarus, Cinderella, and Oedipus.

- The first shape, **Rags to Riches**, is characterised by a rise in the emotional arc. This story shape follows a protagonist who starts in a difficult situation and, through their own efforts, rises to a position of wealth and success. This is like the 'Rising Action' stage in the Story Spine model.
- **Riches to Rags**, is characterised by a fall in the emotional arc. This story shape follows a protagonist who starts in a position of wealth and success and, through their own mistakes or external factors, falls into a problematic situation. This is like the 'Falling Action' stage in the Story Spine model.
- **Man in a Hole** is characterised by a fall followed by a rise in the emotional arc. This story shape follows a protagonist who falls into a problematic situation. Still, through their own efforts, they rise out of it. This is like the 'The Event' and 'The Climax' stages in the Story Spine model.
- The fourth shape, **Icarus**, is characterised by a rise followed by a fall in the emotional arc. This story shape follows a protagonist who rises to a position of success or power but, through their own mistakes or external factors, falls from that position. This is like the 'Middle' stage in the Story Spine model.
- The **Cinderella** shape is characterised by a rise, fall, and rise in the emotional arc. This story shape follows a protagonist who rises from difficulty to success, falls back to hardship, and then rises again to final victory. This is like the 'Beginning', 'Middle' and End' stages in the Story Spine model.
- The sixth shape, **Oedipus**, is characterised by a fall, rise, and fall in the emotional arc. This story shape follows a protagonist who falls into a difficult situation, rises out of it, but then falls again to a final difficult situation. This is like the 'The Event' and 'The Climax' stages in the Story Spine model.

Vonnegut's Shape of Stories model is a more general framework covering various stories. In contrast, the Story Spine model is more specific in storytelling for brands and ad campaigns.

Both models provide a structure for creating a story that follows an emotional arc, which is the change in the emotional state of the characters and the audience throughout the story. The emotional arc is used to create tension and suspense and to guide the audience through the story. Both frameworks can be used together to create a compelling story that resonates with the audience and leaves a lasting impression.

MODEL: 3D STORYTELLING

The 3D Storytelling model utilises one or a combination of the three dimensions of time, place and character to connect with the target audience, keep their attention and ultimately change their minds about a particular subject. By strategically using these dimensions, writers can craft a story that informs, captivates, and transforms the reader.

- The **time** dimension helps writers to create a sense of progression and development and infuse their story with tension and suspense.
- The **place** dimension can transport readers to a different time and place, creating a deeper connection with the characters and their actions.
- Finally, the **character** dimension can create empathy, relatability, and connection with the readers, making them care about the story and invest in the outcome.

By manipulating the way time is presented and experienced, writers can create a sense of tension, suspense, and emotional impact that can be difficult to achieve with shorter formats. The following provides suggestions of when to use these constructs and the Author's intent.

Examples of contexts in which to each the time dimension:

Table 12. Time Dimension Examples

TIME	CONTEXT
Chronological	Dramatic and high-profile stories that unfold quickly
Flashback	Adding a historical context to the story
Non-linear	Jumping back and forth in time to reveal information and build suspense

Use of the **place dimension** to write long-form content can create a sense of setting, atmosphere and mood. Writers can transport readers to a different time and place and create a deeper connection with the characters and their actions by describing the physical surroundings and location.

Examples of contexts in which to each the place dimension:

Table 13. Contexts for Place Dimensions

PLACE	CONTEXT
Places	Stories connected to the characters and the actions they take or are forced to take
Setting-driven	Creating a vivid and immersive setting and atmosphere
Travelogue	Describing a journey through different places and how they relate to the story

The **character dimension** can be applied to long-form content to create a sense of empathy, relatability and connection with the readers. By describing the characters, their motivations, emotions and actions, writers can make readers care about the story and invest in the outcome.

Examples of contexts in which to each the character dimension:

Table 14. Contexts for Character Dimensions

CHARACTER	CONTEXT
Character-driven	Telling the story from the perspective of one or more characters
Psychological	Exploring the inner thoughts, emotions and motivations of the characters
First-person	Telling the story through the eyes of the main character and giving readers a more personal experience

By using the **character-driven** dimension to structure your story, you can make your message more relatable and engaging for your audience.

For example, suppose you tell a story about a customer that overcame a major challenge. In this story structure, the **plot** is the story's overarching narrative, the **action** is the specific events and actions taken by the characters, and the **development** is the gradual progression of the story, including the evolution of the characters and the resolution of conflicts. Focusing on the customer's steps to solve the problem and the lessons they learned helps to illustrate the central message of your content and make it more relatable and engaging for your audience.

> The protagonist responds to the sudden negative or positive change in the balance of life in whatever way is appropriate to character and world. A refusal to act, however, cannot last for very long, even in the most passive protagonists of minimalist Nonplots.

Story
Robert McKee

Focusing on the character's challenges can also create a sense of empathy, relatability, and connection with the readers, making them care about the story and invest in the outcome. This approach can be particularly useful when you want to influence the behaviour of your target audience by providing them with a relatable and inspiring story to follow.

By combining these dimensions in a well-thought-out manner, the 3D Storytelling model can create a powerful and engaging story that informs, inspires, and motivates the readers.

Following are various examples of how these tools have been used successfully in marketing.

CASE IN POINT: JOHNNIE WALKER'S *THE MAN WHO WALKED AROUND THE WORLD* VIDEO

The Johnnie Walker *The Man Who Walked Around The World* video illustrates the **time dimension** approach. This 6-minute short film for Johnnie Walker whiskey featuring Robert Carlyle tells the story of a man's journey of self-discovery and exploration through time manipulation.

The film uses a non-linear narrative, jumping back and forth in time, to reveal information and build suspense. The viewer experiences the main character's struggles and regrets but also sees flashbacks of his past experiences, both good and bad, that have led him to where he is now.

This approach adds depth and meaning to the main character's journey. It helps the audience understand and relate to his motivations and emotions. The non-linear narrative creates a sense of progression and development that generates tension and suspense, keeping the audience engaged throughout the film. The story's resolution comes when the character realises that he must take responsibility for his past and move forward. It is a powerful message communicated through the clever use of the time dimension.

CASE IN POINT: BUDWEISER SUPERBOWL AD *BEST BUDS* (2014)

The character-driven approach can be illustrated with the Budweiser 2014 Superbowl ad **Best Buds**. This ad tells the story of the bond between a Clydesdale horse and a Labrador Retriever puppy through a series of scenes that show their friendship and adventures. The ad's central message is the bond between the horse and the puppy and how they are best friends.

The ad uses the character-driven approach to make the audience identify with the main characters, a Clydesdale horse and a Labrador Retriever puppy. By focusing on the characters, their actions, emotions, and motivations, the ad creates a sense of empathy and relatability with the audience, making them care about the story and invest in the outcome.

The ad starts with the puppy's first steps with the horse helping the puppy to stand up and walk, showing the audience how the relationship between the two characters started. Then, through various scenes, we see the puppy and the horse playing together, going through different challenges and adventures, and ultimately, the puppy growing up and having to say goodbye to his best friend.

This approach is particularly effective because it uses relatable and likeable characters, a puppy and a horse, to communicate a powerful message about friendship and loyalty. Making the audience identify with the characters creates a deeper emotional connection to the story and a memorable impact on the audience.

Another case of using likeable characters to elicit an emotional response is Lyndon Johnson's *Daisy* ad (1964).

CASE IN POINT: LYNDON JOHNSON'S *DAISY* AD (1964)

The **Daisy** ad, also known as the *Peace, Little Girl* ad, is a political ad used during the 1964 United States presidential campaign of Lyndon B. Johnson. The ad is known for its use of storytelling and emotive imagery to appeal to the audience's emotions and create a sense of fear.

The ad features a young girl picking petals off a daisy while counting, as another ominous voice counts down from ten. As the countdown reaches zero, the ad cuts to a nuclear explosion and a voiceover from Lyndon B. Johnson warns against the dangers of nuclear war. The ad ends with the tagline *Vote for President Johnson on November 3. The stakes are too high for you to stay home.*

The ad was created during a time of great fear and uncertainty about the possibility of nuclear war. The ad taps into that fear by using the image of a young girl and the countdown to a nuclear explosion to create a sense of dread and urgency. Using a young, innocent girl to represent the atomic war victims was a powerful visual metaphor that helped drive home the ad's message.

The ad is a classic example of using likeable but powerless characters to stimulate the audience's emotions. The use of the young girl in the ad was a powerful emotional trigger that played to the existing sense of fear and urgency in the country and drove people to vote for Lyndon Johnson. The ad's use of storytelling and emotive imagery was highly effective and is still remembered as one of the most potent political ads in American history.

CASE IN POINT: VISIT SCOTLAND: *THE SPIRIT OF SCOTLAND* VIDEO (2016)

An example that illustrates the place dimension can be the **Visit Scotland: The Spirit of Scotland** video campaign. This campaign uses stunning footage of Scotland's landscapes and natural beauty to create a sense of place and atmosphere that transports the viewer to Scotland. The video takes the viewer on a journey through different locations in Scotland, showcasing the country's natural landscapes, cities, and culture.

The place dimension is used to create a sense of setting and atmosphere that evokes the spirit of Scotland. By describing the physical surroundings and location, the video creates an immersive experience that makes viewers feel like they are in Scotland. In addition, the visuals and the footage of the different locations, such as the rugged coastlines, the rolling hills, and the bustling cities, convey Scotland's diversity.

The place dimension also helps to create a deeper connection with the characters and their actions, as the different locations reflect the different aspects of Scottish culture, such as their traditions, history, and way of life. The video also showcases the different activities that can be experienced in Scotland, such as hiking, skiing, and cultural events.

Overall, the use of the place dimension in this campaign helps to create a powerful and evocative video that captures the spirit of Scotland and makes the viewer want to visit the country. It also helps to create a deeper emotional connection with the audience and make the campaign's message more relatable and engaging.

STORYTELLING FORMAT: ENTERTAINING VIDEOS

The combination of storytelling and video is a particularly powerful and effective tool for content marketing. The entertaining content that can result can engage your audience and create unique and shareable content.

There are several key elements to consider when using storytelling in entertaining videos. A description follows.

CORE NARRATIVE

The first step in crafting a compelling story for your video is to identify the **core narrative** you want to share. This could be a personal story, a case study, or a narrative that illustrates a particular point or concept.

> The archetypal story unearths a universally human experience, then wraps itself inside a unique, culture-specific expression.

<mark>Story</mark>: Style, Structur...
Robert McKee

Some stories are universal. Examples:

- We all want someone to love us and be loved in return. We want to hear stories of people finding love and experiencing the joy and fulfilment that comes with it. One famous love story is that of Romeo and Juliet, two young lovers from feuding families who struggle to be together despite the challenges and obstacles in their way.
- We all want our children to be healthy and successful. We want to hear stories of children overcoming challenges and achieving success in their personal and, later, in their professional lives. One famous story of a successful child is that of Malala Yousafzai, a Pakistani activist for female education who, at the age of 17, became the youngest Nobel Prize laureate.
- We all want to feel that we are doing a good job. We want to hear stories of people feeling proud and satisfied with their work and the positive impact they have on others. One famous story of someone feeling proud and satisfied with their work is that of Marie Curie, a pioneering scientist who made ground-breaking discoveries in the fields of physics and chemistry, including the discovery of radium and polonium.
- We all want to be paid just a little bit more than we think we are worth. We want to hear stories of people negotiating and advocating for fair compensation and feeling valued and appreciated for their contributions.
- One famous story of someone negotiating fair compensation is that of Martin Luther King Jr., an American Baptist minister and civil rights activist who led the civil rights movement and fought for the rights of African Americans, including the right to fair wages and equal pay.

> People don't want what you
> make They want what it will do
> for them. They want the way it
> will make them feel.

This Is Marketing
Seth Godin

Here is a script summary for an entertaining video for the buyer persona Emily:

Script Summary:

In this video, Emily shares her story of how she discovered meal delivery services and their impact on her life as a busy working mother.

The video opens with a shot of Emily looking stressed and overwhelmed at her desk. Then, as she talks to the camera, she explains that she is always running from one task to the next and barely has time to catch her breath.

Cut to a shot of Emily scrolling through social media, where she sees an ad for a meal delivery service. She is hesitant at first but then starts thinking about all the time and energy she spends on grocery shopping and meal planning. Finally, she decides to give the service a try.
Cut to a montage of shots showing Emily receiving her meal delivery, cooking and eating the meals with her family, and enjoying the convenience and time-saving benefits of the service.

The video ends with Emily sitting at the kitchen table with her family, looking relaxed and happy. She smiles and says, 'Meal delivery has been a game-changer for me as a working mother. It's saved me so much time and energy, and I can spend more quality time with my family. I highly recommend it to any other busy working mothers out there.'

This script summary illustrates how to identify the core narrative of a story and use it to craft a compelling video. By sharing her personal story, Emily can engage her audience and illustrate the benefits of meal delivery services for busy working mothers.

COMPELLING VISUALS: WIDE SHOTS, CLOSE-UPS, POINT-OF-VIEW SHOTS, AND B-ROLL

Visuals are a crucial element of storytelling in videos. Use a variety of shots and angles to keep the viewer interested and to help illustrate your points.

Here are some examples of compelling visuals that could be used in the entertaining video for the buyer persona Emily:

- Wide shots: Using wide shots of Emily's home, office, or other relevant locations can help set the scene and give the viewer a sense of place.
- Close-ups: Close-ups of Emily's face can be used to show her emotions and reactions and help the viewer connect with her on a personal level.
- Point-of-view shots: Point-of-view shots can be used to put the viewer in Emily's shoes and help them experience her story first hand. For example, a point-of-view shot of Emily scrolling through social media and discovering the meal delivery service can help the viewer understand her initial hesitation.
- B-roll footage: B-roll footage, such as shots of the meal delivery arriving, Emily cooking the meals, or her family enjoying the meals, can illustrate the points in the video and keep the viewer interested.

STRONG AUDIO: MUSIC, SOUND EFFECTS, AND VOICEOVERS

In addition to compelling visuals, it is crucial to use strong **audio** in your videos. This could include using music to set the tone, sound effects to enhance the story, and clear, concise voiceovers to guide the viewer through the content.

Here are some examples of strong audio that could be used in the entertaining video for the buyer persona Emily:

- Using **music** to set the tone can create an emotional connection with the viewer and enhance the overall impact of the video. For example, you could use upbeat, energetic music during the montage of Emily receiving and cooking the meals to create a sense of excitement and positivity.
- **Sound effects** can enhance the story and bring it to life for the viewer. For example, you could use the sound of a doorbell ringing to signify the arrival of the meal delivery or the sound of a sizzle to enhance the cooking scenes.
- Clear, concise **voiceovers** can help guide the viewer through the content and ensure the message is conveyed effectively. For example, Emily could use a voiceover to explain her initial hesitation about the meal delivery service and how she eventually decided to try it.

By using strong audio elements such as music, sound effects, and voiceovers, you can create a more immersive and engaging video experience for the viewer.

HUMOUR: SARCASM, SELF-DEPRECATION, AND PHYSICAL HUMOUR

> People are generally interested in watching the same things: personalities, games, pop music, sport, entertainment, and humor.
>
> Video Marketing like a PRO
> Clo Willaerts

Humour is a great way to engage your audience and make your content more entertaining. Use it sparingly and appropriately, and make sure it fits with your video's overall tone and message.

Here are some examples of humour that could be used in the entertaining video for the buyer persona Emily:

- Using **sarcasm** playfully and appropriately can add a touch of humour to the video. For example, Emily could say something like, *'Who has time to plan and prepare meals every day? Definitely not me. That's why I decided to try out this meal delivery service. It's like having a personal chef, but without all the awkward small talk.'*
- Using **self-deprecating humour** can be an excellent way to connect with the viewer and show that you are relatable. For example, Emily could say something like, *'I'm not the best cook in the world. In fact, I've been known to burn water. But with these meal delivery kits, even I can make a decent meal. It's like magic'.*
- Using **physical humour** can add levity to the video and make it more entertaining. For example, you could include a shot of Emily pretending to be a superhero as she unboxes the meal delivery or show her pretending to be a chef and waving a spatula around as she cooks the meals.

By using humour sparingly and appropriately, you can add an element of fun and entertainment to your video and engage your audience. Just make sure that the humour fits with the overall tone and message of the video.

CASE IN POINT: OLD SPICE GUY

In 2010, the Old Spice brand launched a content marketing campaign that featured actor Isaiah Mustafa as the handsome, witty, and chisel-chested *Old Spice Guy*. The campaign launched just before the 2010 Super Bowl. It quickly became a viral video sensation, with the ads being shared and viewed millions of times on social media. The campaign, which used short, rapid-fire monologues to promote the Old Spice brand, became a pop culture phenomenon and helped to drive massive brand awareness and positive sentiment towards the Old Spice brand.

The *Smell Like a Man, Man* campaign is a perfect example of how humour can be effectively used in content marketing. The campaign, which featured actor Isaiah Mustafa delivering rapid-fire monologues in a humorous and over-the-top fashion, quickly became a viral sensation. The ads were shared and viewed millions of times on social media.

One of the critical factors that contributed to the campaign's success was the use of humour. By injecting a healthy dose of humour into their ads, Old Spice was able to create content that was not only memorable but also highly shareable. This helped to drive massive brand awareness and positive sentiment towards the Old Spice brand.

Another key element of the campaign's success was its ability to tap into popular cultural trends and sentiments. By positioning Old Spice as a product for the modern, confident man, the brand connected with its target audience in a meaningful and relevant way.

STORYTELLING FORMAT: EDUCATIONAL VIDEOS

Educational videos can be a powerful tool for content marketing professionals as they allow them to communicate complex ideas and concepts in a way that is easy to understand and engage with. Educational videos capture viewers' attention and keep them engaged by providing a visual and auditory representation of a concept or idea. Additionally, videos can be used to demonstrate a product or service in action, which helps showcase the benefits of a product or service and make it more relatable to the viewer.

Content marketing professionals can use educational videos in various ways to achieve their marketing goals:

- To build **brand awareness** by creating engaging and memorable content that aligns with their brand message.
- To **generate leads** and **drive conversions** by including a call to action (CTA) at the end that encourages viewers to take a specific action, such as visiting a website or signing up for a newsletter.
- To establish **thought leadership** and position a company as an expert in their industry. By creating educational content that provides value to viewers, companies can establish themselves as credible sources of information in their industry and become a go-to resource for their target audience.
- To increase website traffic and improve SEO by incorporating keywords and phrases in the video's title, description, and tags. This can help boost the video's visibility in search engines, which can lead to increased traffic to the website.

Using **animation** as a format for educational videos can be particularly bene-ficial because it allows for creating illustrations and graphics that may not be possible with live-action footage. Animation can also be used to create char-acters and storylines that can make complex concepts more relatable and en-gaging for viewers. Additionally, animation can create a consistent visual style across a series of videos, which can help establish a brand identity.

Many tools are available for making educational videos with animation, such as Adobe After Effects, Powtoon, Animaker, GoAnimate, Adobe Animate, Au-todesk Maya, and more. These tools can be used to create animations, visual ef-fects, compositing, motion graphics, and other types of animated content. The choice of tool will depend on factors such as the complexity of the animation, the budget, and the skill level of the animator.

CASE IN POINT: THE STORY OF STUFF

In 2007, **The Story of Stuff**, an animated documentary about the lifecycle of material goods, was released on YouTube. The 20-minute film was created by Annie Leonard, an environmental activist. It was produced by The Story of Stuff Project, a non-profit organisation focusing on sustainability and con-sumerism. The film quickly went viral, garnering over 20 million views within the first year of its release.

The Story of Stuff is a powerful and thought-provoking film that critically exam-ines the environmental and social impacts of excessive consumerism. The film highlights the negative effects of overproduction and overconsumption on the planet and its inhabitants. It encourages viewers to rethink their relationship with material goods.

Content Tactics Used:

- The film uses **storytelling** to convey its message. It presents facts and information in a relatable and engaging way, making it easy for viewers to understand and relate to the topic.
- The **animation** in the film helps to make the information more accessible and engaging while also allowing for the creative visual representation of the concepts discussed.

- The film provides an **educational** experience by providing information and facts about the lifecycle of material goods, consumerism's environmental and social impacts, and ways individuals can make a difference.
- The film uses **emotional appeal** to connect with viewers, drawing on emotions such as guilt, empathy, and a call to action to create a sense of urgency and inspire viewers to take action.

The Story of Stuff was a ground-breaking video in terms of its ability to spread awareness, and it Is a great example of how videos can be used to educate and engage people on important issues. *The Story of Plastic* (2021) is another video that continues this legacy of raising awareness about plastic pollution and the environment.

STORYTELLING FORMAT: CUSTOMER STORIES

Sharing **customer stories** or **testimonials** is a powerful way to showcase the value of your products or services and build trust with your audience. Customer stories allow potential customers to see how real people have benefited from your offerings and can help to build credibility and trust in your brand.

There are several ways to share customer stories, including written testimonials, video testimonials, and case studies.

WRITTEN TESTIMONIALS

Written testimonials are short accounts of a customer's experience with your product or service. These can be as simple as a few sentences or as long as a few paragraphs, depending on the length and detail of the customer's experience.

You can ask satisfied customers to write a review or testimonial for your website or social media profiles to gather written testimonials. It is an example:

Dear PlateMate user,
We hope you are enjoying using PlateMate to plan and organize your meals. We value your feedback and would love to hear about your experience using our app. We would greatly appreciate it if you could write a review or testimonial for our website or social media profiles. Your words will help other users understand the

value of PlateMate and make informed decisions about whether it is the right meal-planning solution for them.

To leave a review or testimonial, visit our website or social media profiles and follow the prompts to leave feedback. You can also email us at [email address] with your thoughts, and we will be happy to share them on our website or social media profiles.
Thank you for your support and for helping us to continually improve PlateMate. Sincerely, The PlateMate Team

You can also include a call-to-action on your website or email marketing campaigns asking customers to share their experiences with your products or services. To give you an idea:

Thank you for choosing our gym! Please leave a review or testimonial on our website or social media profiles if you have a moment. Your words will help other seniors understand the value of our gym and make informed decisions about whether it is the right fitness solution for them. To leave a review or testimonial, simply use the contact form below. Thank you for your support and for helping us improve.

VIDEO TESTIMONIALS

Video testimonials are like written testimonials but are recorded on video. They can be more engaging and impactful for your audience. Video testimonials allow customers to share their experiences in their own words. They can be more personal and authentic than written testimonials.

To gather video testimonials, you can ask satisfied customers if they would be willing to record a short video sharing their experience with your products or services. You can then use these videos on your website or social media profiles to showcase the value of your offerings. It is an example:

Dear PlateMate user,
We hope you are enjoying using PlateMate to plan and organize your meals. We value your feedback and would love to hear about your experience using our app in a more personal and authentic way.

Can you record a short video testimonial sharing your experience with Plate-Mate? Your video will help other users understand the value of our app and make informed decisions about whether it is the right meal-planning solution for them. To show our appreciation for your time and effort, we would like to offer you a special discount on your next purchase of PlateMate. Simply use the code 'VIDEO-REWARD' at checkout to redeem your discount.

To record your video testimonial, simply use the camera on your smartphone or computer to record a short message (2-3 minutes is ideal). In your video, please share your thoughts on how PlateMate has helped you plan and organize your meals, any specific features you have found particularly useful, and any results or benefits you have experienced from using our app.

Once you have recorded your video, you can email it to us at [email address] or share it via a file-sharing service such as Google Drive or Dropbox.

Thank you for your support and for helping us to continually improve PlateMate. We look forward to sharing your video testimonial with our community and offering you a special discount on your next purchase.

Sincerely,

The PlateMate Team

Incorporating customer stories into content marketing can be an effective way to engage and connect with your audience. However, to create compelling customer stories, it is important to:

- Identify the **core narrative** of your customer story. This could be a personal story or case study that illustrates your product's or service's benefits.
- Use **vivid language** to bring your customer story to life and help readers visualise the events and ideas you describe.
- Include **engaging visuals** such as before and after photos, infographics, and video clips to illustrate your points and make your content visually appealing.
- Ensure that your customer stories are **authentic** and **relatable** to your target audience.

By following these tips, you can create customer stories that effectively convey your product's or service's value and help drive conversions.

CASE IN POINT: NIKE'S ATHLETES

Nike's 'Just Do It' slogan and tagline have become one of the world's most iconic and memorable slogans and a prime example of the power of storytelling in marketing. The slogan was introduced in 1988 and has since been used in many marketing campaigns, including television commercials, print ads, and social media campaigns.

One of the key reasons for the success of Nike's 'Just Do It' slogan is that it tells a powerful and inspiring story. The slogan encourages people to pursue their goals and dreams, no matter their challenges or obstacles. This message resonates with people from all walks of life. In addition, it has helped to build a strong emotional connection between Nike and its audience.

Nike has used other storytelling techniques in its marketing campaigns, in addition to its 'Just Do It' slogan, such as showcasing real people using and enjoying its products and highlighting the company's values and vision. These campaigns have helped to further strengthen the brand's connection with its audience and build brand loyalty.

Overall, Nike's use of storytelling in its marketing campaigns has been a key factor in the company's success and helped establish it as a leading brand in the sports and fitness industry.

STORYTELLING FORMAT: NARRATIVE MEMO

Jeff Bezos, the founder of Amazon, recognized the value of clear and concise written communication in the company's decision-making process. To foster a culture of writing at Amazon, Bezos implemented a strict **no-powerpoint policy** and required meeting owners to write detailed memos, referred to as 'narratives', for attendees to read before the meeting.

According to Jesse Freeman, a former Amazon employee and expert on the company's writing guidelines, these narrative memos follow a specific structure with six components:

1. an introduction
2. goals

3. tenets
4. an overview of the current state of the business
5. lessons learned, and
6. strategic priorities

This tailored process helps to ensure that all relevant information is clearly and thoroughly conveyed to the intended audience.

The emphasis on writing at Amazon highlights the importance of clear and effective communication in content marketing. By following a structured and well-defined process for written communication, companies can make sure that their messaging is consistent and effective in achieving their marketing goals.

The structure of Bezos' narrative memo is like that of a story:

- The introduction, or **hook,** grabs the reader's attention and provides context for what follows.
- The goals and tenets function as the **stakes,** or what is at risk or at stake for the company.
- The state of the business, including the setting and backstory, provides **context** and **background information** that helps the reader understand the situation.
- The lessons learned and strategic priorities make up the memo's **plot, action,** and **development.**

The purpose of a narrative structure is to convey information to the reader in a logical, clear and engaging way that is easy for the reader to understand and remember.

CASE IN POINT: MOONLIT APPAREL'S ANNUAL REPORT

Following is the imaginary company Moonlit Apparel's 2022 Annual Report, written using Bezos's narrative memo structure:

Introduction: a challenging year for Moonlit Apparel

Welcome to the annual report for Moonlit Apparel. This year has been challenging, with the global pandemic affecting nearly every aspect of our business. However, we are proud to share the progress we have made and our plans with you.

Goals: post-pandemic financial stability

Our primary goal for the year was to maintain financial stability and adapt to the changes brought on by the pandemic. This included shifting to a more online-focused business model and implementing cost-saving measures.

Tenets: sustainability, ethical sourcing, and customer satisfaction

At Moonlit Apparel, we prioritise sustainability, ethical sourcing, and customer satisfaction. These tenets have guided our decision-making and actions throughout the year.

State of the business: steady growth

Despite the challenges, we are pleased to report that we have achieved steady growth in our online sales. We have also expanded our product offerings and collaborated with new partners. However, we have faced difficulties in our brick-and-mortar stores, which have had to operate at reduced capacity or close temporarily due to pandemic restrictions.

Lessons learned: adaptability

This year, we have learned the importance of being adaptable and proactive in facing unpredictable circumstances. As a result, we have had to quickly pivot and find new ways to reach our customers and keep our business running.

Strategic priorities: online presence growth

Our top priorities are to continue growing our online presence, expand our partnerships, and invest in sustainability initiatives. We are also focused on finding ways to safely reopen and revitalise our brick-and-mortar stores. By staying true to our values and being proactive, we can weather any challenges and emerge stronger.

Thank you for your support and loyalty. We are grateful for the opportunity to serve you and look forward to continuing to provide high-quality, ethically made clothing.

THE CASE STUDY FORMAT

Case studies are in-depth accounts of how a specific customer used your products or services to solve a particular problem or achieve a specific goal. These can be particularly effective for showcasing the results and benefits of your products or services in a more detailed and comprehensive way.

To create a case study, you will need to interview the customer and gather detailed information about their experience with your products or services. You will also need to include specific details about the problem they were trying to solve and the results they achieved. It is an example to get you started:

1. *What motivated you to start using our gym for seniors?*
2. *What specific health or fitness goals were you trying to achieve when you began using our gym?*
3. *How did you first hear about our gym, and what made you decide to try it out?*
4. *Can you describe your experience using our gym? What specific activities or classes have you participated in?*
5. *Have you noticed any improvements in your health or fitness since starting to use our gym?*
6. *How has being a part of our senior fitness community impacted your overall well-being and quality of life?*
7. *Would you recommend our gym to other seniors looking to improve their health and fitness? Why or why not?*
8. *Is there anything else you would like to share about your experience with our gym for seniors?*

Sharing customer stories can showcase the value of your products or services and builds trust with your audience. Whether you share written testimonials, video testimonials, or case studies, highlight the specific benefits and results your customers have experienced.

TACTIC: SALES PITCH

A **sales pitch** is a specific type of content used to persuade a prospect or customer to buy a product or service. It is a communication tool designed to convey a product's or service's value and convince the listener to take action. Sales pitches can take many forms, such as verbal presentations, written proposals, or video demonstrations.

In content marketing, a sales pitch can be used to generate leads, close deals, and increase revenue. In addition, it is a way for companies to showcase the unique benefits of their products or services and differentiate themselves from their competitors. Sales pitches can also educate prospects about the problem they are trying to solve and how the company's solution can help.

A well-crafted sales pitch should always align with the target audience's pain points and offer a clear call to action. It should also be tailored to the specific decision-maker and include customer testimonials and case studies to build trust and credibility. Additionally, the sales pitch should be delivered in a way that is easy to understand, engaging and memorable.
In summary, a sales pitch is a powerful content tactic that can increase revenue and generate leads. When executed correctly, it can be a valuable tool for convincing prospects and customers to take action and purchase a product or service.

Andy Raskin, a leading authority in the field of strategic messaging, has identified five key factors that define every compelling strategic narrative:

1. Start with a big, undeniable **change that creates stakes**: a deep-rooted belief inside your customer's head that is in full swing and happens without your consent. By highlighting this change, you create opportunities for your product to meet your customers' needs.
2. **Name the enemy**: the person or thing you and your customers are fighting against to make the world better. This is also the right time to define a large enough category you want to dominate and aim for a goal your competitors cannot reach.
3. Tease the **promised land**. At this point, it may be tempting to present your product, but resist this urge. The hero of this story is not your product but your customers. Instead, paint a picture of how the future will look once they arrive in the promised land.
4. Position capabilities as **magic** for slaying **monsters**. Only now do you have permission to position your product as a means towards winning over the status quo. The more mini villains it can defeat, the better.
5. Present your best evidence. Use **testimonials** and **referrals** from customers who've already arrived in the **promised land** to demonstrate the effectiveness of your product.

> What promise are you making? When the marketer shows up with his or her message (in whatever medium), it always takes the form of a promise: "If you do X, you will get Y." That promise is often hidden. It can accidentally be set aside or intentionally camouflaged, but all effective marketing makes a promise.
>
> This Is Marketing
> Seth Godin

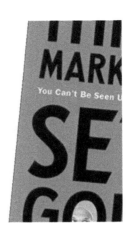

This framework focuses solely on the sales pitch and does not consider any supporting collaterals. However, Raskin believes that when the core narrative is nailed correctly, it will flow naturally into other areas, such as website messaging, content, job descriptions, and investor decks.

It is what the sales pitch for investors from SeniorFit would look like:

1. Start with a big, undeniable change that creates stakes
   The aging population is growing at an unprecedented rate, and with it comes the need for more effective solutions to help seniors stay active and healthy. The status quo of seniors relying on traditional gym memberships or self-motivated workouts is no longer sufficient. The opportunity for SeniorFit to meet this need is undeniable.

2. Name the enemy
   The enemy in this case is the lack of personalised and accessible fitness solutions for seniors. SeniorFit's goal is to dominate this category and provide a solution that addresses the specific needs of seniors, something that traditional gym memberships and self-motivated workouts cannot deliver.

3. Tease the 'Promised Land'
   Imagine a future where seniors have access to personalised workout plans and coaching services tailored to their goals, needs, and abilities. With SeniorFit, seniors can achieve their fitness goals and live a healthy, active, and fulfilling life.

4. Position capabilities as 'magic' for slaying 'monsters'
   SeniorFit is the magic solution for seniors who want to improve their overall health and well-being. Our program is designed to help seniors achieve their fitness goals and improve their quality of life. With our customised workout plans and one-on-one coaching, we can help seniors overcome the obstacles that have held them back in the past.

5. Present your best evidence
   SeniorFit is more than just a concept, it is a proven solution. Our team of certified trainers has helped numerous seniors improve their overall health and well-being. We have testimonials from satisfied customers who have achieved their fitness goals and improved their quality of life thanks to our program. Invest in SeniorFit, and you will be investing in a company with a track record of success and a promising future.

TACTIC: SHOWING THE PERSON BEHIND THE BRAND

Showing the person behind the brand is a content tactic that involves showcasing the **human side** of your business or brand. This can be a powerful way to connect with your audience and create a more personal and authentic experience. By showing the person behind the brand, you can give your audience a sense of who you are and what you are all about, which can help build trust and credibility with your audience.

Here are some examples of how you can show the human side of your brand to your audience:

- Showcase **your team or colleagues** to give your audience a sense of who you are as a company and your culture and what it is like to work with you.
- Share **your values and beliefs** to connect with them on a deeper level and showcase what you stand for as a company, what drives you and what you are all about.
- Share stories about **your personal life** to help them get to know you on a more personal level. These could be stories about your hobbies, family, or any other aspect of your life you want to share.

Here is a list of ideas for more personal stories you could share with your audience:

- Your **current mood or emotion,** like a simple statement about your feelings or a more in-depth exploration of your emotions.
- The **challenges** you are facing or have faced to encourage them to share their own challenges. This could be a personal challenge, or a challenge related to your business or industry.
- Stories about your parents, siblings, children, or any other **family** members you want to share.
- Simple statements of **gratitude** or more in-depth stories about what you are thankful for to inspire and uplift your audience.
- Thank your audience or specific individuals to show appreciation and foster a sense of community. This could be a simple **thank you** message or a more in-depth story about how someone has made a difference in your life.
- Stories about your **hobbies** to connect with your audience personally and showcase your interests and passions. These could be simple or in-depth stories about your hobbies and why you enjoy them.
- Your **life lessons** to inspire and educate your audience. These could be lessons you have learned from personal experiences or lessons you have learned from others.
- Personal **mantras or affirmations** to inspire and motivate your audience. This could be a simple statement or quote that resonates with you or a more in-depth exploration of your personal beliefs and values.
- Glimpses into **your real life**, your daily routine work or other aspects of your life to connect on a more personal level and give them a sense of what you are like in your daily life.
- Share stories about **your local community** or **the places you visit,** like local events, landmarks, or other exciting aspects of your town or city to connect with your audience and showcase your surroundings.
- Share stories about how you **relax** or **unwind** to inspire and motivate your audience. This could be stories about your favourite hobbies or activities or more in-depth explorations of how you take care of yourself and recharge.
- Share **behind-the-scenes** glimpses of your work or daily life to give them a more intimate look at what you do and who you are. These could be stories about your work environment, creative process, or any other aspect of your life you want to share.
- Share **fun or interesting facts** about yourself or your brand to engage your audience and add some personality to your content. This could be anything from trivia about your interests to exciting facts about your business or industry.

- Share stories about **your passions** or what motivates you can to inspire and motivate your audience. This could be stories about your personal or professional goals or more in-depth explorations of what drives you and what you are passionate about.

> Readers will like you if you show that you are human. In a how-to piece, for example, you might write, "This third step is a little hard to master. I ruined six good slides before I got it right. So be smarter than I was; practice on blanks."

100 Ways to Improve Your Writing
Gary Provost

Showing the person(s) behind the brand can be a powerful way to connect with your audience and create a more personal and authentic experience for them. However, when incorporating this tactic into your content strategy, remember to be **genuine** and **authentic** and avoid getting too personal in your content. While it is important to be human and relatable, it is also important to maintain boundaries and respect the privacy of yourself and others.

> Humanize your brand. Having an authentic and human voice lets you take part in conversations naturally. Be human, but never personal.

Digital marketing like a PRO
Clo Willaerts

To **get human but never personal** in the content you post, you can focus on sharing stories about your personal interests, values, and beliefs, rather than sharing too much private or sensitive information. You can also consider showcasing your team or colleagues, as this can give your audience a sense of what it is like to work with you and your company culture.

CASE IN POINT: #FIRST100 ON INSTAGRAM BY JUSTIN TRUDEAU (2015)

#First100 is a campaign launched by Canadian Prime Minister Justin Trudeau on Instagram in 2015. The campaign, which ran for 100 days, chronicled the first 100 days of his leadership through a series of candid behind-the-scenes photos and videos. The campaign was a creative way for Trudeau to connect with Canadians and share his vision for the country.

The campaign was a huge success. It was praised for its storytelling approach and the humanising effect on Trudeau's image, which helped him connect with the younger demographic.

Using Instagram as the primary platform, #First100 was able to take advantage of the visual nature of the platform and the audience engagement it offers. The campaign used a combination of photos and videos to showcase the Prime Minister's daily life and his work. The photos and videos were accompanied by captions that provided context and gave a personal touch to the campaign. This helped to create a sense of intimacy between the Prime Minister and his followers and made the content more relatable and engaging.

Furthermore, the campaign also used Instagram's built-in features like Instagram stories, polls, and live streaming to create an interactive and immersive experience for the audience. This helped to build a sense of community and engagement with the followers. The campaign was a great example of how Instagram can be a powerful storytelling tool for political leaders. It demonstrated how a creative and authentic approach can help humanise political figures, build trust and connect with the audience personally.

FRAMEWORK: PUBLIC NARRATIVE

In his book *This is Marketing*, Seth Godin introduces a framework called **Public Narrative**, which was initially developed by Marshall Ganz, a senior lecturer at the Harvard Kennedy School of Government. The framework is designed to help leaders instil motivation in their followers to pursue a shared set of values and challenge the status quo.

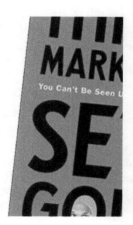

> Marshall Ganz is the brilliant Harvard professor who has worked both with Cesar Chavez and Barack Obama. He has articulated a simple three-step narrative for action: the story of self, the story of us, and the story of now.

This Is Marketing
Seth Godin

To apply this framework to customers, three key elements must be considered:

1. **The story of self** is the leader's personal journey, including the turning points in their life that have led them to where they are today. This can include their family, upbringing, frustrations, or traumas that make them relatable to others.
2. **The story of us** is about how customers can achieve greater synergy by joining the leader's journey. It should answer the question 'Why should we care and join in?' and be bold in sharing the potential benefits of working together.
3. **The story of now** is when the customers are invited to join the leader's journey. It should focus on urgency and creating a sense of peer pressure to take action for the greater good.

It is important to note that these stories are not set in stone and should be changed as the audience and context change. Therefore, it should be viewed as an iterative process rather than a fixed script.

CASE IN POINT: OBAMA 2004 SPEECH AT DEMOCRATIC NATIONAL CONVENTION.

President Barack Obama used the Public Narrative framework at the 2004 Democratic National Convention to connect with his audience and inspire them to join his journey.

1. **The Story of Self** Obama shared his personal story, including his upbringing as the son of a Kenyan father and a Kansan mother and his experiences as a community organiser in Chicago. He shared how these experiences have shaped his values and beliefs and given him the perspective and drive to lead.
2. **The Story of Us** Obama then highlighted how those values and beliefs aligned with the values and aspirations of the American people and how working together, they could achieve a greater good. He spoke about the need for unity and a common purpose and how America's diversity was its strength.
3. **The Story of Now** Obama emphasised the moment's urgency and how the country needed to come together to overcome its challenges. He called on the audience to join him in his journey and take action to create a better future for all Americans.

Using the Public Narrative framework, Obama could connect with his audience on a personal level and inspire them to join his journey for the greater good. He successfully used his own story and experiences to illustrate the shared values and aspirations of the American people and create a sense of urgency.

TACTIC: HELPFUL CONTENT AND EVERGREEN CONTENT

The creation of content that is satisfying and helpful to the reader is of utmost importance in content marketing. Google's August 2022 helpful content update is just one example of how prioritising the needs and interests of the reader can impact search engine rankings. But what does Google mean by 'helpful' content?

According to Google, **helpful content** satisfies users' needs and leaves them satisfied after consuming it. But what does this mean in practice? Google suggests that helpful content is:

- **Created for humans, not search engines**: This means that the content should be easy to read and understand and should not be stuffed with keywords to manipulate search rankings.
- The content should be relevant and **appropriate for the target audience**, considering their needs, interests, and level of knowledge.
- The content should be directly **related to the website's main topic or subject area** and add value to the reader by providing information or insights on that topic.
- The content should be **created by knowledgeable and experienced people in the subject area** and can provide valuable insights and information to the reader.
- The content should demonstrate a **deep understanding of the topic** and explore subtopics or related questions in detail.

For example, if you are a company that sells outdoor gear, creating content that helps your customers choose the right equipment for their next hiking trip or that provides tips on how to properly maintain their gear will be highly valuable to them. Not only will this content help your customers solve a problem or decide, but it will also build trust and credibility for your brand.

Utility means you clearly help your customers do something that matters to them—you help them shoulder their burdens, you ease their pain, or you help them make a decision.

Everybody Writes
Ann Handley

EVERY
WRI

{ Your Go-To Guide
Ridiculously Goo

ANN HAN

> You need to create stuff that will help your clients, you need to become a trusted resource your customers can then look to, and you need to get buyers to take action when they are ready.

Content Rules
Ann Handley, C.C. Chapman, and Davi...

Examples of help content could include:

- **Frequently asked questions (FAQs)** are a common type of help content that provides answers to common questions that customers may have about a brand's products or services. FAQs can help to address common customer concerns and can also provide useful information that customers may not find elsewhere.
- **Tutorials** are a type of help content that provides step-by-step instructions or guidance on how to use a brand's products or services. Tutorials can be useful for customers who are new to a brand's products or services, or who are looking for additional guidance on how to use them.
- **Customer support articles** are a type of help content that provides information and guidance on common customer support issues. These articles can help to address common customer concerns and can also provide useful information that customers may not find elsewhere.

While evergreen content can be useful and informative, it is not necessarily focused on providing support or assistance to customers. It does, however, play a similar role in the Consideration phase of your target audience's customer journey.

> In content marketing, evergreen content is content that ages well and maintains its value over time. Evergreen content is ideal for recycling and repurposing on social media since it does not lose relevance based on the date it's posted.

Pay Attention!
Cassandra M. Bailey and Dana M. Sch...

Evergreen content refers to material that remains valuable and useful for an extended period rather than becoming outdated quickly. Therefore, it remains relevant even if it is only accessed occasionally. By incorporating search engine optimisation (SEO) techniques, evergreen content can achieve high rankings, making it easily discoverable and actively sought out. While evergreen and timely content are important for businesses, evergreen content can generate results even when no new content is published.

> Evergreen content can include how-to guides, frequently asked questions (FAQs), and glossaries.

The Stripped-Down Guide to Content ...
John Egan

Here are some generic examples of evergreen content that could be useful and relevant to a wide range of audiences:

- **How-to guides** are a type of evergreen content that provides step-by-step instructions on how to do something, such as cooking a meal, fixing a leaky faucet, or setting up a home security system. How-to guides are useful because they provide practical and detailed information that can be applied to a wide range of situations.
- **Lists** are a simple and effective way to organise information into a format that is easy to read and understand. Examples of list-based evergreen content could include: ten ways to save money on groceries; five tips for planning a successful vacation; the top 15 must-see attractions in Paris.
- **Infographics** are a visual way to present information and data and can be a useful and engaging form of evergreen content. Infographics can be used to present complex information concisely that can be shared on social media or used in presentations or reports.

A piece of evergreen content generally should be at least 1,000 words.

The Stripped-Down Guide to Content ...
John Egan

TACTIC: INTERACTIVE CONTENT

Creating interactive content such as quizzes, polls, or surveys is a great way to engage and involve your audience. Interactive content allows your audience to actively participate in your content. It helps to create a more personalised and interactive experience.

CASE IN POINT: SNOW FALL AT THE NEW YORK TIMES

Interactive content is an engaging and immersive way for brands to tell stories and connect with their audience. One example of interactive content that stood out in recent years is *Snow Fall: The Avalanche at Tunnel Creek*[1], created by New York Times reporter John Branch. This piece tells the harrowing story of skiers caught in an avalanche, using a combination of text, photographs, videos and other multimedia elements to create an immersive experience for the reader.

The story is divided into several sections, each focusing on a different aspect of the avalanche and its aftermath. The piece begins with a dramatic opening scene, using a full-screen video and scrolling text to set the scene and introduce the characters. As the story progresses, the reader is presented with various multimedia elements, such as photographs, videos and animations which help bring the story to life and make it more engaging.

One of the key features of *SnowFall* is its use of parallax scrolling, which creates a sense of depth and movement as the reader scrolls through the story. This, combined with the multimedia elements, helps to create an immersive experience that keeps the reader engaged throughout the story.

Content marketing creators can learn from this example to create interactive content that tells a story, builds an emotional connection with the audience, and keeps them engaged. Furthermore, it can inspire different industries and niches to create interactive pieces tailored to their audience and resonate with them.

QUIZZES

Creating a **quiz** can be fun and engaging to attract and retain website visitors or social media followers. Quizzes can test your audience's knowledge of a specific topic or help them discover something new about themselves. It can also be a valuable tool for generating leads or gathering data on your audience.

---

[1]   Snow Fall: The Avalanche at Tunnel Creek – Multimedia Feature (2012) https://www.nytimes.com/projects/2012/snow-fall/index.html#/?part=tunnel-creek

To create a quiz:

1. Develop a list of questions and multiple-choice answers. The questions should be relevant to your business or industry, and the answers should be accurate and well-researched. Consider creating a mix of easy and difficult questions to keep the quiz interesting for your audience.
2. Use a quiz-building tool or platform to create the quiz. Many quiz-building tools and platforms that are available, both paid and free, allow users to create and customise their quiz. Some options include Typeform, SurveyMonkey, and Google Forms.
3. Embed your quiz on your website or social media profiles by copying and pasting the provided code. You can also promote your quiz through email marketing or social media to encourage people to take it.

Quizzes can be powerful content marketing tools. Yet, it is essential to use quizzes in a way that your audience values and aligns with your business goals.

POLLS

Polls are a quick and easy way to gather feedback from your audience and involve them in your content. For example, polls can be used to ask your audience's opinion on a specific topic or to gather insights into their needs and preferences.

To create a poll using these tools, you will typically need to follow these steps:

1. Choose a poll-building tool or platform and create an account (if necessary).
2. Choose the type of poll you want to make (e.g., a simple yes/no poll or a poll with multiple-choice answers).
3. Develop your question and list of possible answers.
4. Customise the appearance and functionality of your poll (if desired).
5. Publish your poll and embed it on your website or social media profiles.

There are many tools and platforms available for creating polls with varying ranges of customisation options. Some popular resources include:

- Google.com/forms: An easy-to-use, free tool from Google that allows you to create polls and surveys, as well as other types of forms.

- Crowdsignal.com (formerly Polldaddy): A tool that allows you to create polls, surveys, and quizzes and embed them on your website or social media profiles. Free and paid plans are available.
- SurveyMonkey.com: A tool that allows you to create polls, surveys, and quizzes and gather responses through various channels, including online and via email. Free and paid plans are available.
- Typeform.com: A tool that allows you to create polls, surveys, and quizzes with free and paid plans. Polls and surveys can be embedded in your website or social media profiles.

Remember that polls can be a helpful content marketing tool. Yet, it is important to use them in a way that your audience values and aligns with your business goals.

SURVEYS

Surveys are a powerful tool for gathering insights about your audience and understanding their needs and preferences. They can be used to collect detailed information about your audience's demographics, behaviours, and attitudes. As a result, they can help you make informed decisions about your business or marketing strategy.

Typically, the following steps are needed to create a survey using these tools:

1. Choose a survey-building tool or platform and create an account (if necessary). Many paid and free survey-building tools and platforms allow users to create and to customise their surveys.
2. Choose the type of survey you want to create (e.g. a simple customer satisfaction survey or a more in-depth market research survey).
3. Develop your list of questions and possible answers. The questions should be relevant to your business or industry and the answers should be carefully considered and well-researched. Create a mix of open-ended and closed-ended questions to gather qualitative and quantitative data.
4. Customise the appearance and functionality of your survey (if desired).
5. Publish your survey and embed it in your website or social media profiles.

Surveys can be a helpful content marketing tool. Consider the time and effort required for your audience to complete the survey and provide an incentive (if necessary) to encourage participation. Ensure that your survey is being used in a manner that provides value for your audience and in a way that aligns with your business goals.

TACTIC: PERSONALIZATION

Personalising your content for different audience segments can be a powerful way to create more targeted and relevant content. Create content that resonates more effectively and leads to better engagement and conversion rates by considering the specific needs, preferences, and characteristics of other subsets within your audience.

There are a few different ways you can personalise your content.

PERSONALISATION TOOLS

Personalisation tools allow you to create and deliver personalised content to different audience segments based on various factors, such as location, device type, past behaviour, and more. These tools can be used to create more targeted and relevant content that resonates more effectively with your audience and leads to better engagement and conversion rates.

Some common types of personalisation tools include:

- **Website personalisation tools** allow you to show different versions of your website to visitors based on various factors, such as location, device type, past behaviour, and more. For example, a website personalisation tool can show different product recommendations or calls to action to different visitors based on their interests or behaviours.
- **Email personalisation tools** allow you to personalise the content of your email campaigns based on various factors, such as location, past behaviour, and more. For example, you can use an email personalization tool to send different versions of your newsletter to different subscribers based on their interests or preferences.

- **Customer data platforms (CDPs)** allow you to collect and manage data about your customers and use it to personalise your content and marketing efforts. For example, you can use a CDP to segment your audience into different groups based on common characteristics or interests and then create personalised content or marketing campaigns for each group.

Many personalisation tools, paid and free, can help you create more targeted and relevant content for your audience. However, it is essential to choose the right tools for your business and consider the time and resources required to implement and maintain them.

Here are a few examples of personalisation tools that can be used for content marketing:

- Optimizely.com is a website personalisation tool that allows you to show different versions of your website to different visitors based on various factors, such as location, device type, and past behaviour. You can use Optimizely to test different website versions and see which ones perform best.
- Hubspot.com is a marketing platform that offers a variety of personalisation tools, including email and website personalisation and customer data management. You can use HubSpot to segment your audience into different groups and create personalised content and marketing campaigns for each group.
- Twilio Segment.com is a customer data platform (CDP) that allows you to collect and manage data about your customers and use it to personalise your content and marketing efforts. You can use Segment to segment your audience into different groups based on common characteristics or interests and then create personalised content or marketing campaigns for each group.

DIFFERENT VERSIONS OF YOUR CONTENT

By creating **different versions** of your content for different audience segments, you can tailor your messaging and content to each group's specific needs and interests, resulting in more targeted and relevant content that resonates more effectively with your audience. Just maintain a consistent brand voice and messaging across all versions of your content to ensure that your audience recognises and trusts your brand.

For example, suppose your brand, Moonlit Apparel, sells streetwear clothing and apparel. In that case, you might create different versions of your content for different audience segments, such as segment-focused versions of your email newsletter:

Focus One – trendy, urban-inspired clothing for customers in their 20s:

Subject Line: 'Stay ahead of the trends with Moonlit Apparel'

Hey there,
Are you always on the lookout for the latest and greatest in streetwear fashion? Look no further than Moonlit Apparel! We've got all the trendy, urban-inspired pieces you need to stay ahead of the game.
Check out some of our top picks for the season:
- *Our 'City Nights' graphic t-shirt features a bold, neon design perfect for hitting the town.*
- *Our 'Skater's Paradise' windbreaker, with a retro-inspired design that's perfect for cruising the streets in style.*
- *Our 'Street Art' joggers, with a colourful, graffiti-inspired print, are sure to turn heads.*

Don't miss out on these hot new styles – shop now and stay ahead of the trends with Moonlit Apparel!

Focus Two – more classic timeless pieces for customers in their 30s:

Subject Line: 'Elevate your style with timeless pieces from Moonlit Apparel.'

Hi there,
Are you looking to elevate your style with timeless, classic pieces? Look no further than Moonlit Apparel! We've got a range of high-quality, stylish clothing that will always stay in fashion.
Look at some of our top picks for the season:
- *Our 'Heritage' denim jacket, with a vintage-inspired wash and sturdy construction, will last for years.*
- *Our 'Classic Crew' sweatshirt, with a simple, understated design that can be dressed up or down.*
- *Our 'Sleek Stripes' polo shirt, with a slim fit and stylish stripe pattern that's perfect for work or play.*

Upgrade your wardrobe with these timeless pieces from Moonlit Apparel – shop now and elevate your style!

You could also create regionally focused versions of your website or social media content that highlights local events or promotions, such as.

For Customers in the U.S.:

We're excited to announce that we'll showcase our latest collections at the Streetwear Expo in Los Angeles next month. So be sure to stop by our booth and check out our new arrivals – we'll be offering special discounts and promotions for attendees.
Take advantage of this exciting opportunity to see our new collections in person and save on your favourite pieces. We'll see you at the Streetwear Expo!

For Customers in Europe, where Moonlit Apparel has no physical presence:

We are excited to announce that we will showcase our latest collections through a live-streaming event on our website and social media channels next month. So be sure to tune in and check out our new arrivals and take advantage of special discounts and promotions. Plus, receive a free accessory with purchases over €100. Even though we do not have a physical presence in Europe, we are still excited to bring our collections and promotions to our customers in the region through this online event. So don't miss out on this exciting opportunity to see our new arrivals and take advantage of our special offers.

We look forward to connecting with you online!

SEGMENT YOUR AUDIENCE

Segmenting your audience into smaller, defined groups based on common characteristics or interests is crucial to effectively personalise your content, creating even more targeted and relevant content that resonates more effectively with each group.

For example, suppose your business sells clothing. In that case, you might segment your audience into groups based on age, gender, location and personal style. This would allow you to create content specifically tailored to each group's needs and interests rather than trying to appeal to everyone with a one-size-fits-all approach. The result is more relevant content that resonates more effectively with each group and leads to better engagement and conversion rates.

Some common characteristics or interests that you might use to segment your audience include:

-   Demographic information, such as age, gender, income and education level
-   Geographic location, such as country, region, or city
-   Behavioural data, such as past purchases or website activity
-   Interests and preferences, such as hobbies, lifestyle, or product categories

Remember that personalisation can be time-consuming. So it is essential to strike a balance between personalised and generic content that can be used for all audience segments. It is also important to consider the ethical implications of personalisation and ensure you are not overstepping any boundaries or invading people's privacy.

CHOOSING THE RIGHT DIGITAL CONTENT FORMATS

What format should you choose when creating digital content for the page, stage or screen? As you ponder this question, remember that selecting the appropriate format is crucial in building an effective digital content marketing strategy. Consider your goals, objectives and target audience's preferences and behaviours to make the best choice for your business and maximise the impact of your digital content marketing efforts.

Images, the oldest form of transportable communication, have a universal appeal that transcends language barriers and cultural differences. They have the power to evoke emotions and convey meaning in a way that text alone cannot. However, according to the **Media Naturalness Theory**, writing has only existed for less than 2% of human history, so our brains are not evolved for reading. This means that the absence of vocal and facial cues in written text can make it difficult for readers to fully understand the intended context.

> For our purposes as content creators and brand storytellers, the format is the way that a piece of content is brought to life: the form it takes when it leaves your brain and enters the world, and the means by which our audience can engage with or consume it.

The Content Fuel Framework
Melanie Deziel

Therefore, when creating digital content, consider using images and other visual elements to supplement the written text to ensure the message is conveyed clearly and effectively. Additionally, audio and video formats, such as podcasts or webinars, that can provide vocal and facial cues can be a powerful way to reach your audience and give them the context they need to fully engage with your content.

Some common digital content formats include blog posts, articles, videos, infographics, social media posts, eBooks, whitepapers and webinars. Each of these formats has its own strengths and weaknesses and can be used differently to achieve different goals.

> Customize the content you distribute on each channel. Consider what messages are appropriate for each channel, and create a message you think will resonate with that specific audience.

Content Inc.
Joe Pulizzi

HOW TO WRITE LIKE A PRO

The elements of a text:

1. The **title** is the name or heading of the text. It should be concise and catchy, and it should give the reader an idea of what the text is about.
2. The **introduction** is the first part of the text, and it serves to introduce the topic and provide context for the reader. It should grab the reader's attention and provide a clear overview of what the text will cover.
3. The **paragraphs** are the main body of the text, and they contain the main ideas and supporting details. Each paragraph should have a clear topic sentence that introduces the main idea of the paragraph, and the rest of the paragraph should provide supporting details and examples.
4. The **conclusion** is the final part of the text, and it summarises the main points and conclusions of the text. It should also provide any final thoughts or recommendations.

Other elements that may be included in a written text are subheadings, lists, tables and images. These elements can help to break up the text and make it easier to read and understand.

It is important for a copywriter to consider all these elements when writing a text, as they work together to create a cohesive and effective piece of writing that effectively communicates the intended message to the reader.

TITLE AND HEADLINE

Titles and headlines differ in characteristics and purposes in content marketing. The **title** is the overall subject or theme of the content piece, and it should be concise and accurate. The title is often used as the primary identifier for the content. Therefore, it is displayed prominently at the top of the page or in search results.

The **headline**, on the other hand, is a brief phrase or sentence that appears near the top of the content, grabs the reader's attention and summarises the content's main points or themes. The headline is typically displayed in a larger font than the rest of the text and is often used to entice the reader to read the rest of the content.

> Your headline should promise the reader what you are going to deliver—as specifically as possible. What are readers going to get out of reading this piece? In what way will it inform them, or make their lives better?

Everybody Writes
Ann Handley

Writing compelling headlines and titles is an essential skill in digital content marketing:

- A good headline or title can grab the attention of your target audience and can encourage them to click and read your content.
- A lousy headline or title, on the other hand, can turn potential readers away, resulting in low engagement and poor performance.

> Find the key words — vivid words — in the text and try to get them into the headline.

The Times Style Guide
Ian Brunskill and Times Books

> **Go for titles that solve someone's problem.**
>
> Video Marketing Like a PRO
> Clo Willaerts

> **Brevity and clarity matter more than ever.**
>
> Everybody Writes
> Ann Handley

KEEP IT SHORT AND SWEET

Some tips for writing good titles and headlines:

- Use titles and headlines to grab the reader's attention and effectively communicate your content's main themes or messages.
- Use titles and headlines to increase the chances of your content being read and shared.
- Use titles and headlines to improve engagement and performance.
- Keep titles and headlines easy to read and understand.
- Aim for titles and headlines that are 6-12 words long.
- Avoid titles and headlines that are too long or too short.

> Online we tend to scan more, so shorter words and sentences become even more important.

Everybody Writes
Ann Handley

EVERY
WRI

{ Your Go-To Guide i
  Ridiculously Good

ANN HAN

USE POWER WORDS

Power words can elicit a strong emotional or psychological response from the reader. Some examples of power words include: amazing, incredible, unbelievable and revolutionary. When used in titles and headlines, these words add excitement and interest and encourage the reader to continue reading.

Power words effectively trigger specific emotions in the reader, such as greed, curiosity, trust and lust. By using these words strategically, you can create titles and headlines that grab the reader's attention and effectively communicate your content's main themes or messages.

Cache-focused power words are words or phrases that imply scarcity and exclusivity. They can be used in copywriting to create a sense of urgency and encourage the reader to take action.

Some examples of power words that imply scarcity and exclusivity:

- applications currently closed
- class full
- competitive
- cutting-edge
- early bird
- exclusive
- insider
- just-finished
- login required
- members-only
- never-before-seen
- pilot

- pioneer
- premium
- premiere
- red hot
- request invitation

- revolutionary
- selective
- secret
- waitlist
- VIP

Urgency-focused power words imply speed and time-sensitivity. Here are some examples:

- expiring
- fast
- fast-pass
- hurry
- immediately
- latest
- limited edition
- limited time

- now
- one-time
- only available
- quick
- time-limited
- today
- in X weeks

Here is a list of **low risk** focused power words that imply security and stability:

- 100% satisfaction guarantee
- approved
- authorized Dealer
- certified
- confidential
- dedicated
- fully licensed
- guaranteed

- insured
- no risk
- official
- original
- protected
- safe and secure
- trusted
- verified

Energy-focused power words imply action and transformation:

- accelerate
- boost
- discover
- empower
- grow
- ignite
- introducing
- learn
- life-changing

- magic
- miracle
- profit
- revolutionize
- simplify
- transform
- unlock
- unleash
- win

Here are a few examples for PlatePlanner headlines that use power words:

Transform Your Meal Planning with These 10 Incredible Tips
Revolutionize Your Kitchen with These Amazing Meal Planning Strategies
Discover the Unbelievable Benefits of Meal Planning and Never Go Hungry Again

Here are three examples of headlines for Moonlit Apparel:

Get the Ultimate Street Style with These 10 Amazing Streetwear Trends
Rock Your Wardrobe with These Revolutionary Streetwear Brands
Stay Up to Date with the Latest Incredible Streetwear Trends for Teens

Instead of using vague or general titles and headlines, try to be specific and use concrete details to describe the content of your article or post. This will give readers a clear idea of what to expect and encourage them to read.

> A good title should reveal information, not hide it. Don't write, "Tips on an Important Purchase." Write, "Six Ways to Save Money Buying a House."
>
> 100 Ways to Improve Your Writing
> Gary Provost

DO NOT USE CLICKBAIT

Make sure to avoid using clickbait titles. **Clickbait titles** are headlines and titles that are designed to trick or deceive potential readers into clicking on a piece of content and they are often used to generate clicks and traffic.

'You won't believe what happens next: the most shocking twist in the history of twists!'
'You won't believe what this cat does when it sees a dog!'
'This one simple trick will change your life forever!'

However, they can also result in a poor user experience and damage your brand's reputation and credibility.

Instead of using clickbait titles, focus on creating authentic, engaging and transparent headlines and titles that accurately reflect the content of your article or post.

USE NUMBERS

Including **numbers** in your titles and headlines can be a valuable strategy for making them more specific and engaging. By including a number, you are giving the reader a clear indication of how many tips, ideas, or examples they can expect to find in your content. This can make your titles and headlines more attractive and give the reader a better understanding of what to expect.

> Numbers set expectations for readers. I like oddball numbers (like 3½, or 19, or 37).
>
> Everybody Writes
> Ann Handley

For example, a title such as 10 *Tips for Improving Your Content Marketing Strategy* is more specific and engaging than *Tips for Improving Your Content Marketing Strategy*, as it gives the reader a clear indication of the number of tips they can expect to find in the article. This can make the content more organized and structured and encourage the reader to continue reading.

Numbers can also help improve your content's search engine optimisation (SEO). Search engines often prioritise more specific and detailed content and including numbers in your titles and headlines can signal to search engines that your content is relevant and valuable to the reader.

INCLUDE SEO KEYWORDS

Including relevant **keywords** in your titles and headlines can help improve your content's search engine optimisation (SEO) and make it more visible to potential readers.

> Use relevant keywords. Determine these by asking: which product/ service do you offer and how do your potential customers search for that service/product?
>
> Digital marketing like a PRO
> Clo Willaerts

Here is how this might look for Moonlit Apparel:

The Ultimate Guide to Streetwear Trends for Skateboarding and Rap-Loving Teens: Find the Best Sneakers and Hoodies Here

Keywords that accurately reflect the main themes and content of the blog post have been used in the title to make it clear what readers can expect in the article. Keywords also help it to rank high in search results, increasing its visibility.

TOOL: COSCHEDULE HEADLINE ANALYZER

CoSchedule's Headline Analyzer (coschedule.com/headline-analyser) is a free online tool that helps content marketing professionals analyse the length and effectiveness of their titles and headlines. It is designed to help users create titles and headlines that are more compelling, engaging and effective at grabbing the reader's attention.

To use Headline Analyzer, users simply enter their title or headline into the tool. Then, it generates a score based on various factors including length, readability, emotion and SEO. Suggestions for improving the headline, including recommendations for shorter, more specific and more SEO-friendly headlines are also provided.

The Headline Analyzer is particularly useful for content marketing professionals looking to create titles and headlines that are easy to read and understand while still being able to grab the reader's attention and effectively communicate their content's main themes or messages. By using the tool to analyse and optimise their titles and headlines, content marketers can improve the chances of their content being read and shared and ultimately increase engagement and performance.

Here is a list of alternative tools that can help you create shorter titles and headlines:

1. **Title Generator** creates titles and headlines based on keywords you enter. It can help to provide ideas for short and specific titles and headlines.
2. **Headline Analyzer** by Advanced Marketing Institute is a tool that analyses the emotional impact of your headlines and provides a score based on factors such as length, readability and emotion. It can help you to create headlines that are more compelling and effective at grabbing the reader's attention.
3. **Headline Studio** is a tool that helps you to create and optimise headlines for SEO. It provides suggestions for shorter, more specific and more SEO-friendly headlines based on keywords that you enter.
4. Portent's Title Generator: Portent's Title Generator is a tool that generates titles and headlines based on keywords you enter. It provides a range of options, including shorter and more specific titles. It can help to provide ideas for headlines that are easy to read and understand.

INTRODUCTION

A compelling **introduction** is an essential element of any written piece, as it sets the tone and purpose of the content and helps to engage and persuade the reader to continue reading. Following are some tips for writing a compelling introduction.

START WITH A HOOK

A **hook** grabs the reader's attention and draws them into the content. There are many hooks, including rhetorical questions, statistics, quotes, anecdotes and suspenseful statements. Choose a hook appropriate for your content and audience and use it to draw the reader in and make them want to read.

CLEARLY STATE THE PURPOSE

Make the **purpose** of your content clear to the reader and **what they can expect to learn from it**, within the first sentence or two of your introductory paragraphs. This will set the tone and direction of your content.

> Listen to customer service inquiries. Watch how customers behave. See what problems they have. "Look for patterns.

Everybody Writes
Ann Handley

> Do not try to cram in too much information; but do not wait until paragraph six to answer those obvious questions: who, where, what, why, when?

The Times Style Guide
Ian Brunskill and Times Books

PROVIDE CONTEXT

Depending on the content of your article or post, providing some **context** or background information may help the reader understand what you are writing about. This can be particularly important if you are writing about a complex or unfamiliar topic.

> There should be enough description so the audience will see, hear, taste, smell, and feel everything going on.

The Art of Storytelling
John Walsh

NAIL YOUR INTRO WITH THE INVERTED PYRAMID STYLE

In content marketing, using the inverted pyramid style can effectively structure your writing and grab the reader's attention. This style involves placing the most important or critical information at the beginning of the article, followed by supporting information and background information.

The **inverted pyramid style** is commonly used in journalism to ensure that readers can quickly and easily understand the key points of a story. By starting with the most essential information and gradually providing more detail, the inverted pyramid style helps keep the reader engaged.

To apply the inverted pyramid style to your content marketing

- Start by clearly stating the main point or takeaway of your article or blog post in the title and the first few sentences. This will help to grab the reader's attention and quickly communicate the key points of your content.
- Then, use the rest of the article to provide supporting information and background context. This will help readers easily understand and retain the main points of your content, even if they only read the first few sentences.

Overall, using the inverted pyramid style in content marketing can effectively structure your writing and ensure that your key points are clearly communicated and easily understood by your reader.

> Writing in the pyramid style means getting to the point at the top, putting the "who, what, when, where, and why" in the first paragraph, and developing the supporting information under it.

100 Ways to Improve Your Writing
Gary Provost

SUBHEADINGS AND PARAGRAPHS

When creating content for a newsletter or article, consider how your audience will be scanning the text. Use **subheadings** and **paragraphs** to break up the text into easily digestible chunks to optimise attention. This serves to optimise readers' attention because they can easily and quickly scan the content and find the information they are looking for.

Incorporating other visual elements such as **bullet points**, **images** and **infographics** can make your text more scannable and engaging. By formatting your content in a way that is easy to scan, you can increase the chances that your audience will engage with and retain the information you are trying to communicate.

Limit each paragraph to one topic.

> Make the paragraph the unit of composition: one paragraph to each topic.

The Elements of Style
William Strunk Jr.

> Create transitions between paragraphs. Good transitions greatly improve the feel and reader-friendliness of any work. The best writing flows from paragraph to paragraph, creating progression and cadence. Good transitions are like fine stitching, turning disconnected writing into a seamless whole.

Everybody Writes: Your Go-To Guide ...
Ann Handley

STYLE

In content marketing, the **writing style** that you use can have a significant impact on the effectiveness of your message and the overall success of your content.

> Good writing serves the reader, not the writer. It isn't self-indulgent. Good writing anticipates the questions that readers might have as they're reading a piece, and it answers them.
>
> Everybody Writes
> Ann Handley

Many different writing styles can be used in content marketing, each with unique characteristics and purposes. Some common writing styles:

1. **Persuasive writing** is designed to convince the reader to take a specific action or to adopt a particular point of view. It often uses strong, emotive language and concrete evidence to support the writer's argument.
2. **Descriptive writing** is designed to describe something in detail, often using sensory language to help the reader visualise or experience the subject. This style is often used in travel writing, food writing and other forms of content that aim to paint a vivid picture of a place or experience.
3. **Narrative writing** tells a story, often using dialogue and descriptive language to bring the story to life. This style is commonly used in fiction writing. Still, it can also be used in content marketing to create engaging and immersive content.
4. **Expository writing** is designed to explain or inform the reader about a particular topic. It often uses a logical, step-by-step structure to present information clearly and concisely.
5. **Creative writing** is any writing that is not purely informative or factual. It can include elements of poetry, fiction and other forms of artistic expression and is often used to create engaging and imaginative content.

Overall, many different writing styles can be used in content marketing. The best style for your content will depend on your goals and the needs of your audience. This is an example of what persuasive writing might look like for Moonlit Apparel:

> *Are you sick of wearing the same old hoodies and sneakers as everyone else? Are you looking for something unique, stylish and high-quality? If so, then our line of hoodies and sneakers is perfect for you!*
>
> *Our hoodies are made from top-notch materials and have cool, attention-grabbing designs that make you stand out. They're also super comfy, so you can wear them all day without feeling weighed down or restricted.*
>
> *Our sneakers are just as awesome, with a sleek, modern design and unbeatable comfort. They're great for casual wear, showing off your style when skateboarding, or listening to your favourite rap songs. And they're made from durable materials that will last a long time, so you won't have to worry about replacing them anytime soon.*
>
> *Do not just take our word for it – see why our hoodies and sneakers are the best. Check out our collection today and feel the difference. We promise you will be satisfied!*

Here are some tips for crafting a strong and persuasive writing style:

- Rather than being vague or abstract, make sure to be **specific** and provide **concrete details** in your copy. This will help make your writing more engaging and believable and make it easier for the reader to understand and relate to your content.

> Your writing will be faster, livelier, and clearer if you write short paragraphs. The reader will welcome the break and the white space.
>
> 100 Ways to Improve Your Writing
> Gary Provost

- **Short sentences and paragraphs** are easier to read and understand and can help keep the reader engaged and interested in your content. Avoid using long, complex sentences or paragraphs, as they can be challenging to follow and may cause the reader to lose interest.
- When writing persuasively, you must present your topic confidently and support your idea with **factual evidence**. This can include statistics, examples, case studies, or expert testimony, which will help make your writing more credible and convincing.

By following these tips and focusing on crafting a strong and persuasive writing style, you can create content that is engaging, accessible and effective at persuading your reader to take the desired action, whether that be making a purchase, signing up for a newsletter, or simply continuing to read and engage with your content.

GRAMMAR

It is essential to pay attention to **grammar** and **language** used to create clear and compelling content. Here are some tips for improving your grammar and making your writing punchy and to the point:

- Writing is more direct and engaging when written in the **active voice**, meaning that the subject of the sentence performs the action. For example, 'The cat chased the mouse' is in active voice, while 'The mouse was chased by the cat' is in passive voice.

Use the active voice.

The Elements of Style
William Strunk Jr.

- **Simple present tense** describes actions or states that are currently happening or are always true. Using simple present tense can make your writing more concise and to the point, as it eliminates the need for verb conjugations. For example, 'I write' is in the simple present tense, while 'I am writing' is in the present continuous tense.

> Active is better than passive, concrete better than abstract, positive usually better than negative.

The Times Style Guide
Ian Brunskill and Times Books

By paying attention to grammar and language usage and using active voice and simple present tense, you can create punchy, to-the-point and engaging content for your reader.

> As every writer knows, if you want to be a writer, you have to be a reader first.

Show Your Work!: 10 Ways to Share Y...
Austin Kleon

Here are some ways that content marketing professionals can improve their grammar skills:

- **Reading** can help to expose you to different writing styles and grammatical structures and can help to improve your language skills and understanding of grammar.
- Many **online classes and workshops** are available to help you learn more about grammar and improve your writing skills.
- Use a **grammar checker**: Tools like Grammarly or Hemingway App can help you to identify and correct common grammatical mistakes in your writing.
- Asking for **feedback** from colleagues or professional editors can help you to identify areas where you can improve your grammar skills and receive guidance on how to do so.
- Use **reference materials**: Many books and online resources are available to help you improve your grammar skills. Some popular reference materials include *The Elements of Style* by William Strunk Jr. and E.B. White, *The Chicago Manual of Style* and *Merriam-Webster's Collegiate Dictionary*.

Be a critical reader and look upon all that you read as a lesson in good writing.

100 Ways to Improve Your Writing
Gary Provost

Overall, there are many ways that content marketing professionals can improve their grammar skills and the best approach will depend on your individual needs and learning style.

VOCABULARY: KEEP IT SIMPLE

Effective copy is clear and concise and complex or jargon-heavy language is avoided. Keep your language straightforward and uncomplicated.

Apple's advertising and marketing materials are known for their clever and concise use of language. They often use metaphors and other literary devices to create a strong emotional connection with their audience.

For example, one of Apple's famous slogans is 'Think Different', a simple yet powerful message that encourages people to think outside the box and challenge the status quo.

> No one will ever complain that you've made things too simple to understand.
>
> Everybody Writes
> Ann Handley

> Create transitions between paragraphs. Good transitions greatly improve the feel and reader-friendliness of any work. The best writing flows from paragraph to paragraph, creating progression and cadence. Good transitions are like fine stitching, turning disconnected writing into a seamless whole.
>
> Everybody Writes
> Ann Handley

Here are some additional vocabulary tips for copywriters:

- **Active verbs** are verbs that show action, such as run, jump, or create. Using them can make your writing more dynamic and engaging and help to convey a sense of movement or progress.
- Avoid using **Filler words**, like very, really, or sort of. They do not add any meaning or value to the text and can make your writing seem vague or unconvincing.
- Use **Strong nouns**, specific and descriptive words that convey a clear image or concept, such as ocean, diamond, or sunset. Using strong nouns can add depth and detail to your writing and make it more evocative and memorable.
- **Vary your vocabulary** to keep your writing fresh and engaging. Repeating the same words and phrases can make your writing feel monotonous and boring.
- Use **contractions**, words that are formed by combining two words and abbreviating them, such as 'don't,' 'won't,' or 'can't.' Using contractions can make your writing sound more natural and conversational and help to create a more personal and engaging tone.

> So write with a combination of short, medium, and long sentences. Create a sound that pleases the reader's ear. Don't just write words. Write music.

100 Ways to Improve Your Writing
Gary Provost

LISTS AND TABLES

Lists and **tables** are helpful tools for improving the readability and organisation of your content. Here are some ways that lists and tables can help:

- Lists and tables can **break up long blocks of text**, making it easier for the reader to scan and understand the content.
- Lists and tables help to **organise information** clearly and logically, making it easier for the reader to understand and process.
- Lists and tables can **highlight key points or takeaways** from your content, making it easier for the reader to quickly grasp the main points.
- **Make complex information more digestible**: Lists and tables can help present complex or technical information in a more digestible format, making it easier for the reader to understand and retain the information.

CONCLUSION AND CALL-TO ACTION

The **conclusion** of your content is a crucial element that can help to summarise your main points and drive home your message.

> Don't leave your readers just standing awkwardly in the middle of the dance floor after the music stops. What do you want them to do next?

Everybody Writes
Ann Handley

EVER\
WRI

{ Your Go-To Guide
  Ridiculously Goo

ANN HAN

Here are some tips for writing a solid conclusion and call to action:

- Conclude your writing by **summarising your main points** and restating your key message. This will help to remind the reader of the key takeaways from your content and will help to drive home your argument.
- In your conclusion, consider **stating the obvious** or drawing out the implications of your main points. This helps clarify your message and make it more meaningful for the reader.
- Your conclusion is an excellent opportunity to encourage the reader to take a specific action, such as signing up for a newsletter, making a purchase, or leaving a comment. Ensure to include a clear and compelling **call to action** that motivates the reader to take the desired action.

> Use a clear call to action if you want your followers to do something.
>
> Everybody Writes: Your Go-To Guide ...
> Ann Handley

EVER)
WRI

Your Go-To Guide
Ridiculously Good

ANN HAN

Considering these tips and crafting a strong and persuasive conclusion, you can create engaging, memorable and compelling content driving your reader's desired action.

TOOL: GRAMMARLY

Grammarly is a tool that helps you write better. It checks your writing for mistakes in spelling, grammar and punctuation. It also gives you suggestions for how to make your writing clearer and more engaging. Grammarly can even help you avoid accidentally copying someone else's words by checking for plagiarism. Plus, you can customise it to fit your own writing style and the type of writing you are doing. You simply type your writing into Grammarly and it will give you feedback and suggestions to help you improve.

Grammarly is a popular tool for creating textual content because it helps users produce error-free writing. It uses artificial intelligence and natural language processing technology to check writing for grammar, spelling, punctuation and other errors. It also offers suggestions for improving word choice and sentence structure to make writing more effective and engaging. Additionally, Grammarly integrates with many popular writing platforms and applications, making it easy for users to check their writing as they work. Overall, Grammarly's comprehensive error-checking capabilities and writing suggestions make it a valuable tool for anyone looking to create high-quality textual content.

On the downside, Grammarly currently only offers corrections for one language: English.

Grammarly offers an extensive English grammar guide:

- grammarly.com/grammar

Some of the top alternatives to Grammarly include:

- ProWritingAid.com offers similar features to Grammarly, including grammar and spelling checks, style and tone suggestions and a plagiarism checker. It also has additional features, such as a readability checker and a thesaurus.
- WhiteSmoke.com offers a range of writing enhancement features, including grammar and spelling checks, style suggestions and a translation tool. It also has a unique feature that allows users to customise their writing based on their audience and purpose.
- Ginger (gingersoftware.com/grammarcheck) offers grammar and spelling checks, as well as sentence rephrasing suggestions to improve clarity and readability. It also has a unique feature that allows users to translate their writing into over 40 different languages.

These are just a few examples of the many alternatives to Grammarly available. Other popular options include Hemingway, After the Deadline and Language-Tool.

BLOG POSTS

> Blog posts remain among the most popular forms of content in the content marketing universe.

The Stripped-Down Guide to Content ...
John Egan

Blog posts are an effective way to share in-depth information on a specific topic and establish your business as a thought leader in your industry. They are a versatile and customisable format for content marketing that can be shared and distributed through various channels.

Blogs can benefit businesses by:

- improving conversion rates;
- fostering customer relationships;
- increasing revenue;
- promoting brand awareness; and
- improving search engine rankings.

Businesses can also establish themselves as friendly, knowledgeable and helpful by writing informative, well-written blogs, which can build trust and confidence in their brand.

Regular blogging can also be beneficial for search engine optimisation (SEO). Adding new content to your blog regularly can improve your chances of ranking higher in search engine results, which can drive more traffic to your website.

There are many sources of inspiration for blog posts and the best ones depend on the business, the audience and the goals of the content marketing strategy. Some common sources of inspiration for blog posts include:

-   **Customer feedback and insights** Businesses can learn about the needs, challenges and preferences of customers by listening to and engaging with them. This feedback can be used to create blog posts that are relevant, valuable and engaging to them.
-   **Industry trends and developments** Businesses that track business intelligence can create blog posts that are timely, informative and insightful and showcase their expertise and leadership in their field.
-   **Competitor analysis and research** Analysis and research of competitors' strategies and content can help businesses to learn about their strengths and weaknesses and allow them to create blog posts that are unique, different and better than their competitors.
-   **Internal expertise and knowledge** can be leveraged by businesses to create blog posts that are authentic, credible and authoritative and that can showcase their unique perspectives and value propositions.

When writing blog content, it is essential to consider the format of your post. This includes:

-   the length of the post;
-   the use of headings and subheadings; and
-   the inclusion of images and other media.

A well-formatted blog post is easy to read and can help to keep your readers engaged.

There are many sources of inspiration for blog posts. Businesses can use a combination of these sources to create blog posts that are relevant, valuable and engaging to their audience and that can help to achieve their marketing and business goals.

Here are some blog post ideas that can help to establish you and your business as the authority in your niche, while being of help to your audience:

-   A **list post** is a type of blog post that includes a numbered or bullet-pointed list of items, tips, or resources. It is easy to read and can be a great way to provide concise information.
-   A **how-to post** is a tutorial that walks readers through a process or task step by step. It can help demonstrate your expertise and provide value to your audience.

- A **tips and tricks post** is a blog post that includes a list of recommendations or advice on a particular topic. It can help provide value to your readers and demonstrate your expertise.
- A **case study post** is a detailed analysis of a specific situation or problem, along with the steps taken to solve it. This type of post can be a powerful way to demonstrate the value of your products or services.
- A **problem/solution post** addresses a specific problem your audience is facing and provides solutions or recommendations for managing it. It can help to establish you as an expert in your field and provide value to your readers.
- An **FAQ post** is a collection of frequently asked questions about a particular topic, along with answers to those questions. It can provide information and address common questions and concerns.
- An **SAQ post** is a blog post that includes a list of questions customers or prospects should ask but may not think to ask. It can provide valuable information and address common concerns or questions.
- A **research post** is a blog post that summarises and analyses research or data on a particular topic. This post can help to establish you as an expert in your field and provide valuable insights to your readers.
- A **checklist post** is a list of steps or items readers can use to complete a task or achieve a specific goal. It can provide guidance and ensure readers have all the necessary information.
- An **ultimate guide post** is a comprehensive resource that covers all aspects of a particular topic. It can provide in-depth information and establish your business as your niche's go-to source of information.
- A **definition post** is a blog post that defines a specific term or concept. This type of post can provide clarity and understanding to readers who may be unfamiliar with the topic.
- A **series post** is a set of blog posts that are related to a specific topic and are published over time. It can provide in-depth information and keep readers engaged over an extended period.
- A **stats post** is a blog post that includes statistics or data on a particular topic. This type of post can provide information and demonstrate the significance of a particular issue or trend.
- A **pillar post** is a comprehensive, in-depth blog post that covers a particular topic in detail. This post is a go-to resource for readers and can help establish you as an authority in your niche.
- A **video review** post is a blog post that includes a review of a particular product or service in the form of a video. It can provide visual content and demonstrate your expertise in one area.

- A **tools post** is a blog post that includes a list of tools or resources that can be helpful for a particular task or goal. This post can provide recommendations and demonstrate your knowledge of valuable resources in your field.

These are just a few ideas for blog posts that can establish you and your business as the authority in your niche and provide value to your audience.

Your blog posts do not need to be all about you! By writing posts that focus on other people or brands, you can showcase your interests outside your brand and provide value to your audience by sharing useful or interesting content.

Here are some additional blog post ideas that put other brands or people in the centre of attention:

- Write posts **highlighting other people or brands** you admire or think your audience would be interested in. This can be a great way to build relationships and showcase your interests outside your brand.
- Write a **profile post about an influential person** in your industry or niche. This can be a great way to introduce your audience to someone they may need to become more familiar with and to showcase the expertise of others in your field.
- A **link roundup post** includes a collection of interesting links or articles you've come across recently. This can be a great way to provide value to your audience by sharing useful or interesting content that you have found online.
- A **pick of the week post** highlights a product, service, or resource you have been enjoying recently. This can be a great way to share your recommendations and showcase your interests outside your brand.
- A **crowdsourced post** includes contributions from multiple people or sources. This can be a great way to get input from others and showcase the expertise of various people in your field.
- A **quote post** includes a collection of quotes that you find inspiring or thought-provoking. This can be a great way to inspire and motivate your audience.
- A **people-to-follow post** includes a list of people or brands you recommend following on social media or elsewhere. This can be a great way to introduce your audience to new voices or perspectives and to build relationships with others in your industry.

- An **interview post** includes an interview with someone in your industry or niche. This can be a great way to introduce your audience to new voices and showcase the expertise of others in your field.
- A **best of the web** post includes a collection of the best articles or resources you have come across recently. This can be a great way to provide value to your audience by sharing useful or interesting content that you've found online.

CORPORATE BLOGS

Corporate blogging can be a powerful tool for businesses of all sizes. By regularly updating a company blog with informative and engaging content, businesses can attract and retain a loyal audience, establish themselves as thought leaders in their industry and drive traffic and revenue to their websites.

Here are some key principles for writing for a company blog:

- **Stick to what you know** by focusing on the facts and anecdotes you know first-hand rather than trying to stretch the story to fit a particular narrative or make grandiose claims that cannot be supported. This will help you build credibility and authenticity with your audience.
- **Focus on the human element** by sharing stories about people's experiences, whether a customer's experience with your product or a team member's personal journey. These stories can help you connect with your audience on a deeper level.
- **Use descriptive language and technique**s structured to create an engaging and immersive experience for the reader. This can bring your content to life and make it more compelling.

By following these principles, you can create compelling content that resonates with your audience and helps to establish your company as a thought leader in your industry.

Here are some blog post ideas for a company blog:

- A **company update post** includes news and updates about your company, such as new products, projects, or initiatives. This post can help keep your audience informed and engaged with your business.

- A **year-in-review post** looks back at the highlights and accomplishments of your company over the past year. It can provide a snapshot of your business and reflect your progress.
- A **project showcase post** highlights a project or initiative your company has completed. This post can help demonstrate your capabilities and expertise.
- A **presentation post** includes a video recording or slides from a presentation given by an employee. It can help share knowledge and insights with your audience.
- A **product update** post includes news and updates about a particular product. This post can help keep your audience informed and engaged with your products.
- A **product tips post** includes tips and tricks for using a particular product. It can help provide value to your customers and demonstrate your product knowledge.
- A **comparison post** compares the features and benefits of your product to those of your competitors. It can help demonstrate the value of your product and highlight its unique features.
- A **best-of post** includes a list of your company's best products, projects, or initiatives. This post can highlight your best work and showcase your capabilities.
- A **trend post** analyses a current trend in your industry and discusses its implications for your business. This post can inform your audience about trends and demonstrate your expertise in your field.

In summary, writing for the company blog is a powerful way to engage and inform your audience and establish your company as a thought leader in your industry. By focusing on what you know, highlighting the human element and using effective language and structure, you can create content that resonates with your audience and helps to build relationships and credibility.

CASE IN POINT: MICROSOFT START BLOG

The Microsoft Start Blog at blogs.msn.com provides small business owners and entrepreneurs information and resources.

The blog includes a wide range of content, including:

- tips and best practices for small businesses;
- profiles of successful entrepreneurs; and
- updates on new products and services from Microsoft.

Many blog posts also include advice and resources for using Microsoft products and services in a small business setting.

Overall, the content on the Microsoft Start Blog is geared towards providing value to small business owners and entrepreneurs while promoting the products and services offered by Microsoft. By providing valuable and informative content, the blog may attract and retain a loyal audience of small business owners and entrepreneurs, which could lead to increased sales and revenue for the company.

WEBSITE ARTICLES

Publishing valuable, relevant and engaging content on your website is an essential part of a content marketing strategy because it allows you to showcase your expertise, values and offerings and to attract, engage and retain your audience.

Websites can host a wide range of content, such as blog posts, articles, videos, images, etc. They can be optimised for different audiences, devices and platforms. Like blog posts, **articles** are often shorter and more focused on news and current events.

> Create content that is high quality and in-depth, and that covers a range of angles related to your subject. Website content needs to be useful, engaging, informative and credible – this is more important than the length (word count). It also needs to be current, fresh and original. Content is still king!

Digital Marketing Like a PRO
Clo Willaerts

Websites are well-suited for engaging with audiences on social media because they provide a central hub for content and interactions and allow businesses to control the design, branding and functionality of their online presence.

You can showcase your expertise and establish yourself as a thought leader in your industry by regularly publishing articles on your website. This can help to build trust and credibility with your audience and, ultimately, lead to increased sales and revenue.

Publishing articles on your website can also improve its search engine ranking, making it more likely for potential customers to find your business through search engines like Google.

Here is an example of a website article for a meal-planning app called PlatePlanner:

Welcome to PlatePlanner! Our meal-planning app makes it easy to plan healthy, delicious meals for the week. Simply select your dietary preferences and restrictions and our app will generate a personalised meal plan for you. You can also use our shopping list feature to ensure you have all the necessary ingredients. So, start meal planning today and take control of your health and wellness. Sign up now and see the difference it can make in your daily routine.

EBOOKS

eBooks are digital books that can be read on electronic devices like computers, tablets and e-readers. As a result, eBooks have become a popular format for delivering content to audiences, especially in the context of content marketing.

BENEFITS OF EBOOKS

eBooks offer several benefits as a content marketing tool:

1. **They are portable** and easily accessed on a wide range of devices, making them convenient for users who are on the go or who prefer to read digitally.

2. eBooks can include **interactive features**, such as hyperlinks, videos and audio clips, which can enhance the user experience and make the content more engaging.
3. eBooks are generally **less expensive** to produce and distribute than print books, making them a cost-effective content marketing tool.
4. They can be easily customised to fit different needs and audiences, making them a **versatile** content marketing tool.
5. eBooks can be easily **tracked and measured** which can help businesses and organisations understand the effectiveness of their content marketing efforts.

Other content that can be presented in a PDF format includes:

- **Booklets** Small, concise documents that provide information on a specific topic. They are often used for marketing purposes or as educational materials.
- **Guides** Detailed documents that provide step-by-step instructions or advice on how to do something. They can be used for various purposes, such as providing guidance on how to use a product or service or teaching a skill.
- **Lookbooks** A collection of images and descriptions showcasing a company's products or services. They are often used in fashion and retail to promote a new collection or season.
- **Catalogues** A comprehensive list of company products or services, often with detailed descriptions and images.
- **Magazines** Periodical publications containing various articles and features on various topics. They can focus on a specific industry or subject matter or be more general.
- **Planners** Documents that help individuals or teams organize and schedule tasks and events. They often include calendars and to-do lists and a section for notes.
- **Organisers** Like planners, organisers provide a way to structure and organise information. They can keep track of contacts, appointments, or other important details.
- **Checklists** Lists of items or tasks that need to be completed, often used to ensure that all necessary steps are taken in a process.
- **Instructions** Detailed descriptions of how to use a product or perform a task. They are often provided with products to help users get the most out of them.

- **Patterns** Detailed descriptions and diagrams showing how to create a specific item, such as clothing or a craft project.
- **Templates** Pre-designed documents or files that can be easily modified and used for various purposes, such as creating a brochure or a resume.
- **Worksheets** Documents that provide a structure for organising and recording information, often used in education or training settings.
- **Thought leadership eBooks** are digital publications designed to showcase your expertise and thought leadership in a particular subject area. By sharing your knowledge and insights through storytelling, you can engage your audience and establish yourself as a trusted authority.

> A thought leader is an individual or firm that is recognized as an authority in a specialized field. Their expertise is often rewarded and sought after in TV station interviews, guest posts on big blogs, opinion pieces in trade or industry magazines or newspapers, and speeches at conferences and events.
>
> Digital Marketing Like a PRO
> Clo Willaerts

STORYTELLING TACTICS FOR EBOOKS

Incorporating storytelling tactics can be an effective way to engage and connect with your audience when it comes to using eBooks as a tool for thought leadership. Storytelling allows you to communicate your message in a more relatable and memorable way, making it easier for your audience to understand and remember your core narrative. In this context, there are several key elements to consider when using storytelling in a thought leadership eBook:

- Identify the **core narrative** you want to share in your thought leadership eBook.
- **Structure** the story in a way that is easy to follow and engaging for your audience, using chapters or sections, headings and subheadings.

- Use **vivid language** to bring the story to life and help readers visualise the described events and ideas.
- Include **specific details** and **sensory language** to make the story more relatable and immersive for the reader.
- Tailor the story to the **interests** and **needs** of your audience.

In a content marketing context, PlatePlanner, an imaginary meal planning app, can use Emily's story as an example in a thought leadership eBook on time and money-saving strategies for working mothers.

Emily is a working mother in her 30s looking for ways to save time and money while still being able to provide for her family. She discovers meal delivery services, which provide convenience and cost savings by saving her time on grocery shopping and meal planning and reducing the amount she spends on eating out.

Here is what the text on this eBook's first page could look like:

As a busy working mother, finding ways to save time and money can be a constant challenge. Of course, you want to provide for your family and ensure their well-being. Still, you also want the time and resources to enjoy quality moments together and care for yourself. At PlateMate, we understand the struggles and demands of modern parenting. We want to help you find practical solutions that allow you to save time and money without sacrificing the things that matter most to you. In this eBook, we will share the story of Emily, a working mother like you and how she was able to save time and money by using meal delivery services. We hope Emily's story will inspire you to try new strategies, simplify your life and make the most of your time and resources.

Emily's story demonstrates the benefits of meal delivery services for busy working mothers who want to save time and money while still caring for their families. Emily can print the eBook at work as a physical reminder of these strategies.

eBook Structure

Once you have identified your story, it is important to structure it in a way that is easy to follow and engaging for your audience. This could involve using chapters or sections to break up the content, headings and subheadings to help readers navigate the material.

Here is an example of how to structure the story for the buyer persona Emily:

Chapter 1: Introduction to Emily's struggles as a working mother
Emily's busy schedule and the challenges she faced trying to balance work and family life.
The importance of finding ways to save time and money while still providing for her family.

Chapter 2: Emily discovers meal delivery services
The benefits of meal delivery services for busy working mothers
Emily's initial hesitation and how she overcame it

Chapter 3: Emily's experience with meal delivery services
The convenience and time-saving benefits of having meals delivered to her door.
The cost savings compared to eating out or buying takeout.

Chapter 4: Conclusion and tips for other working mothers
Emily's overall experience with meal delivery services and the positive impact it has had on her life.
Suggestions and recommendations for other working mothers looking to save time and money.

By structuring the story this way, the content is broken up into easy-to-follow chapters and sections and the use of headings and subheadings helps readers navigate the material and stay engaged with the story.

To bring your story to life, it is important to use vivid language that paints a clear picture for your readers. Use descriptive words and phrases to help readers visualise the events and ideas you describe. Here is an example of how to use vivid language for the buyer persona Emily:

Emily is a working mother, whose schedule has always been jam-packed. Between her job, taking care of her children and managing the household, she barely had time to catch her breath. She was constantly running from one task to the next and the thought of planning and preparing meals on top of everything else was overwhelming.

One day, while scrolling through social media, Emily stumbled upon an ad for a meal delivery service. At first, she was hesitant. The thought of having someone else choose her meals and cook for her felt strange and indulgent. But as she con-

tinued to scroll, she saw posts from other working mothers raving about meal delivery's convenience and time-saving benefits.

Finally, Emily decided to give it a try. She signed up for a weekly delivery of healthy, home-cooked meals and was amazed at the difference it made in her life. She no longer had to spend hours at the grocery store or in the kitchen preparing meals. Instead, she was able to focus on other tasks and spend more quality time with her family.

The descriptive language in this example helps readers visualise Emily's busy schedule and the challenges she faced as a working mother. It also helps readers understand the convenience and time-saving benefits of meal delivery services and how they positively impact Emily's life.

In addition to using descriptive language, it is also helpful to include exciting visuals in your thought leadership eBook. This could consist of charts, graphs, images, or other media that help illustrate your points and make your content more engaging for readers.

Here are some examples of engaging visuals that could be included in a thought leadership eBook for the buyer persona Emily:

- An infographic could illustrate the benefits of meal delivery services for busy working mothers. The infographic could include statistics on the time and money saved by using meal delivery and quotes from other working mothers who have had success with the service.
- Including photos of the meals being delivered or of Emily and her family enjoying the meals could help bring the story to life and make it more engaging for readers.
- Charts and graphs could be used to visually compare the cost of meal delivery versus eating out or buying takeout. This could help illustrate the cost savings of using meal delivery services.

Including these types of visuals can add depth and interest to your thought leadership eBook and make it more engaging for readers.

CASE IN POINT: ADOBE'S EBOOKS

Adobe has a wealth of knowledge and expertise in digital creativity and design. Adobe shares this valuable resource with its customers via eBooks. Adobe's eBooks can be purchased and downloaded from adobepress.com/store/browse/ebooks.

Adobe's eBooks cover a wide range of topics, such as design best practices, tips and tricks for using Adobe's products and trends and insights into the creative and design industries.

By producing eBooks as part of its content marketing efforts, Adobe can demonstrate its expertise and position itself as a thought leader in the creative and design space. Additionally, these eBooks can help educate and inform customers and prospects about the value and capabilities of Adobe's products, ultimately helping to drive sales and customer loyalty.

EBOOKS FOR B2B AUDIENCES

A wide variety of audiences enjoy downloading and reading eBooks, including B2B (business-to-business) audiences. Some common types of B2B audiences that may be interested in downloading and reading eBooks include:

1. **Business professionals**, such as managers, executives and entrepreneurs, may be interested in eBooks that offer practical tips, best practices and industry insights to help them improve their skills and grow their businesses.
2. **Marketing and sales professionals** may be interested in eBooks that guide lead generation, customer acquisition and sales strategy.
3. **IT professionals** may be interested in eBooks that cover technical topics, such as data analytics, cybersecurity and software development, to help them stay up to date with the latest trends and technologies.
4. **HR professionals** may be interested in eBooks that cover topics such as employee engagement, training, development and leadership.
5. **Procurement professionals** may be interested in eBooks that guide supplier management, sourcing strategies and cost optimisation.

B2B audiences are often looking for eBooks that offer practical, actionable and relevant information that can help them improve their skills, grow their businesses and stay up to date with the latest trends and technologies. By creating eBooks that align with the needs and interests of these audiences, businesses and organisations can effectively reach and engage these audiences through content marketing.

CASE IN POINT: HUBSPOT'S EBOOKS

HubSpot is a software company specialising in marketing, sales and customer service tools. The company is well known for its comprehensive content marketing strategy, which includes a blog, webinars, eBooks and other resources that help businesses grow and succeed.

HubSpot uses eBooks as part of its content marketing efforts which is centred around providing valuable and informative content to its target audience of businesses and marketing professionals. The company's content is available as blog posts, webinars, eBooks and other resources designed to help businesses grow and succeed.

One key component of HubSpot's content marketing strategy is its use of e-Books. They offer eBooks on various topics, including marketing, sales, customer service and business growth. This provides users with practical and actionable information to help them improve their skills, achieve their goals and build brand loyalty,

HubSpot also uses its eBooks as a lead generation tool. Its eBooks are offered as gated content, meaning HubSpot can collect valuable contact information from users who download eBooks and build a targeted list of potential leads to nurture through the sales funnel.

HubSpot also includes calls to action and links to its products and services within its eBooks that align with its target audience is needs and interests. HubSpot's eBooks serve to generate additional leads and, ultimately, to drive the growth of their business.

GUIDELINES

Writing **guidelines** are rules or guidelines that help ensure that your content is clear, concise and practical. They can be handy when working with a team or writing content for a specific audience or purpose.

Here is an example of guidelines for finding your streetwear and apparel style, written as if an influencer that Noah looks up to (like a rap artist) wrote them:

Yo, what's good, Noah? It's [Influencer] here and I'm here to help you find your own style in streetwear and apparel.

- *First things first, you gotta know what you like. Take some time to consider what brands and styles you typically gravitate towards. For example, are you more into a laid-back, casual vibe, or are you all about that edgy, trendy look? By understanding your style, you can more effectively find brands and products that fit your preferences.*
- *Next up, do some research. There are tons of streetwear and apparel brands out there and each one has its own unique style and aesthetic. Take some time to check out different brands and see what they offer. Look at their website and social media pages, read reviews and testimonials and see what other people say about them. This will help you narrow your options and find brands that align with your personal style.*
- *Don't be afraid to experiment with different styles and brands. Whether it's trying on a new pair of sneakers or a new t-shirt, you will know what works for you once you try it out. So be open to new things and don't be afraid to step outside your comfort zone.*
- *Finally, don't be afraid to mix and match different pieces to create your own unique style. This could mean pairing a streetwear t-shirt with a pair of classic jeans or layering a trendy hoodie over a more traditional button-up shirt. Mixing and matching different pieces allows you to create a look that is uniquely your own.*

Hope these tips help you find your own personal style, Noah. Stay fresh.

HOW-TO INSTRUCTIONS

Writing practical how-to instructions is essential for content creators, as it allows you to guide readers clearly and concisely through a process or task. Here are some tips for writing practical how-to instructions:

- Know your audience and tailor your instructions to their level of knowledge and experience.
- Define your purpose for writing the instructions.
- Use clear and concise language and avoid jargon or complex language.
- Organise information using numbered or bullet point lists.
- Include visuals such as images or diagrams to help illustrate the instructions.
- Use a military manual or airline instructions style of visuals, which are simple, clear and concise.

Here is an example for our skater boy Noah. Following these instructions, Noah will be prepared and confident for his date night.

DATE NIGHT PREPARATION INSTRUCTIONS

1. *Choose your outfit: Select an outfit that is appropriate for the occasion and reflects your personal style. Consider factors such as the location and time of the date, as well as your preferences and comfort level.*
2. *Groom yourself: Take the time to groom yourself according to your personal preferences and the expectations of the occasion. This could include showering, shaving, hair styling and applying personal care products.*
3. *Plan your transportation: Determine how you will get to and from the date and make any necessary arrangements. If you are driving, ensure your vehicle is clean and in good working order. If you are using public transportation or a ride-sharing service, make sure you know the route and have the necessary information.*
4. *Prepare any necessary items: Depending on the specifics of the date, you may need to bring certain items with you. Make a list of required items and pack them in a bag or wallet before leaving.*

Here are some ideas for images or diagrams that could help demonstrate the steps in Noah's dating preparation process:

- An image of a wardrobe full of clothes, with a red circle around Noah's chosen outfit.

- A series of images showing different grooming steps, such as showering, shaving and styling hair.
- A diagram of different transportation options, such as driving, public transportation, or ridesharing, with a red arrow pointing to Noah's chosen option.
- An image of a bag or wallet, with a checkmark next to each item on Noah's list of necessary items.

USING VISUALS AND VIDEOS EFFECTIVELY

Using visuals and video effectively is an essential skill in digital content marketing. Visuals and videos can make your content more engaging and capture your target audience's attention.

> There's no point in spending time and money creating nice videos if you don't know what you want to achieve with them or what your ultimate goal is.

Video Marketing Like a PRO
Clo Willaerts

Consider the types of visuals and videos and choose the one that is most appropriate for your target audience and goals:

- **Educate** them with infographics or explainer videos.
- **Entertain** them using memes or funny videos.
- **Inspire** them with motivational quotes or images. For example, if you are writing a blog post about personal growth, you might use an image of a mountain with a quote about perseverance.
- **Inform** them using graphs or charts. For example, if you are writing a blog post about market trends, you might use a bar chart to illustrate the data.
- **Persuade** them through testimonials or case studies. For example, if you are writing a blog post about the benefits of a particular product, you might use a video testimonial from a satisfied customer to support your argument.

Here is a list of general visual content ideas:

- Sharing **behind-the-scenes** glimpses of your work or daily life can be an excellent way to give your audience a more intimate look at what you do and who you are. This could be photos or videos of your work environment, creative process, or any other aspect of your life you want to share.
- **Before and after** photos or videos can be an excellent way to showcase the transformation or progress of a product, service or process. This could be a before and after of a home renovation, a product being used, or any other situation where there is a noticeable difference between before and after.
- Sharing **tutorials or how-to videos** can be an excellent way to educate and inform your audience. This could be a step-by-step guide on using a product or service or a general tutorial on a particular topic.
- Sharing **inspirational quotes or messages** can be an excellent way to motivate and inspire your audience. This could be quotes from industry leaders, well-known personalities, or your own affirmations or mantras.
- Sharing photos or videos of **you or your team at work** can be an excellent way to give your audience an authentic sense of your work environment and what it is like to work with you. This could include candid shots of you working or more formal photos or videos of your team in action. Additionally, sharing photos or videos of your work life can help your audience understand what it is like to work with you and your work environment. This could include glimpses into your daily routine, work environment, or other aspects of your work life that you want to share with your audience.

- Sharing **photos or videos of your product** can be an excellent way to showcase its features and benefits and give your audience a sense of what it is like to use your product. These could be photos or videos of the product being used in staged or real-life situations.
- Sharing photos or videos of your **service in action** can be an excellent way to showcase what it is like to work with you and what you offer. These could be photos or videos of your team providing the service or more general shots of the service being provided.
- Sharing **sneak peeks** of new products, services, or projects can be an excellent way to generate buzz and anticipation for your audience. These could be photos or videos of prototypes, early versions of your products or services or more general glimpses of your work.

TOOL: CANVA.COM

Canva is a free online design platform launched in 2013 with the goal of enabling anyone to create professional-looking designs. The platform offers a simple drag-and-drop user interface and a vast range of templates for creating various types of visual content, such as presentations, social media graphics and posters. Canva also has a large library of fonts, stock photography, illustrations, video footage and audio clips that users can incorporate into their designs. It is available on desktop, web, iOS and Android.

Canva is a popular tool for creating visual content because it is easy to use, even for those with little to no design experience. It offers a wide range of templates, graphics and images that users can customize to create professional-looking designs. It also has various useful features, such as adding text, resizing and cropping images, filters and effects. Additionally, Canva offers a free plan, making it affordable for businesses and individuals looking to create visual content. Canva's user-friendly interface and extensive design capabilities make it an excellent tool for creating visual content.

Canva has its own design school and YouTube playlist with tutorials on how to design like a pro, explore typography, design trends, colour and more.

- canva.com/designschool/
- youtube.com/@canva

Some of the top alternatives to Canva include:

- **Adobe Spark** offers similar features to Canva, including a range of templates, graphics and images for creating visual content. It also has additional features, such as the ability to animate graphics and add video clips.
- **create.microsoft.com** Create designs that inspire Design unique and beautiful content for social posts, videos, presentations, flyers and more. No design experience required.
- **Visme** offers a range of templates, graphics and images for creating visual content, as well as the ability to add animation and interactive elements. It also has a unique feature that allows users to create presentations, infographics and other visual content in one place.
- **Piktochart** focuses on creating infographics, offering a range of templates and customizable graphics and images. It also has additional features, such as the ability to add maps and charts and to collaborate with others on a single project.

These are just a few examples of the many alternatives to Canva available. Other popular options include Crello, Stencil and Adobe Illustrator.

IMAGES

In content marketing, **images** can be a valuable tool for improving the readability and effectiveness of your content.

Many different types of images can be used in content marketing, each with its unique characteristics and benefits. Some common types of images include:

- **Photos** are images that depict real-life subjects or scenes. They can be used to illustrate a concept or to add visual interest to your content.
- **Illustrations** are images created using drawing, painting, or digital design techniques. They can be used to represent abstract concepts or to add a creative touch to your content.
- **Graphics** are images that are created using computer software and are used to visualise data or illustrate concepts. They can make complex information more digestible and engaging for the reader.

- **Infographics** are images that combine graphics, text and other visual elements to present information clearly and concisely. They can be used to summarise key points or to present data in an easy-to-understand format.
- **Screenshots** are images that capture a snapshot of what is currently displayed on a computer screen. They can be used to illustrate a concept or to provide a visual reference for the reader.

PHOTOS

Creating your own photos for content marketing can be a cost-effective way to add visual interest and authenticity to your content. Subjects could include:

- your **products in use** or being worn by customers;
- **before and after** transformation photos;
- your team or employees **at work or in action** publicly or behind-the-scenes;
- professional **headshots** of your team;
- landscape or **location shots** related to your business or industry;
- **customer testimonial** photos or quotes;
- **event** or trade show photos;
- product or service **tutorials** or **demos** in video or photo form; and
- products laid out flat on a surface photographed from straight above, **flat lay photos**, which can be an excellent way to showcase products or items as aesthetically pleasing and visually appealing.

Here are some tips for creating relevant, engaging and compelling content photos with limited resources:

- If you do not have access to a high-quality camera, **use your smartphone to capture photos**. Modern smartphones have improved photography components that can produce professional-looking photos.
- Use **props and backgrounds** creatively to add context and interest to your content photos. For example, you might use everyday objects as props or shoot your photos in an unusual location to add visual appeal.
- Pay attention to **lighting and composition** when capturing your content photos, as they can significantly impact the quality and appeal of the photo. Use natural light whenever possible and try different angles and compositions to find the best shot.

Lighting and composition are essential elements of photography that can significantly impact the quality and appeal of a photo.

Lighting options:

- Use **natural light** whenever possible. Natural light is often the most flattering and can help to create a sense of depth and dimension in your photos.
- Avoid using **flash**. Flash can produce harsh shadows and wash out your photos' colours.
- Experiment with different **lighting conditions**, such as morning light, afternoon light and evening light.

Composition options:

- The **rule of thirds** is a fundamental principle of composition that divides the frame into nine equal parts with four intersections points. Placing your subject along one of these intersections can create a more balanced and visually appealing photo.
- Experiment with different **angles** to find the most appealing and compelling composition for your subject. For example, you might try shooting from a high angle, a low angle, or from the side.
- Use **leading lines** in a photo that draws the viewer's eye toward a particular point in the frame. Leading lines, such as roads, fences, or rivers, can help guide the viewer's eye and create a more dynamic and engaging photo.

Basic **photo editing techniques** can significantly improve the appeal of your photos. Some examples:

- **Cropping** involves removing unwanted areas from the photo and adjusting the composition. Cropping can focus the viewer's attention on the photo's subject and improve the photo's overall balance and appeal.
- Adjusting brightness and contrast. **Brightness** refers to a photo's overall lightness or darkness, while **contrast** refers to the difference between the light and dark areas of a photograph. Adjusting a photo's brightness and contrast can help improve its overall appearance and make the subject stand out.
- **Removing blemishes** involves using photo editing software to remove blemishes, such as scars, acne, or wrinkles, from the subject of a photo. This can improve the overall appearance of the subject and create a more polished and professional-looking photo.
- **Adjusting a photo's colour** can help improve its overall appeal and mood. For example, you might use photo editing software to adjust a photo's hue, saturation, or temperature to create a particular effect.
- **Sharpening** a photo involves enhancing the detail and clarity of the image. This can help to make the photo's subject stand out and improve the photo's overall quality and appeal.

By following these tips, you can create relevant, engaging and compelling content photos with limited resources, time and budget and add visual interest and authenticity to your content.

ILLUSTRATIONS

Illustrations are essential to any type of content, whether a book, a website, or a presentation. They can convey complex ideas or concepts visually, making them easier for readers or viewers to understand. Illustrations can also add a creative touch to your content, making it more engaging and visually appealing.

Many different techniques and approaches can be used to create illustrations.

- Some prefer to work with traditional media such as pencils, paints and markers.

- In contrast, others use digital tools such as graphic design software or drawing tablets.

Many tools can help you create illustrations, whether you prefer to work with traditional media or digital tools.

Digital tools such as graphic design software and drawing tablets allow you to create illustrations on a computer or other device. In addition, these tools often offer a range of features and effects to help you create professional-quality illustrations.

Whether you are working with traditional media or digital tools, it is essential to **pay attention to details** and make sure that your illustration is **accurate and visually appealing**.

This might involve using techniques such as shading or highlighting to add depth and dimension to your illustration or incorporating elements such as colour and texture to bring it to life.

Maybe it is easier for you to use images that were created by others. If you are looking for illustrations to use in your own content, there are many places where you can find and select illustrations. Some options include:

Stock illustration websites offer a range of illustrations you can purchase and use in your own content. These websites often have a wide selection of illustrations, making it easy to find something that fits your needs:

- **Shutterstock** is a popular stock illustration website that offers a wide range of illustrations, including vector graphics, photos and more.
- **iStock** is another popular stock illustration website that offers a wide range of illustrations, including vector graphics, photos and more.
- **Adobe Stock** is a stock illustration website that offers a wide range of illustrations, including vector graphics, photos and more. It is particularly popular with those who use Adobe Creative Cloud software, as it integrates seamlessly with these tools.

If you are looking for something specific or want to work with a particular artist, you can hire a **freelance illustrator** to create custom illustrations. You can find freelance illustrators through online marketplaces or by reaching out to artists directly. Some examples of online marketplaces include:

- **Upwork** is an online marketplace that connects freelancers with clients looking for their services. It includes a wide range of categories, including illustrations. It allows you to browse through profiles and portfolios of different illustrators to find the right fit for your project.
- **Fiverr** is an online marketplace that connects freelancers with clients looking for their services. It includes a wide range of categories, including illustrations. It allows you to browse through profiles and portfolios of different illustrators to find the right fit for your project.
- **99designs** is an online marketplace specializing in design services, including illustration. It allows you to post a project and receive submissions from various illustrators, making it easy to find the right fit for your project.
- **Illustration agencies** represent a variety of artists and offer a range of illustrations you can purchase and use in your content. They often have a wide selection of styles and approaches and can help you find a suitable illustration for your needs.

Many illustrators share their work and offer their services on online and social media platforms. You can find and connect with illustrators in these communities, such as:

- **DeviantArt** is an online community popular with artists and illustrators. It allows users to share their work and connect with other artists, making it a great place to find and connect with illustrators.
- **Instagram** is a social media platform popular with artists and illustrators. Many illustrators share their work on Instagram and use it to connect with potential clients.
- **Pinterest** is a social media platform popular for sharing and discovering creative ideas, including illustrations. Illustrators often share their work on Pinterest to connect with potential clients.

GRAPHICS, CHARTS AND GRAPHS

Graphics are an essential aspect of content marketing, as they can help to illustrate complex concepts and make them more easily understood by readers. Whether you are creating graphics for a blog post, social media, or a presentation, they can be a powerful tool for engaging and informing your audience.

There are many types of graphics that you can use in content marketing, including charts, diagrams, infographics and more. These graphics help to visualise data and make it more digestible for the reader or illustrate abstract concepts more concretely. Points to consider to optimise use of graphic content:

- First identify what you want to convey and how you want to present the information. This might involve gathering data and creating a plan for how you visualise it or sketching rough ideas for illustrating a concept.
- Next, begin to work on the actual graphic. This might involve using computer software such as graphic design software or a spreadsheet program to create charts or diagrams or working with a designer to create more complex graphics.
- It is essential to pay attention to design elements such as colour, typography and layout when creating graphics for content marketing. These elements can make your graphics more visually appealing and convey your message most effectively.

Microsoft **Excel** is a powerful spreadsheet program that can be used to create a variety of charts and diagrams for content marketing. Here are some steps to follow to create charts and diagrams in Excel:

1. Open Excel and create a new spreadsheet.
2. Enter your data into the spreadsheet. Make sure to include column and row labels to clearly identify what each piece of data represents.
3. Select the data that you want to include in your chart or diagram. You can do this by clicking and dragging your mouse over those cells.
4. Click on the 'Insert' tab in the top menu and select the chart or diagram you want to create. Excel offers various options, including bar charts, line charts, pie charts and more.
5. Excel will automatically create a chart or diagram based on your selected data. You can customise the appearance of the chart or diagram by clicking on it and using the options in the 'Design' and 'Format' tabs in the top menu.
6. Suppose you want to include additional data or customize the layout of the chart or diagram further. You can use the options in the 'Layout' and 'Format' tabs in the top menu.
7. Once you are happy with your chart or diagram, you can save it as a separate image file or embed it in your content marketing materials. To do this, you can use the 'Save As' option in the 'File' menu and select a file format such as JPEG or PNG.

Creating charts and diagrams in Excel is a simple process that lets you quickly visualize and present data in your content marketing materials. By following these steps and using the options in the program, you can create professional-quality charts and diagrams that engage and inform your audience.

INFOGRAPHICS

Infographics are a visual format that can be used to present complex information in an easily understandable way. Infographics can be a useful tool in content marketing for several reasons:

- Infographics help to make complex information more easily digestible for the audience.
- They can increase the shareability of a piece of content, leading to increased reach and website traffic.
- Infographics can improve a business's search engine optimization by including relevant keywords and phrases.
- They can break up large blocks of text and make it easier for readers to understand key points.
- Infographics can be especially useful for businesses dealing with complex topics or data-heavy information.

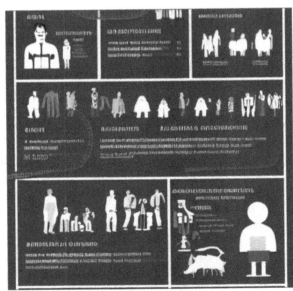

To create an infographic, follow these steps:

1. Identify the **topic** or **message** that you want to convey with your infographic. This will help to guide the design and content of the infographic.
2. Gather relevant **data** and **information** to include in the infographic. This could include statistics, facts, or other information that supports your topic or message.
3. Choose a **design style** for your infographic. This could be a more traditional bar or pie chart design, or it could be a more creative and visual design that uses illustrations or graphics.
4. Use a **graphic design tool**, such as Canva or Adobe Illustrator, to create the infographic. Begin by laying out the structure and flow of the infographic, including the placement of text, data and graphics.
5. **Add the data and information** to the infographic, using charts, graphs and other visual elements to represent the information clearly and accurately.
6. Add any **additional text or captions** to the infographic to provide context or explanation for the data and information.
7. **Review and revise** the infographic to ensure that it is accurate, well-designed and effectively conveys the topic or message.
8. **Save and export** the infographic in a suitable file format, such as a PDF or JPEG, for sharing or publishing.

> The best infographics are entertaining, educational, and intrinsically useful. Ask yourself: How will this help my audience? Will they find this applicable to their business? Will they be fascinated enough to spend a few minutes with it, then pass it around?

Everybody Writes
Ann Handley

Infographics can be helpful in a content marketing strategy as they can help to make complex information more accessible, increase the shareability of content and enhance a business's SEO efforts.

TOOL: VISUAL.LY

Visual.ly is a tool that allows users to create professional-quality infographics quickly and easily. Infographics are a popular and effective way to present data and information in a visually appealing and easy-to-understand format.

To create an infographic using Visual.ly, users can select from various templates and design elements to create a custom infographic that meets their needs. In addition, the tool offers a range of customisation options, including adding charts, graphs and other visual elements to the infographic.

Visual.ly also offers a range of other features, including the ability to create data visualisations, social media graphics and other types of visual content.

Visual.ly is a powerful and user-friendly tool that can be a valuable resource for content marketers looking to create professional-quality infographics. Using Visual.ly, content marketers can save time and effort in the infographic creation process and focus on other aspects of their content marketing efforts.

Here are some alternatives for creating infographics:

- **Canva** is a graphic design platform that is easy to use and offers a wide range of templates and tools for creating infographics. It has a drag-and-drop interface that makes it easy to create professional-quality infographics, even if you need to gain design experience.
- **Piktochart** is a tool specifically designed for creating infographics. It offers a range of templates and design tools that make it easy to create professional-quality infographics, even if you need to gain design experience.
- **Adobe Illustrator** is a powerful graphic design software popular with professional designers. It offers a wide range of tools and features that make it easy to create professional-quality infographics, including vector graphics, text and layout tools. It is a more advanced tool and may require some design experience to use effectively.

SCREENSHOTS

Screenshots, or images of what is currently displayed on a computer screen, are an essential tool in content marketing. They can help to illustrate concepts and provide visual references for readers.

For example, you can use screenshots to illustrate how to use a particular software or website or to show an example of a specific concept or idea. Screenshots can be particularly useful for explaining technical concepts or procedures. They provide a visual reference to help readers understand the information more easily.

You can use the built-in screenshot tools on your computer or device or a third-party screenshot tool to create a screenshot. For example, many devices have a built-in screenshot tool that allows you to capture a screenshot by pressing a specific key combination or using a particular function on the device.

To take a screenshot with your iPhone, follow these steps:

1. Go to the screen that you want to capture.
2. Press and hold the Side button on the right side of your iPhone.
3. While holding the Side button, click the Volume Up button on the left side of your iPhone.
4. Release both buttons.

Your iPhone will take a screenshot and save it to your Photos app. You can then edit or share the screenshot as needed. You can also take a screenshot by pressing the Side and Home buttons on older iPhone models.

Once you have captured a screenshot, you can edit it using graphic design software or a simple image editing tool. This might involve cropping the image, adding text or graphics, or making other changes to enhance the image.

When using screenshots in content marketing, it is essential to consider how they will be used and their purpose. You should create clear and concise screenshots that effectively illustrate the concept or idea you are trying to convey.

MEMES

Memes are a popular and effective way to engage with audiences on social media. They are often humorous and shareable, making them well-suited for content marketing campaigns.

> A meme is a concept or idea that spreads virally from one person to another via the Internet. An Internet meme could be anything from an image to an email or video file; however, the most common meme is an image of a person or animal with a funny or witty caption added to it.
>
> Video Marketing Like a PRO
> Clo Willaerts

Many examples of memes have been used as marketing campaigns, either intentionally or unintentionally. Here are a few examples:

- *The Most Interesting Man in the World* (Dos Equis beer) This meme, featuring an older man with a debonair demeanour, was used in a series of commercials for Dos Equis beer. The campaign successfully created a memorable and enduring meme that helped increase brand awareness and sales.
- *Gonna Tell My Kids* (Netflix) This meme, which features a person holding a photo and saying, *Gonna tell my kids this was [X]* (where X is something absurd or unlikely), was used in a campaign by Netflix to promote its original series *Stranger Things*. The campaign was successful in generating buzz and increasing viewership for the series.
- *Baby Yoda* (Disney+): This meme, featuring a character from the Disney+ series, *The Mandalorian*, became popular shortly after the show was released. It featured the character, Baby Yoda and quickly became a cultural phenomenon and was used in various marketing campaigns by Disney and other companies.

Here are a few tips for creating memes:

- Memes are typically based on a single image with a caption added to the top and bottom of the image. **Keep your memes simple** and focused, with a clear message that is easy to understand.
- Familiar memes are often more effective than less well-known ones. Consider using **popular memes** as a starting point for your creations, or search for relevant memes to your content marketing efforts.
- While using popular memes can be effective, **adding your own twist** can help to make your meme stand out. Consider how you can spin a popular meme or create a new meme that is unique to your brand or message.
- Memes should be **relevant** to your audience and content marketing efforts. Consider what your audience will find funny and engaging and tailor your memes accordingly.
- While memes are often used for humour, consider your branding and **how your memes reflect your brand**. Make sure that your memes align with your brand's values and tone.

Creating memes can be a fun and effective way to engage with your audience on social media. By following these tips, you can create entertaining and relevant memes.

TOOL: IMGFLIP'S MEME GENERATOR

Imgflip's Meme Generator (imgflip.com/memegenerator) is a tool that allows users to create and share their own memes or search for popular memes to share on social media. The tool is free to use and offers a simple and intuitive interface for creating memes.

To create a meme using Imgflip's Meme Generator, users can select a template from the tool's library of popular memes or upload their own image. They can then add text to the top and bottom of the image to create the meme. Once the meme is complete, it can be shared on social media platforms or saved for later use.

In addition to creating memes, Imgflip's Meme Generator also allows users to search for and browse popular memes that have been created by others. This can be useful for finding relevant memes for your content marketing efforts or having fun.

> Videos allow people to connect on a more human level than a faceless email or a more generic video. Video communication enables empathy. It will enable real people to tell real stories in ways that text or pictures simply can't.
>
> Video Marketing Like a PRO
> Clo Willaerts

VIDEOS

Videos are a popular format for storytelling and entertainment because they:

- provide a more immersive and engaging experience than other formats;
- easily accessible and consumable on various devices;
- are highly shareable on social media, increasing reach and website traffic;
- are attention-grabbing and increase the likelihood of a desired action from the viewer; and
- they help to build trust and credibility with the audience, establishing the business as a thought leader in the industry.

> Video allows you to create a human connection with your audience while building trust.
>
> Video Marketing Like a PRO
> Clo Willaerts

Many different video formats can be used in content marketing, depending on the goals and objectives of the business:

- **Explainer** videos are short videos that explain a product or service in simple, easy-to-understand terms. Explainer videos are often used to introduce a new product or service or explain the benefits of an existing product or service.
- **Tutorial** videos provide step-by-step instructions for using a product or service. Tutorial videos can be particularly useful for businesses that sell complex or technical products, as they can help to reduce customer support inquiries and improve the user experience.
- **Customer testimonial** videos are videos in which satisfied customers share their experiences with a product or service. They can build trust and credibility with the audience, providing real-life examples of how the product or service has benefited others.
- **Product demonstration** videos showcase the features and capabilities of a product or service in action. Product demonstration videos highlight a product's or service's unique features. They can be an effective way to differentiate the business from its competitors.
- **Talking head** videos feature an individual speaking directly to the camera, often used for interviews or presentations.
- **Slide show** videos are a group of images or slides, often accompanied by music or narration.
- **Screencast** videos capture the action on a computer screen and are often used to demonstrate how to use software or navigate a website.
- **Behind the scenes** videos feature a company or production process.
- **Interview** videos feature an individual or group answering questions from a moderator or interviewer.
- **Q & A** videos features a question-and-answer session with an expert or industry leader.
- **TED-style talk** videos feature a speaker presenting on a particular topic in the style of a TED talk.
- **Presentation** videos feature a speaker presenting on a particular topic.
- **Graphic recording** videos capture a live event or presentation using hand-drawn visual notes.
- **Trailer/preview** is a short video that previews a product or service, often used to generate interest or anticipation.
- **Webcast recording** is a video of a live event or presentation broadcast online.

- **Live event recording** is a video of a live event or presentation captured on-site.
- **Hyperlapse** is a time-lapse video that features smooth, flowing camera movements.
- **GIF** is a looping video file that consists of a short sequence of images or clip that automatically repeat.

> The content marketing plan should answer the following questions: What types of content the company intends to post and promote on social media? Who will create the content? How often will the company post content? What is the target audience for each type of content? How you the company promote the content?
>
> Social Media Marketing: A Practitio...
> Marc Oliver Opresnik, Philip Kotler...

VIDEO PRODUCTION METHODS

Traditional **video production methods** refer to the techniques and processes used to create videos using more traditional media, such as film or video cameras. These methods involve various steps, including pre-production, production and post-production. They can create multiple videos, including movies, television shows, music videos and more.

- **Pre-production** is the planning stage of traditional video production, where you determine the video's concept, script and overall direction. This might involve creating a treatment or outline, casting actors and scouting locations.
- **Production** is the actual filming of the video, where you use a camera and other equipment to capture the footage. This might involve setting up lighting and sound, rehearsing and blocking and capturing takes.
- **Post-production** is traditional video production's editing and refining stage, where you take the raw footage and turn it into a finished video. This

might involve cutting and arranging the footage, adding sound effects and music and colour grading.

More modern video production methods include screen recording and animation, allowing you to create videos using computer software and digital tools. These methods are often faster and more flexible than traditional video production methods. They can be used to create a wide variety of videos.

- **Screen recording** involves using a computer program to capture a video of what is happening on your computer screen. This can be useful for creating tutorials, demos, or videos to show viewers how to use a particular software or website.
- **Animation** involves creating a video by creating and arranging digital graphics and other visual elements. This can be done using various software and techniques, including 2D or 3D animation. Animation can create many videos, including explainer videos, commercials and more.

Overall, these methods are often faster and more flexible, allowing you to create professional-quality videos using computer software and digital tools.

BEST PRACTICES FOR VIDEO PRODUCTION

Here are some best practices when creating video for content marketing purposes:

1. Start by identifying the purpose and target audience of the video. This will help you determine the best format and style for the video and ensure that it effectively communicates your message.
2. When creating a video, paying attention to the **production values**, such as lighting, sound and composition, is essential. These elements can make your video more visually appealing and professional and enhance the overall effectiveness of the video.
3. Once you have a clear idea of what you want to create, you can begin planning and producing the video. This might involve scripting, storyboarding and gathering equipment and resources.

SCRIPTING

Scripting is an essential step in creating a video, as it helps ensure that the video is clear, well-organised and effective at communicating your message. When scripting a video, you should create a written plan that includes the video's dialogue, action and overall structure.
A script should include all the elements that will be included in the video, such as characters, dialogue, action and transitions. It should also include the overall structure of the video, including the beginning, middle and end and how the different elements will be arranged.

Creating a script is important in making a video clear, well-organised and effectively communicating your message. A script can also serve as a roadmap for the production process, helping you plan the necessary steps and resources for creating the video.

Here is a generic scripting template that content marketers can use to create a written plan for their video:

1. Introduction: This is the video's opening, where you introduce the topic and set the stage for the rest of the video.
2. Body: This is the main section of the video, where you present the main information or message of the video. You can divide the body into multiple sections or segments as needed.
3. Conclusion: This is the video's closing, where you summarise the main points and call to action.
4. Transitions: These elements connect the different sections of the video and help create a smooth flow.
5. Dialogue: This is the spoken word in the video, including any dialogue between characters or narration.
6. Action: This is the visual element of the video, including any movement, gestures, or visual effects.
7. Special effects: These are any additional elements you want to include in the video, such as music, sound effects, or graphics.

Using this template, you can create a written plan for your video that includes all the necessary elements and helps ensure that the video is clear and well-organised. You can then use this script as a roadmap for the production process, allowing you to create a professional-quality video that engages and informs your audience.

STORYBOARDING

Storyboarding is an essential step in creating a video, as it helps to visualise the look and flow of the video and serves as a guide for the production process. A storyboard is a visual representation of the video, often in the form of sketches or illustrations, that shows the different scenes and elements of the video.

Here is how to create a storyboard:

1. Start by sketching out the different scenes and elements of the video. This might include characters, dialogue, action and transitions. You can also include notes or descriptions to help explain the different elements of the storyboard.
2. Once you have a rough sketch of the storyboard, you can refine it and add more detail. This might involve adding more detailed illustrations or notes to explain the different elements of the video.

A storyboard can be a valuable tool for visualising the look and flow of the video and it can make sure the video is clear and well-organised. It can also guide the production process, allowing you to plan the necessary steps and resources for creating the video.

Overall, storyboarding is an essential step in creating a video, as it helps to visualise the look and flow of the video and serves as a guide for the production process. You can create a professional-quality video that engages and informs your audience by creating a detailed storyboard.

EQUIPMENT AND RESOURCES

Gathering **equipment** and **resources** involves acquiring any necessary items or materials that you will need to create the video, such as cameras, lighting and props. This might include purchasing or renting equipment or securing access to locations or other resources.

> Today most of us have a phone in our pockets that can perfectly capture decent quality videos.
>
> Video Marketing Like a PRO
> Clo Willaerts

There are many different types of equipment and materials that you might need to create a video, depending on the kind of video you are making and the production method you are using. Some common items that you might need include:

- Depending on your video type, you might need a **camera** to capture the footage. This could be a traditional video camera, a digital camera, or a smartphone.
- Proper **lighting** is essential for creating a professional-quality video, as it can help to set the mood and tone of the video and make the footage look more appealing. Use a range of lighting equipment, such as lamps, softboxes, or reflectors.

- Good audio quality is essential for creating a professional-quality video, as poor audio can distract from the content of the video. Use various **audio equipment**, such as microphones, sound recorders and headphones.
- Depending on the type of video you are making, you might need to use **props** to help illustrate your message or create a particular atmosphere. This could include objects, costumes, or other materials.
- Once you have captured your footage, you need to edit it to create the finished video. This might involve **video editing software** like Adobe Premiere or Final Cut Pro.

Overall, you need many different types of equipment and materials to create a video. However, gathering the necessary items and resources can create a professional-quality video that engages and informs your audience.

CASE IN POINT: PATAGONIA'S VIDEOS

Patagonia is an outdoor clothing and gear company known for its storytelling campaigns focusing on environmental and social issues. The company uses a variety of storytelling formats to engage with its audience and inspire them to take action on these issues.

One of the main storytelling formats that Patagonia uses is video. The company produces a range of videos that tell stories about environmental and social issues, such as climate change, conservation and sustainability.

These videos are often emotionally powerful and visually appealing. One of the key strategies that Patagonia uses in its videos is to focus on real people and their experiences. The company often tells the stories of individuals working to make a difference in the world, whether through environmental conservation efforts, social justice activism, or other causes. By showcasing these inspiring stories, Patagonia can connect with its audience and inspire them to take action and make a difference in their lives.

In addition to featuring real people, Patagonia's videos often include visually appealing elements, such as stunning landscapes and breath-taking shots of nature. These elements help to create a sense of awe and wonder and further enhance the emotional impact of the videos.

In addition to video, Patagonia uses other storytelling formats, such as written content, social media posts and live events, to engage with its audience and convey its message. The company's website, for example, features a section called 'The Footprint Chronicles,' which tells the stories of the company's sustainability efforts and the impact of its products on the environment.

Storytelling is a key element of Patagonia's marketing and branding efforts and has helped the company build a loyal and engaged audience passionate about environmental and social issues.

PODCASTS

Podcasting can be an effective content marketing tactic for businesses looking to reach and engage with their target audience in a more personal and interactive way.

PODCAST LISTENING AUDIENCE

Podcasts can appeal to many people with different demographics, interests and needs. However, some general characteristics of people who tend to enjoy podcasts include the following:

- Podcasts are typically consumed through digital platforms such as smartphones or tablets, so people who enjoy podcasts tend to be **tech-savvy** and comfortable with technology and digital media.
- Podcasts are a convenient way to consume media, as they can be listened to anytime and anywhere, whether during a commute while working out or doing other tasks. As a result, people who enjoy podcasts tend to be **busy** and looking for ways to multitask and stay entertained.
- Podcasts cover a **wide range of topics**, from news and politics to sports, entertainment and more, so people who enjoy podcasts tend to be curious and interested in various subjects.
- Many podcasts are hosted by individuals or small teams and tend to be more conversational and personal. As a result, people who enjoy podcasts tend to value **authenticity** and **personal connection** and prefer more authentic and genuine content.

By considering your target audience's demographics, interests and needs, you can tailor your podcast content and format to appeal to people who are likely to enjoy listening to podcasts.

PODCAST TOPICS AND FORMATS

Podcasts can cover a wide range of topics, so choosing a topic that will interest your target audience and align with your business goals is essential. Some popular podcast topics include:

- **Current events and news** reports can be a great way to keep your audience informed and engaged.
- **Business and finance** news and features can be a valuable resource for entrepreneurs and professionals looking to stay up to date on industry trends and best practices.
- **Personal growth and development** can be popular topics with audiences looking to improve their lives and careers.
- **Sports** can be a great way to stay up to date on your favourite teams and players and be popular with sports fans.
- **Entertainment and pop culture** can be a great way to keep your audience entertained and engaged.

It is also important to select a format that best suits your topic and audience. Some popular podcast formats include:

- **Interviews** with experts or interesting people, these can be a great way to provide valuable insights and perspectives to your audience.
- **Solo shows** that feature a single host discussing a particular topic can be a great way to provide a personal perspective and build a connection with your audience.
- **Panel discussions** that feature a panel of experts or interesting people discussing a particular topic can be a great way to provide a variety of perspectives and engage with your audience.
- Podcasts that use **storytelling** as a format can be a great way to engage and captivate your audience with compelling narratives and interesting characters. This format can effectively tell personal stories, historical accounts, or fictional tales. It can be a powerful way to connect with your audience and convey your message.

PLAN AND OUTLINE YOUR EPISODES

Planning and outlining your podcast episodes is essential for creating a successful podcast series. Here are some key considerations for planning and outlining your podcast episodes:

1. Before planning your episodes, you must clearly understand the **main points** you want to cover. This might include topics, themes, or issues you wish to explore in depth.
2. Interviews can be a powerful way to provide valuable insights and perspectives to your audience. Consider the **guests or experts** you want to interview and how they can contribute to your main points.
3. In addition to interviews, you may also want to include other **supporting material** in your episodes, such as articles, videos, or images. Gather any material you need ahead of time to ensure you have everything you need for your episodes.
4. Once you have identified your main points and gathered any supporting material, start **outlining** your episodes. Consider the structure and flow of your episodes, including any intro and outro segments and any breaks for commercials or sponsors.
5. After you have completed your outlines, **review and revise** them as needed to ensure that they are clear, concise and effective. Consider getting feedback from others to ensure that your outlines are on track.

Here is an example of a podcast episode outline for Moonlit Apparel's podcast series Moonlit Conversations.

I. *Introduction*
    - *Welcome to Moonlit Apparel's podcast*
    - *Introduce today's guest, MC Grind*
    - *Introduction to the topic: Eco-Friendly Skateboarding Sneakers Designed by MC Grind*

II. *Interview with MC Grind*
    - *Introduction to MC Grind and his background in skateboarding and streetwear design*
    - *How did the idea for the eco-friendly skateboarding sneakers come about?*
    - *Can you tell us more about the materials and processes used to create these sneakers?*

- *How do these sneakers compare to traditional skateboarding sneakers in terms of performance and durability?*

III. *The importance of eco-friendliness in streetwear and skateboarding*
- *Why is it important for the streetwear and skateboarding industries to be more environmentally conscious?*
- *What impact do you hope these sneakers will have on the industry and on consumers?*
- *Are there any other eco-friendly initiatives you are working on or planning?*

IV. *Closing thoughts*
- *Recap of key points from the interview*
- *How can listeners learn more about the eco-friendly skateboarding sneakers and purchase them?*
- *Thank you to MC Grind for joining us today*
- *Thank you to listeners for tuning in*

V. *Outro*
- *Announcement of next week's guest and topic*
- *Farewell and invitation to follow Moonlit Apparel on social media and subscribe to the podcast.*

PODCAST RECORDING EQUIPMENT

An investment in quality equipment to record, edit and distribute your episodes is needed to produce a professional-sounding podcast. Essential equipment for creating podcasts:

- A good quality **microphone** for recording high-quality audio for your podcast. Consider purchasing a USB microphone that is easy to use and produces clear crisp audio.
- **Headphones** for monitoring your audio as you record and can help you identify any issues or mistakes in real time. Consider purchasing a pair of closed-back headphones that will block out background noise and provide a clear, accurate representation of your audio.
- Many different **recording software** options are available, ranging from free to paid. Consider your budget and needs when selecting recording

software. Look for one that is easy to use and has features such as multiple tracks, effects and editing tools.

- **Audio editing software to polish your audio** by removing mistakes, adding music or sound effects and applying other enhancements to your audio.
- A **podcast hosting platform to distribute** your podcast episodes. Many different options are available, ranging from free to paid, so consider your budget and needs when selecting a hosting platform.

A typical equipment setup for Moonlit Apparel's podcast series on a low budget might include:

1. Options include a **USB microphone**, such as the Blue Yeti, or a traditional **XLR microphone** with an audio interface.
2. Any headphones with a good frequency response will work, but it is best to **avoid earbuds** or headphones with bass-boosting features.
3. Recording software: options include Audacity (free) or Adobe Audition (paid).
4. A **pop filter** helps to reduce plosives (hard 'p' and 'b' sounds) that can distort the audio. A simple and inexpensive option is a foam windscreen.
5. A laptop or desktop **computer** is necessary for running the DAW and storing audio files.
6. A **stable internet connection** is necessary for hosting and distributing the podcast online.

This equipment setup should be sufficient for recording and producing a high-quality podcast on a low budget.

TOOL: SPOTIFY FOR BROADCASTERS (PREVIOUSLY ANCHOR.FM)

When Anchor.fm got acquired by Spotify, it was a popular platform that allows content marketers to easily create and publish podcast episodes. Now it's been renamed to Spotify for Broadcasters, it still offers a range of features such as audio editing tools, show notes and distribution to various platforms.

Other options for creating and publishing podcast episodes include Buzzsprout, Podbean, Transistor, Spreaker and Simplecast, which also offer a range of features and tools for podcast creation. Content marketers can use these platforms to build their brand and reach new audiences through podcasting.

GIFS

GIFs (short for Graphics Interchange Format) are short, looping videos that can be used to add visual interest or illustrate a concept in content marketing. In addition, GIFs often convey emotions, reactions, or ideas quickly and memorably. As a result, they can be an effective tool for engaging and informing your audience.

The content of your GIF is crucial to its effectiveness, so you should choose the material that is visually appealing and relevant to your message. This might involve selecting a video or series of well-shot, visually compelling images and effectively conveying your message.

You can make effective GIFs that communicate your message by selecting appropriate content, choosing a suitable GIF-making tool, setting appropriate looping and timing options and editing and refining the GIF.

Here are three popular GIF-making tools that you might consider using:

1. Giphy.com is a popular online platform that allows you to create, share and discover GIFs. You can use Giphy to create GIFs from video files or images. It offers a range of options for customising your GIFs, including looping and timing settings, text overlays and more.
2. Adobe Photoshop is a professional image-editing software that allows you to create a wide range of graphics and visuals, including GIFs. You can use Photoshop to create GIFs from video files or images, offering a range of advanced editing and customisation options.
3. Ezgif.com is an online GIF-making tool that allows you to create GIFs from video files or images. It offers a range of options for customising your GIFs, including looping and timing settings, text overlays and more. It also allows you to edit and refine your GIFs using cropping, resizing and colour adjustments.

These are just a few examples of the many GIF-making tools that are available. You can choose the tool that best meets your needs and preferences based on your specific goals and requirements.

ENSURING THE QUALITY AND ACCURACY OF YOUR CONTENT

High-quality, accurate content helps to establish trust and credibility with your audience. As a result, it can increase the reach and impact of your content.

Always **edit** and **proofread** your copy to ensure that it is free of errors and typos and that it is clear and easy to understand.

> "Is it good? Does it work? Why not? Should I cut? Add? Reorder?"

Story
Robert McKee

Follow best practices to ensure the quality and accuracy of your content, such as:

- remove unnecessary words
- use spelling and grammar checkers
- fact-check your information
- use reliable sources
- avoid plagiarism and copyright infringements

TRIMMING THE FAT

Editing your content is an important step in the writing process. One key aspect of editing is **trimming** the bloat and fat from your text. This means looking for ways to say things more concisely and eliminating unnecessary words or phrases.

> Trim the bloat and fat. Are you potentially using far too many words to say things that might be said more concisely?

Everybody Writes
Ann Handley

Here is how to trim the fat from your content:

1. Read through your text and identify areas where you use far **too many words** to convey your message. These may include long wordy sentences or unnecessary filler words.
2. Rephrase these sections more **concisely**. This may involve breaking long sentences into shorter ones, eliminating unnecessary words, or using more precise language.
3. It is also helpful to **read your text out loud**, as this can help you identify areas where you are using too many words or where your writing could be more comfortable.

> Cross out every sentence until you come to one you cannot do without. That is your beginning.

100 Ways to Improve Your Writing
Gary Provost

By trimming the bloat and fat from your content, you can make your writing clearer and more concise, making it easier for your readers to understand and engage with your message. So, keeping your content as concise as possible is always better.

USING SPELLING AND GRAMMAR CHECKERS

The quality and accuracy of your written materials are crucial to your success in content marketing. One way to ensure that your content is error-free and easy to read is by using **spelling and grammar checkers**. These tools can help you identify and correct mistakes in your writing, allowing you to produce professional-quality content that engages your audience and effectively communicates your message.

Many different spelling and grammar checkers are available, ranging from simple browser extensions to more advanced software programs. Some popular options include Grammarly.com, ProWritingAid.com and HemingwayApp.com.

> A few misspelled words will jar the reader's concentration, and a lot of misspelled words will wreck your credibility.
>
> 100 Ways to Improve Your Writing
> Gary Provost

These tools scan your text for errors and suggest corrections or improvements. Some also offer additional features, such as style suggestions and the ability to check for plagiarism.

Using a spelling and grammar checker is straightforward.

1. Simply copy and paste your text into the tool or write directly in it if it has a built-in editor.
2. The tool will then scan your text and highlight any errors or potential improvements.
3. You can then review the suggestions and choose whether to accept or ignore them.

While spelling and grammar checkers can be extremely helpful, it is important to remember that they are not fool proof. They may only catch some mistakes and sometimes make incorrect suggestions. Therefore, double-checking your work and using your judgment when reviewing the recommendations is always a good idea.

FACT-CHECKING YOUR INFORMATION

In content marketing, it is important to ensure that the information you share is accurate and up to date. Fact-checking your information is a crucial step in this process, as it helps you verify the reliability of your sources and ensure that your content is based on solid evidence.

There are many ways to fact-check your information, depending on the type of content you are creating and the sources you are using. Some general best practices to follow include:

1. It is a good idea to **consult multiple sources** when researching a topic rather than relying on a single source. This can help you get a more balanced perspective and increase the reliability of your information.
2. **Verify the credibility of your sources**: Make sure that your sources are reputable and reliable. Look for sources that are well-known in their field or that are affiliated with a reputable organisation.
3. It is also important to **double-check your work** to ensure that you have understood everything correctly. Make sure you accurately represent the information you have gathered and be prepared to adjust it if necessary.
4. **Check for accuracy**: Ensure the information you use is accurate and up to date. Use tools to verify facts and be cautious of information that seems too good to be true.

Different tools are available help you verify facts, including:

- Google is a powerful search engine that can help you find information on various topics. Simply type your question or keywords into the search bar and browse through the results to find reliable sources of information.
- Snopes.com is a fact-checking website that investigates and verifies the accuracy of various claims and rumours. You can use the site to search for specific topics or browse through the most popular or recent fact checks.
- FactCheck.org is a non-partisan fact-checking website that investigates and verifies the accuracy of claims made by politicians and public figures. The site also offers a library of fact checks on various topics and tools and resources for checking facts on your own.
- Leadstories.com is a fact-checking website that investigates and verifies the accuracy of claims made on social media and the internet. The site has a team of fact-checkers who research and verify the accuracy of claims. It also offers a library of fact-checks on various topics.

USING RELIABLE SOURCES

When creating content for your marketing efforts, it is essential to use reliable sources of information to ensure the accuracy and credibility of your content. Reliable sources are trustworthy, authoritative and based on verifiable evidence.

Using reliable sources is essential for several reasons:

1. It helps to ensure that the information you share is **accurate** and **up to date**.
2. It helps to build **trust** with your audience, as they can be confident that the information you share is based on solid evidence.
3. Using reliable sources can help increase your content's **credibility**, making it more effective at achieving your marketing goals.

> Wikipedia is not a credible source—even according to Wikipedia itself.

Everybody Writes
Ann Handley

So how can you find reliable sources for your content marketing efforts? Here are a few tips to follow:

- When researching a topic, find **renowned and respected authorities**. These sources are likely more reliable, as they have a reputation to uphold.
- **Check the credibility of your sources**. Before using a source, check to see if it is credible. Look for sources affiliated with reputable organisations or with a long track record of producing reliable content.
- When possible, use **primary sources**, such as original research papers or government reports, rather than secondary sources, such as news articles or blog posts. Primary sources are typically more reliable as they are based on original research or data.
- Be careful of sources that are **biased** or have a vested interest in the topic you are researching. These sources may need to present a balanced view of the topic and their information may not be as reliable.

- When using a source, make sure it is based on **verifiable evidence**. Look for sources that provide citations or references to back up their claims and verify that the evidence they present is reliable.

> Proper citation is rooted in respect for other people's work and it allows your readers to refer to the original source of your information if they so wish. Think of it as a giant thank you to the people who said something before you did, or helped advance your thinking on an issue.
>
> Everybody Writes
> Ann Handley

By following these tips, you can make sure that the sources you use in your content marketing efforts are reliable and credible. This can increase your content's accuracy and effectiveness and build trust with your audience.

AVOIDING COPYRIGHT INFRINGEMENTS AND PLAGIARISM

Respecting copyright and intellectual property laws is crucial when creating and sharing content online. This means obtaining the necessary licenses and permissions for any images or other content you use to avoid potential legal and financial consequences.

One of the best ways to avoid plagiarism and copyright infringements is to use original content that is created by you or your team. This means writing your own articles, creating your own videos, or using your own images and graphics in your content. By using original content, you can make sure that your content is unique and does not infringe on anyone else's copyright.

Additionally, you can solicit feedback and input from others, such as colleagues or experts in your field, to help you improve the quality and accuracy of your content. By implementing these strategies, you can create trustworthy and compelling content to achieve your goals.

Copyright is a legal concept that gives creators of original works, such as art, music, writing and photographs, the exclusive right to use and distribute their work. This means that only the creator of the work can decide who can use it and how it can be used.

Regarding content marketing, it is important to respect copyright laws by obtaining the necessary permissions and licenses to use someone else's work in your content. This includes things like images, music and writing. If you use someone else's work without permission, you could break the law and face legal consequences.

> View permission requests as an opportunity to build relationships: people will appreciate that you admire their work, which is a great way to begin a conversation.

Everybody Writes
Ann Handley

EVER\
WRI

{ Your Go-To Guide
  Ridiculously Goo

ANN HAN

To sum it up, copyright means that creators have the right to control how their work is used and shared. Therefore, respecting these rights by getting permission before using someone else's work in your content is essential.

Suppose you need clarification about the copyright status of an image. In that case, it is best to purchase a license or use a royalty-free image. To clarify the copyright status of an image, there are a few steps you can take:

1. Check the **terms of use** for the image. Many websites that host images will include information about the copyright status of the images they offer. This information may be included in the website's terms of use or in the image's metadata.
2. **Contact the image creator** or copyright holder. If you need help finding information about the copyright status of an image, try reaching out to the creator or copyright holder directly. They can provide you with the necessary permissions or inform you of any restrictions on using the image.
3. If you need to use an image for commercial purposes, you may need to **purchase a license**. This will typically involve paying a fee to the copyright holder in exchange for permission to use the image.
4. If you cannot obtain the necessary permissions or do noy want to pay for a license, you can consider using a **royalty-free image**. Many websites offer royalty-free images, such as Pexels.com, Unsplash.com and Pixabay. com. These images can be used without paying royalties or obtaining permission. Still, it is essential to check the terms of use to ensure proper use. Some restrictions may include crediting the creator and not altering the image.

Plagiarism is using someone else's work or ideas without proper attribution or permission. It is a serious issue that can have significant consequences, including legal action and damage to your reputation.

As a content marketer, it is essential to avoid plagiarism by properly citing your sources and obtaining permission to use someone else's work. Here are a few tips for avoiding plagiarism:

1. **Cite your sources** When using someone else's work or ideas, give proper credit by citing your sources. This can be done through in-text citations and a list of references or a bibliography.
2. **Use quotation marks** If you are directly quoting someone else's words, be sure to use quotation marks to indicate that the words are not your own.
3. **Paraphrase** If you are using someone else's ideas, try to rephrase them in your own words rather than copying and pasting their work.

4. **Obtain permission** If you want to use someone else's work in your own content, be sure to obtain permission from the copyright holder. This may involve paying a fee or obtaining a license.

> (Tools like Son of Citation Machine [citationmachine.net] can spit out a properly formatted citation after you plug in some basic information about what you're referencing and where you found it.)

Everybody Writes
Ann Handley

EVERY
WRI

{ Your Go-To Guide
Ridiculously Goo

ANN HAN

By following these best practices, you can avoid plagiarism and ensure that you are creating original and ethical content. This will not only help you build trust with your audience, but it will also help you present a more professional image and increase the effectiveness of your content.

Ø4

DISTRIBUTING AND PROMOTING YOUR DIGITAL CONTENT

Distributing and promoting your content allows you to reach a wider audience and ultimately achieve your goals for creating the content in the first place. This could include raising awareness about a particular issue, promoting a product or service, or simply sharing information with others.

IDENTIFYING THE RIGHT CHANNELS FOR YOUR CONTENT

Identifying the right **channels** for your content is essential to ensuring that your message reaches the right audience. To do this, you need to consider both the type of content you are creating and the audience you are trying to reach.

Here are a few steps to help you identify the right channels for your content:

- Start by thinking about the **type of content** you are creating. Is it a blog post, video, podcast, or something else? Each type of content is best suited to different channels, so it is essential to consider this when choosing where to distribute your content.
- What is your content's home? Your **content home** is the primary platform or channel where your brand's content lives and is published. This could be

your brand's website, blog, or social media page, or it could be a third-party platform like YouTube or Medium. Ideally, this is part of your Owned Media – specifically your website and/or blog.

- Next, consider the **audience** you are trying to reach. Who are they and what channels do they typically use? For example, suppose you are trying to get young adults. In that case, you should focus on social media channels like Instagram and TikTok. On the other hand, LinkedIn may be a better choice if you are trying to reach professionals.

> Customize the content you distribute on each channel. Consider what messages are appropriate for each channel, and create a message you think will resonate with that specific audience.

Content Inc.
Joe Pulizzi

In our example target audience:

- Emily, our working mother in her 30s who lives in an urban area and has a household income of over $75,000 per year. Some potential digital channels that this group may be active on include social media platforms (such as Facebook, Instagram and Pinterest), online forums and discussion boards related to parenting and motherhood and blogs and websites focused on parenting, family and lifestyle.
- Noah, our teenager who is interested in skateboarding and streetwear fashion. Some potential digital channels that this group may be active on include social media platforms (such as Instagram and TikTok), online forums and discussion boards related to skateboarding and streetwear and blogs and websites focused on skateboarding, fashion and street culture.
- Retired yet active seniors like Iris and John may be active on social media platforms (such as Facebook and LinkedIn), online forums and discussion boards related to fitness and health and blogs and websites focused on fitness, nutrition and wellness.

Facebook is still popular with older millennials and up. Facebook is King of the 40+ demographic!

Video Marketing Like a PRO
Clo Willaerts

Research the different channels available to you. There are many different channels, and it can be overwhelming to try and choose the right ones. To make this easier, consider looking at what other people in your industry are doing. Which channels are they using and how successful are they? This can give you a good starting point for choosing your own channels.

Social media, websites, and YouTube are the most popular distribution channels for video content.

Video Marketing Like a PRO
Clo Willaerts

Test out different channels to see which ones work best for your content. It is important to remember that only some channels will work for some pieces of content, so feel free to experiment. Try distributing your content on several channels and see which ones perform the best. This will help you identify the most effective channels for your content and audience.

> Less is always more. Be great at one or two channels instead of mediocre at four or five.

Content Inc.
Joe Pulizzi

Use the ICE Matrix to choose the most efficient digital channels for publishing and distributing your content marketing. Create a table like the one below and give each digital channel a score out of 10 for 3 criteria: Impact, Confidence and Ease.

Table 15. ICE Matrix

DIGITAL CHANNEL	IMPACT	CONFIDENCE	EASE	ICE SCORE
Blog				
eBook				
White Paper				
Infographic				
Video				
Podcast				
Webinar				
Email Newsletter				
Social Media (e.g. Facebook, Instagram, Twitter)				
Search Engine Optimisation				
Content Distribution Platforms (e.g. Medium, LinkedIn)				
Influencer Marketing				

You would give it a high score for **Impact**, if for example, implementing a blog significantly impacts growth. If you are confident that it will work as expected, you would give it a high score for **Confidence**. If it is easy to implement, you would give it a high score for **Ease**.

The average of Impact, Confidence and Ease scores is the **ICE score** for each channel. The channel with the highest ICE score gets priority in your digital marketing efforts.

- Consider each criterion when choosing digital marketing channels.
- Assess potential impact, confidence in success and ease of implementation.
- Monitor competitors' digital channels to gather insights into their strategies.
- Test new channels or tactics for at least 3 months before re-evaluating their effectiveness.

PUBLISHING AND DISTRIBUTING YOUR CONTENT: 80/20

The **80/20 distribution approach** is a popular way to think about the balance between creating and promoting content.

Jonathan Aufray, cofounder and CEO of Growth Hackers, an agency that specializes in digital marketing and lead generation, thinks 20 percent of your time should be spent on creating content and 80 percent on promoting it.

The Stripped-Down Guide to Content ...
John Egan

This approach suggests that you spend 80% of your time and efforts on promotion, while only 20% should be spent on creating the content itself.

This is because it is often easier and more effective to promote existing content than to continually develop new ideas. Of course, the exact balance will depend on your specific goals and audience, so it is important to consider how you distribute and promote your content.

One of the most effective ways to distribute content is through **owned media channels**. Owned media refers to the digital assets and channels a company has direct control over, such as its website, blog, email and newsletters. Businesses have more control over the message they are communicating and the audience they are reaching by distributing content through these owned channels.

-   A well-designed **website** optimised for conversions is crucial for distributing content. This includes creating landing pages, blog posts, product pages and lead magnets tailored to your target audience's specific needs and interests. In addition, by tracking website metrics such as bounce rate, pages per session and time on site, businesses can gauge the effectiveness of their website in driving traffic and conversions.
-   Your **blog** is another powerful tool for distributing content, as it allows you to reach your target audience in a more personal and engaging way. Businesses can increase traffic, engagement and lead generation by creating informative and interesting blog posts, infographics, videos and podcasts. In addition, by measuring metrics such as page views, unique visitors, bounce rate, time on page, comments and shares, businesses can evaluate the performance of their blog and adjust their strategy accordingly.
-   **Emails** and **newsletters** effectively connect with your audience, promote new content and drive conversions. You can increase open rates, click-through rates and conversions by sending out newsletters and promotional emails to your subscribers. Businesses can gauge the effectiveness of their email campaigns and adjust their strategy accordingly by tracking metrics such as open rate, click-through rate, conversion rate and unsubscribe rate.

Owned media channels such as websites, blogs, emails and newsletters are valuable assets for distributing content. By utilising these channels effectively, businesses can reach and engage their target audience, increase conversions and track their performance to adapt and optimise their strategy.

Table 16. Owned Media

OWNED MEDIA	TYPES OF CONTENT TO DISTRIBUTE	TARGET KPIS	METRICS TO CHECK
Website	Landing pages, blog posts, product pages, lead magnets, pillar pages	Traffic, conversions, engagement	Bounce rate, pages per session, time on site, conversion rate
Blog	Blog posts, infographics, videos, podcasts	Traffic, engagement, lead generation	Pageviews, unique visitors, bounce rate, time on page, comments, shares
Emails and Newsletters	Newsletters, promotional emails, transactional emails	Open rate, click-through rate, conversions	Open rate, click-through rate, conversion rate, unsubscribe rate

Here are some content promotion tips that you can try out, but it is advisable to use them sparingly:

- Use a link-shortening service such as Bitly.com or TinyURL.com to create a cleaner look for your URL. Include this shortened link in your email signature, at the bottom of invoices or receipts, or your business card.
- Use a tool like HelloBar.com or OptinMonster.com to create an exit-intent pop-up on your website. This pop-up should display a link to your latest content when a visitor is about to leave your website.
- After someone completes a form or makes a purchase on your website, use a tool like Leadpages.com or Unbounce.com to redirect them to a thank you page with a link to your latest piece of content.
- Use a tool like Boomerangapp.com to include a link to your latest content in your out-of-office auto-responder message.
- Use in-app messaging tools such as OneSignal.com or Airship.com to send in-app notifications to your app users with a link to your latest content.
- Use a QR code generator like QRCode-Monkey.com or QR-Code-Generator. com to create QR codes linking to your latest content. Place these QR codes in strategic locations like billboards, buses, flyers, or other print material.

Remember to use these tips sparingly, as over-promoting your content can come across as spammy and can negatively impact your audience's experience with your brand.

HOW OFTEN AND WHEN SHOULD YOU POST?

One of the most important decisions regarding content marketing is how often to publish content. Studies have shown that for B2C companies, more than a quarter publish content daily. In the B2B space, about one in five companies publish content daily.

While there is no definitive answer on how often to publish content, it is generally recommended to aim for **consistency**. Regularly posting content will help keep your audience engaged and increase the chances of your content being seen and shared. However, it is also important to leave your audience with enough content. It is better to publish high-quality content less frequently than low-quality content more frequently.

In addition to the frequency of content publishing, consider the optimal days and times to publish content. Generally, it is best to refrain from posting on weekends, as engagement and reach tend to be lower. On the other hand, weekdays, specifically Wednesdays and Thursdays, tend to have the highest engagement rates. The best time of day to publish varies depending on the audience and the platform. However, studies show that the best time to post on social media is between 12-1pm and 3-4pm.

The frequency of content publishing, the day of the week and the time of day are all important factors to consider when creating a content marketing strategy. Aim for consistency while avoiding overwhelming your audience with too much content. Additionally, it is beneficial to publish on weekdays and during peak engagement hours to maximise reach and engagement. Finally, remember that what works for one company may not work for another. Test different strategies and track the results to find your business's ideal content publishing schedule.

TOOL: BUFFER

Buffer.com is a tool that allows users to schedule and automate their social media posts across multiple platforms, including Twitter, Facebook and LinkedIn. It is a valuable tool for content marketers looking to distribute their content across multiple social media channels efficiently and effectively. Buffer's features:

- allow users to schedule social media posts in advance;

- provide analytics and insights to help users understand the performance of posts and optimise content distribution strategy; and
- offer conveniences such as social media scheduling for teams, customisable posting schedules and integration with content management systems.

CROSS-POSTING ON EARNED PLATFORM PLATFORMS

Earned media refers to a company's coverage and exposure through unpaid channels, such as social media, medium.com, guest posts, forums and communities and review websites. The coverage is generated by the audience, not by the company.

Using earned media to promote your content can be a powerful way to increase brand awareness, reach and audience engagement. By distributing your content through these channels, you can tap into the power of social proof and word-of-mouth marketing.

Cross-posting is the practice of publishing the same content on multiple platforms. It can be valuable to reach a wider audience and drive traffic to your website. Cross-posting permits you to reach a wider audience and drive traffic back to your website. Here are some ideas:

Table 17. Types of Content to Distribute

TYPES OF CONTENT TO DISTRIBUTE	TARGET KPIS	METRICS TO CHECK
Social Media Accounts	Brand awareness, audience engagement, reach	Followers, likes, shares, comments, click-through rate
Medium.com	Brand awareness, audience engagement, reach	Views, reads, claps, comments, shares
Guest Posts	Brand awareness, reach, backlinks	Views, clicks, comments, shares
Forums and Communities	Brand awareness, audience engagement, reach	Views, clicks, comments, shares

Republish your long-form text content on Medium.com to reach a bigger audience with minimal effort. Include a powerful image immediately after the headline.

Digital marketing like a PRO
Clo Willaerts

Digital Marketing lik
Prepare. Run. Opti

YOUR SOCIAL MEDIA ACCOUNTS

Sharing your content on **social media accounts** is an example of cross posting that can increase your reach and engagement with your target audience. Monitoring metrics such as followers, likes, shares and comments lets you gauge the effectiveness of your social media strategy and adjust it accordingly.

Cross-post your content to social media platforms like Facebook, Twitter and LinkedIn to reach a wider audience. LinkedIn, for example, allows you to write and share status updates directly from the platform. If you want to share a blog article, you can use the full editor by clicking on the 'Write an article on LinkedIn' button. This will launch the editor and give you access to all the features you need to create and publish a professional-quality blog post. This can help increase exposure for your business and make connections with potential customers who may not have otherwise been aware of it.

MEDIUM.COM

Medium.com is a popular blogging platform that allows anyone to publish articles on various topics. Publishing your content on medium.com can increase your reach and engagement with a broader audience and drive traffic back to your website. Monitor metrics such as views, reads, claps, comments and shares to evaluate the performance of your content on the platform.

GUEST POSTING

Guest blogging involves writing an article for someone else's blog or website in exchange for backlinks to your website to boost the awareness and reach of your brand. By tracking metrics such as views, clicks, comments and shares you can gauge the effectiveness of your guest post strategy.

FORUMS AND COMMUNITIES

There are many **online communities**, such as forums and discussion groups, where you can share your content and engage with other users.

Participating in relevant forums and communities can increase brand awareness and engagement with your target audience. In addition, by monitoring metrics such as views, clicks, comments and shares, you can evaluate the performance of your content within these communities.

Make sure to follow best practices, such as **crediting the original source** and avoiding duplicate content, to ensure that your content is compelling and respected by others.

Duplicate content: remove, or revise the content to avoid duplication.

Digital Marketing Like a PRO
Clo Willaerts

Some platforms and search engines may penalise you for publishing **duplicate content**. To avoid this, you can use canonical tags to tell search engines that the original content is on your own website, or you can make slight adjustments to the content to make it unique.

Canonical tags are HTML tags used to indicate a web page's original or preferred version. They are typically used when there are multiple pages on a website with similar or duplicate content. Using canonical tags, you can tell search engines which page you want them to index and show in search results.

SHARING THE LINK TO YOUR CONTENT

Whether it is a blog post, web article, or eBook, you've put in a lot of hard work, and it is time to share it with the world. Here are some strategies to promote your content and get it in front of as many people as possible.

REACH OUT WITH YOUR NEWSLETTER

Emailing your **newsletter** subscribers is a highly effective tactic for driving traffic to your website and promoting your new content. If you have a newsletter, send an email to your subscribers announcing your new content and providing a link for them to read it.

Newsletters (monthly, bi-monthly – i.e., mails sent on a regular basis) give a quick overview of the most important things that are going on such as special deals, company news, industry best practices, and compelling content pieces.

Digital Marketing Like a PRO
Clo Willaerts

A great way to avoid sounding too self-centred is to mix the promotion of your content with content from other places on the web. This tactic is called Content Curation.

TACTIC: CONTENT CURATION

Content curation is a marketing tactic that involves gathering and sharing relevant, high-quality content from various sources. It can be useful for businesses to keep their audience informed and engaged by sharing a diverse range of relevant content to their industry or niche.

> Content Curation—The easiest way to begin a relationship through sending a powerful social signal while fulfilling the never-ending need to publish authentic content through your social channels at no cost.
>
> The Age of Influence
> Neal Schaffer

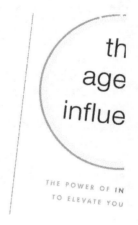

Many types of content can be curated, including:

- **Industry trends** and thought leadership content: Sharing your industry's latest trends and insights can help position your business as a thought leader and keep your audience up to date on the latest developments.
- **Infographics** and other visual content can effectively present information clearly and engagingly.
- Sharing **news related to your industry** can help keep your audience informed and show that your business is up to date on the latest developments.
- Sharing **helpful tips and guides** can be a valuable resource for your audience and position your business as an expert in your field.

- Sharing **entertaining or eye-catching content** can be a good way to engage your audience and break up more serious or informational content.
- Sharing **quotes from industry experts and personalities** can be a great way to add credibility to your content and show that your business is connected to influential figures in your field.
- Sharing **relevant research and studies** can add credibility to your content and show that your business is informed about the latest developments in your industry.

Here are some steps to follow when curating your content:

1. **Identify** the type of content that would be most relevant and engaging for your audience. This may include industry trends, thought leadership content, visual content such as infographics, news related to your industry, tips and guides, entertaining or eye-catching content, quotes from industry experts, or relevant research and studies.
2. **Search** for relevant content online using tools and resources like Google Alerts, industry-specific blogs and news sites and social media platforms.
3. **Select** the most relevant and engaging content to share with your audience.
4. **Share** the content with your audience across various channels, such as your website, social media accounts, email newsletters, or other platforms.

Businesses can create a well-rounded and engaging content marketing strategy by carefully curating a mix of these types of content,

> A robot can aggregate content, but only a human can tell me why it matters. Your curated content might not be original to you, but you should deliver an original experience that adds unique value.
>
> Everybody Writes
> Ann Handley

OUTREACH TO ONLINE COMMUNITIES AND INFLUENCERS

- Look for **online communities or forums** where your target audience hangs out. Consider sharing a link to your content there. Just follow any rules or guidelines for posting links and avoid spamming.
- If your content is relevant to a particular **influencer or industry expert**, consider reaching out to them and asking if they would be willing to share your content with their followers. This can be a great way to get your content in front of a larger audience.

By following these strategies, you can effectively promote your freshly published content and get it in front of as many people as possible. Remember to be consistent and patient, as it can take time for your content to gain traction. But with a little effort, you can effectively share your content and reach your target audience.

TACTIC: UPFRONT VALUE

Promoting your content in online communities like LinkedIn, Quora or Reddit can be tricky. Many professional groups or Q&A forums have strict rules against self-promotion and the community often ignores or downvotes posts that are clearly self-promoting. However, there is a way to effectively promote your content while still adding value to the community: by providing **upfront value**.

One way to do this is by creating a post that offers valuable information or resources to the community and then slipping in a subtle call-to-action (CTA) for your own content at the end.

For example, suppose your business is a content marketing agency. In that case, you could create a post that lists the top 10 strategies for creating high-performing blog posts. This post provides valuable information for the community and establishes you as an authority on the topic. Then, in the comments or at the end of the post, include a CTA for newsletter or website.

Another example is a content marketer who wrote a detailed guide on creating a successful email marketing campaign. This post provided valuable information for the community and established the content marketer as an authority on the topic. They then added a CTA at the end promoting their agency's services.

On the other hand, a poor way to promote your content on LinkedIn or Reddit is by creating a post about yourself and making no attempt to add value to the community. An example is a marketer who made a post asking the community to visit their website without providing any context or value. A better approach would be to create a post with a title that promises upfront value, such as *5 Proven tactics to increase website traffic* and then include a subtle CTA for your services or products at the end.

SHARE IT ON SOCIAL MEDIA

Promoting your content on social media accounts is a powerful way to increase brand awareness, reach and audience engagement. Be mindful of the social media platforms you choose to share your content on, how often you post and the value your posts bring to your followers or the wider community.

Here are some tips on how to effectively promote your content on social media:

- **Bio link** include a link to your latest piece of content in your bio on social media platforms like Twitter, Instagram and LinkedIn. This way, visitors to your profile can easily access your latest content.
- Consider reaching out to your followers with a **private message** promoting your latest content. This can be done through direct messages on platforms like Instagram, Twitter, or LinkedIn.
- Share a **status update** on platforms like Facebook, LinkedIn and Instagram that includes a link to your latest piece of content.
- **Image/Advertisement** Use eye-catching images or graphics to make your post stand out on social media platforms, whether a standalone or an advertisement.

While it is essential to promote your content and get it in front of as many people as possible, it is not advisable to post on social media platforms where you are not actively engaged with other users. Posting on platforms where you do not have a presence or a following can be perceived as spammy. It could harm your reputation rather than help it.

Instead, focus on building a strong presence on a few key social media platforms where your target audience is active and where you can consistently provide valuable and engaging content. This will help you build a loyal following and effectively promote your content without sounding spammy.

LINK POSTING ON SOCIAL MEDIA WEBSITES

Here is an overview of the various strategies you can use to share links to your content on Facebook, Twitter, LinkedIn, Reddit and Quora.

Facebook:

- Post a link to your content on your personal or business Facebook page.
- Share the link in relevant Facebook groups or communities.
- Consider using Facebook ads to promote your content and reach a wider audience.

LinkedIn:

- Share a link to your content on your personal or business LinkedIn profile.
- Share the link in relevant LinkedIn groups or communities.
- Consider using LinkedIn ads to promote your content and reach a wider audience.

Twitter:

- Tweet a link to your content, a catchy headline and relevant hashtags.
- Share the link in relevant Twitter chats or communities.
- Consider using Twitter ads to promote your content and reach a wider audience.

Reddit:

- Share a link to your content in a relevant subreddit (a community within Reddit focused on a specific topic).
- Engage with other users in the subreddit and participate in discussions before sharing your content.
- Follow Reddit is rules and self-promotion guidelines to avoid being spammy.

Quora:

- Share a link to your content in a relevant Quora thread or as a response to a question.
- Engage with other users in the thread and add value to the discussion before sharing your content.
- Follow Quora's rules and self-promotion guidelines to avoid being spammy.

By following these strategies, you can effectively share links to your content on Facebook, Twitter, LinkedIn, Reddit and Quora and reach a wider audience. Just be sure to be respectful of the community guidelines and avoid coming across as spammy.

LINK SHARING ON INSTAGRAM, TIKTOK AND SNAPCHAT

Instagram does not allow hyperlinking in post captions unless you run paid advertising. However, you can still share links to your content on Instagram through the following methods:

- **Links in bio** You can include clickable links in your Instagram bio that directs users to your website or content.
- **Link in Instagram Stories** You can use the 'Link' sticker in Instagram Stories to include a clickable link that directs users to your website or content.
- **Link in Instagram Direct Messages** You can send a direct message to individual users or groups with a link to your website or content.

It is not possible to provide a clickable link within the caption of a video on **TikTok**. Instead, you can use the following methods to share links to your content on TikTok:

- **Link in bio** If you have fewer than 10,000 followers, you can include a clickable link in your TikTok bio that directs users to your website or content.
- **Link in TikTok stories** If you have more than 10,000 followers, you can add clickable links to your TikTok stories that direct users to your website or content.

You can add a link to your **Snapchat** story by tapping on the paperclip icon while customising your snap. Snapchat will allow you to add a link you've shared before, search for the link, or paste in a completely new one.

PINNING YOUR CONTENT TO PINTEREST

Pinterest is a visual search engine allowing users to discover and save ideas for their interests and hobbies. It can be a powerful platform for driving traffic to your website or blog, especially if you have visually appealing content such as infographics, photos, or videos. Here are some tips for using Pinterest to promote your content:

1. You must create a **business account** to use Pinterest to access analytics and other features that can help you track your performance and reach on the platform.
2. **Set up your profile**, including a clear and concise bio that describes what your business or blog is all about and a link to your website to make it easy for users to find and visit your site.
3. Pinterest is all about visuals, so make sure to **create high-quality pins** that are visually appealing and will catch the eye of users as they scroll through their feeds. You can use tools like Canva or Adobe Spark to create professional-looking pins.
4. **Hashtags** on Pinterest work differently than on other social media platforms. Instead of using them to join a conversation, you should use them to make your content more discoverable by users who are searching for specific topics.
5. Pinterest is a community-driven platform, so make sure to **engage with your audience** by commenting on their pins, responding to comments on your own pins and sharing their content. This will help to build relationships and drive more traffic to your website or blog.

Following these tips, you can effectively use Pinterest to promote your content and drive traffic to your website or blog. Remember to consistently and regularly post new and engaging content to keep your audience engaged and coming back.

REPURPOSING YOUR CONTENT: COPE, GARYVEE AND 4R MODELS

As a content creator, you likely spend a lot of time and effort crafting high-quality pieces of work. However, as your audience grows and evolves, it can be helpful to find new ways to repurpose your content to reach a wider audience and keep them engaged.

One way to repurpose your content is to take a long-form piece, such as a blog post or article and break it down into smaller, bite-sized pieces of content, such as social media posts or infographics. This can help to make your content more accessible and easily digestible for your audience.

The **COPE (Create Once, Publish Everywhere)** content distribution tactic is about maximising your content's value by repurposing and recycling it effectively. For example, instead of creating new content from scratch every time you want to share something with your audience, you can start with a base format, such as an eBook, whitepaper, video, or research report and then break it out into smaller assets that can be shared across different channels and platforms.

GaryVee's Content Model was created by Gary Vaynerchuk, a digital marketing expert and entrepreneur. It is still being determined precisely when he created this model. Still, it has been widely discussed and referenced in his various books, talks and media appearances over the past several years. It is a powerful example of how businesses can leverage the COPE tactic to amplify their content and reach a wider audience. The model suggests creating a 'pillar' piece of content, such as an in-depth blog post or video and then repurposing and distributing it across various channels and formats.

For example, a business might create a video about social media marketing strategies and then use that video to make shorter, edited versions for Instagram, Facebook and LinkedIn. They might also create a video transcript to create a series of blog posts or newsletters. The business can reach a wider audience and generate more leads and conversions by breaking out the content into smaller, more digestible pieces.

The COPE tactic is a great way to maximise the value of your content and ensure that it reaches as many people as possible. In addition, by repurposing and recycling your content, you can extend its shelf life and continue to engage and educate your audience.

By using the COPE content distribution tactic, you can save time and resources while still providing valuable and relevant content to your audience. It also allows you to reach a wider audience, share your content across different platforms and channels and adapt it to other formats and styles.

To make the most of the COPE content distribution tactic, create high-quality, in-depth content that can be repurposed effectively and to have a clear plan for how you will share and promote your content across different channels and platforms. It is also important to track and analyse the performance of your content and to adjust your strategy based on what works and doesn't. By following these best practices, you can make the most of your content marketing efforts and achieve your business goals.

View all of the pieces of content you plan to create as expressions of a single bigger idea. Or, alternatively—if you are starting with something larger, like a white paper or ebook—think about how you can create smaller chunks of shareable content from that single content asset.

Content Rules
Ann Handley, C.C. Chapman, and Davi...

Another content model that can be effective for promoting your content is the 4R model. The **4R model**, also known as the Repurpose, Repost, Remix and Reinvent model, is a strategy for getting the most out of your content.

- **Repurpose** suggests taking your pillar piece of content and repurposing it onto other mediums, such as a podcast or an infographic. This allows you to reach new audiences and increase the longevity of your content.
- **Repost** suggests to re-share your content every so often. This allows you to reach new audiences who may have missed it the first time.

- **Remix** suggests changing how you deliver the content via different formats. This could mean creating a video or a slide presentation from a blog post. This allows you to create new and exciting ways to showcase your content.
- **Reinvent** suggests taking the piece of content and saying it differently. This could mean creating a summary video or a different blog post covering the same subject matter. This allows you to create new and fresh content around the same topic.

The following list illustrates how you can apply these content distribution models to a piece of long-form content in the form of an e-book.

- **Infographic**: The information from the eBook can be condensed and illustrated in a visual format for easy understanding and sharing on social media.
- The information from the eBook can be broken down into smaller, more focused pieces and used as a series of **blog posts** on a website.
- **Social Shares**: Quotes or key takeaways from the eBook can be used as social media updates to promote the book and drive sales.
- The **expert quotes** from the eBook can be pulled out and used as standalone quotes in a blog post, press release, or social media update.
- The eBook can be converted into a **physical print book** and sold through traditional bookstores.
- The eBook can be **translated into other languages** to reach a wider audience.
- **Vertical eBook** content can be reorganised into subtopic-specific eBooks to appeal to different niche audiences.
- The book's content can be recorded as **audiobooks** and sold online or through streaming services.
- **Video Series** content can be used to create a series of videos, which can be hosted on a website or shared on social media platforms.

The 4R model is a great way to get the most out of your content and make it more shareable. It allows you to reach new audiences and increase engagement with your existing audience. Combined with the Create Once, Publish Everywhere and GaryVee's Content Model, it can help maximise your content's potential.

TOOL: REPURPOSE.IO

Repurpose.io is a platform that allows content marketers to easily repurpose their existing content for different platforms and formats. Its range of features makes it simple to turn a single piece of content into multiple pieces without the need to create new content from scratch.

One of the key features of Repurpose.io is the ability to customise multiple connections between content sources and destinations, allowing you to create a workflow that fits your specific needs. So, whether you want to repurpose content for your website or social media channels, you can easily achieve that.

Additionally, Repurpose.io offers a vast library of templates that you can use to adapt your content for every destination, ensuring that it looks great no matter where it is published. You can also create unlimited clips from videos, burn captions and headlines into videos and automatically resize videos into vertical and square formats.

Repurpose.io offers three pricing plans, each with different features and functionalities and the ability to connect to different social media platforms. There is also a 14-day free trial available for you to test it out before committing.

Some alternative platforms for repurposing content include Chopcast, Invideo, Kapwing and Vidyo.ai.

- Chopcast.io is a podcast editing and repurposing tool that allows you to create new episodes, clips and social media snippets from existing podcasts.
- Invideo.io is a video creation platform enabling you to repurpose existing videos into different formats and sizes.
- Kapwing.com is a content creation and editing tool that can repurpose images, videos and GIFs.
- vidyo.ai is an AI-driven video platform that allows you to automatically repurpose existing videos into different formats and sizes.

UPDATE AND REPUBLISH OLD CONTENT

Finally, you can repurpose your content by **updating and republishing old pieces**. This can be especially useful for evergreen content that is still relevant and useful to your audience. You can breathe new life into your old content and continue to engage your audience by updating the information and giving it a fresh spin.

> Content repurposing requires altering a piece of content to make it fresh by changing the angle or switching up the format. Integrating repurposing into your strategy can lower costs, advance production, expand audience reach, and provide myriad additional benefits,
>
> Content Inc.
> Joe Pulizzi

Repurposing your content can be an excellent way to reach a wider audience, keep them engaged and continue to grow as a content creator. By finding creative ways to adapt your content for different platforms and formats, you can continue to provide valuable and interesting content for your audience.

TRANSLATE YOUR CONTENT

Translating your content for different audiences can be a powerful way to reach new markets and expand your reach. By repurposing your written content for other languages and cultural contexts, you can tap into new pools of potential customers and increase the impact of your marketing efforts. In this chapter, we will explore some key considerations and best practices for translating your content.

The target language itself is one of the first things to consider when translating your content. Suppose you are targeting a non-English-speaking audience. In that case, you will need to use a **professional translation service** that has experience in your market to ensure that your content is accurately and effectively communicated.

In addition to the language itself, you will also need to consider the **cultural context** of your target audience. Different cultures have different values, beliefs and communication styles and it is essential to consider these differences when repurposing your content. This might involve adapting your tone and style to better suit your audience or including local examples and references that resonate with your target market.

Another essential factor to consider when translating your content is the **platform** on which it will be published. Different platforms may have additional formatting requirements and you will need to ensure that your content is formatted correctly and optimised for each platform. This might involve adapting your layout, using different graphics or images, or adjusting your use of headings, bullet points and other formatting elements.

Finally, it is important to remember that translation is not a one-time process. As your business grows and your target audience evolves, you will need to continually **update and translate** your content to ensure it remains relevant and effective. This might involve conducting regular audits of your translated content, seeking feedback from your audience and making any necessary updates or changes.

TOOL: DEEPL

DeepL Translate is a powerful tool that allows you to translate your written content quickly and easily into multiple languages. Here is how to use it:

1. Visit the DeepL Translate website (deepl.com/translator) and select the language you want to translate your content from and the language you want to translate it into.
2. Copy and paste your content or upload a document file into the input field.
3. Click the 'Translate' button to begin the translation process. DeepL Translate will use artificial intelligence and machine learning to translate your content accurately and effectively.
4. Review the translated content to ensure that it accurately conveys your message. You can use the 'Edit Translation' feature to make necessary changes or adjustments.

5. Once satisfied with the translation, you can copy and paste it into your desired platform or download it as a document file.

DeepL Translate is a fast and easy way to translate your content into multiple languages. It is handy for those with limited experience with translation or who need to translate large volumes of content quickly. Remember to constantly review your translations carefully to ensure they accurately convey your message.

There are several alternatives to DeepL Translate that you may want to consider, depending on your needs and preferences:

-   Google Translate: One of the most popular translation tools, Google Translate offers fast and reliable translations in over 100 languages. It is free to use and is available as a web or mobile app.
-   Microsoft Translator: Another well-known translation tool, Microsoft Translator, offers translations in over 60 languages. It is free to use and is available as a web application, a mobile app and as an API for developers.

These are just a few examples of the many translation tools and services available. To find the best option for your needs, consider your budget, the languages you need to translate into and the features and capabilities that are most important to you.

EXAMPLE CONTENT PROMOTION CHECKLIST

Day One Amplification on social media, share on:

-   Twitter with a compelling headline
-   Twitter as a thread
-   LinkedIn with a long-form post
-   your Facebook page with a 3-4 sentence summary

Day Two Amplify through native channels:

-   upload and publish as a Medium article
-   upload and publish as a LinkedIn article
-   retweet the original thread from Day One

Day Three Community-driven distribution:

- amplify in a Slack community
- amplify in a Facebook group
- amplify in a Discord channel
- submit to an industry forum (x2)

Day Four Newsletters & mixing things up:

- reshare the link on Twitter
- share a link on your Instagram story
- reach out to 'friendlies' for engagement
- promote internally for employee advocacy
- write scripts for SDRs/BDRs to use for prospects/leads
- add to your email signature for the week

Day Five Influencer outreach efforts:

- reach out to industry newsletters
- direct message industry influencers with a link
- pin post to article at the top of your channels
- respond to influencers' tweets with additional value and a link to your asset
- engage a TikToker to create content about the asset

Day Six Repurposing time. Convert the blog post into a:

- YouTube video
- Instagram carousel
- LinkedIn document
- Slideshare deck
- vertical video.

Note that this is just a sample, not an exhaustive list. It is crucial to track the performance and engagement of your content and adjust your promotion strategy accordingly. Your tools and channels also vary depending on your target audience and industry.

BUILDING AN AUDIENCE AND COMMUNITY

> The best content creators inform, inspire, educate, entertain, and build community all at once.

Video Marketing Like a PRO
Clo Willaerts

Building an audience and fostering a community through your content can be a challenging but rewarding process. Here are a few steps you can take to achieve this:

- Identify your target audience and **create content that resonates with them**. This means understanding their interests, values and pain points and creating content that addresses these issues and provides value to them. The more specific you can be, the easier it will be to create content that resonates with your audience and encourages them to engage with it.

> Create content that is likely to resonate with small groups of friends, rather than content that is aiming for universal appeal across large populations. Ensure the content is something people are likely to chat about offline. Content that close friends share will spread from group to group to group, and can end up reaching millions of people. But you need to specifically design for the small group of friends for the content to spread.

Grouped
Paul Adams

To effectively manage a community, it is important to consistently publish high-quality content and use engagement tactics to encourage interaction with the content. Here are some engagement tactics to consider:

- Interact with your audience by responding to comments, answering questions, and engaging with people who share your content to foster a sense of community.
- Provide exclusive content and offers such as behind-the-scenes insights, early access to new content, or special discounts on your products or services to make your audience feel valued and appreciated.
- Host events, webinars, or online workshops to unite your audience and create a supportive and engaged community around your content.

> The easiest way to turn off your community members is to broadcast the same message across multiple channels.

Content Inc.
Joe Pulizzi

ENGAGING WITH YOUR AUDIENCE THROUGH SOCIAL MEDIA

Engagement as a KPI (key performance indicator) for social media marketing refers to the level of interaction and participation that a brand's audience has with its content on social media. This can include:

- likes, comments, shares and clicks on a post and
- actions such as signing up for a newsletter or visiting a brand's website.

> Content drives conversations. Conversation engages your customers. Engaging with people is how your company will survive and thrive in this newly social world.
>
> Content Rules
> Ann Handley, C.C. Chapman, and Davi...

Measuring engagement as a KPI is important for social media marketers because it provides insight into how well their content resonates with their audience.

- High levels of engagement indicate that a brand's content is interesting, valuable and relevant to its audience, which helps to build trust and loyalty.
- Low levels of engagement indicate that a brand's content is not resonating with its audience and may need to be adjusted.

Creating content that gets a lot of social media engagement can be a challenging and rewarding task. To create content that will engage your audience, you need to understand your audience and what they are looking for. Some tips include:

- Focus on **providing value** to your audience. This could mean sharing helpful information, entertaining them, or giving them a unique perspective. Whatever form your content takes, it should be something that your audience will find exciting and engaging.
- **Consistency is key!** This means posting regularly and on a schedule that your audience can rely on. This can help to build trust and loyalty with your audience, as they will know when to expect new content from you.
- Focus on creating **visually appealing content**, like high-quality images, videos, or graphics to enhance your posts and make them more engaging.

> Half of blogging is consistency, or just showing up on a regular basis.
>
> Everybody Writes
> Ann Handley

EVER)
WRI

{ Your Go-To Guide !
  Ridiculously Goo

ANN HAN

Here are some tips for boosting engagement on your content posts:

- **Asking a question** in your post can encourage your audience to comment and engage with your content. This can be a simple question about their thoughts or a more open-ended question that encourages them to share their experiences or insights.
- Asking your audience for **advice** or their opinions on a particular topic can be an excellent way to encourage engagement. This can be a simple question asking for their thoughts on a specific issue or a more open-ended question asking for their advice on a particular problem.
- **Adding a GIF** to your post or comment can be a fun way to add some personality and humour to your content. This can make your content more engaging and memorable for your audience.
- Use **'This or That'** or **'Would You Rather'** prompts. These can be a fun way to engage your audience and encourage them to share their opinions. For example, ask your audience to choose between two options or choose which option they prefer.
- **Creating a poll or survey** can be a good way to gather feedback from your audience and encourage them to engage with your content. This can be a simple poll asking for their opinions on a specific topic or a more comprehensive survey gathering more detailed feedback.
- Use **'If You Could'** or **'Fill in the Blank'** prompts. These prompts can be a fun way to encourage your audience to share their thoughts and ideas. For example, you could ask your audience what they would do if they could do anything or ask them to fill in the blank with their thoughts or ideas.

- Use '**Mad Libs'** style prompts: These prompts involve asking your audience to fill in the blank with a specific word or phrase to create a humorous or entertaining story or message. This can be a fun way to engage your audience and encourage them to share their thoughts and ideas.
- **Controversial topics** can be an interesting way to spark discussion and engage your audience. However, it is important to approach controversial topics with sensitivity and respect, as they can also be divisive and potentially offensive to some people.
- Offering a **free download or resource** can be a good way to encourage your audience to engage with your content. This could be a white paper, an eBook, a template, or any other resource your audience might find valuable.
- Running a **contest or giveaway** can be an excellent way to engage your audience and encourage them to share your content. This could be a simple contest asking your audience to share a photo or video related to your brand or a more complex contest with specific rules and requirements.

Finally, feel free to experiment and try new things. Social media is a constantly evolving platform and what works today may not work tomorrow. By testing and trying new approaches, you can stay ahead of the curve and continue to engage your audience with fresh and exciting content.

COLLABORATING WITH INFLUENCERS

Influencers have a large and dedicated following on social media, and they can help promote a brand's products or services to their audience.

> While brands struggle to influence through content, influencers, who intrinsically are content creators, are masters at it.

The Age of Influence
Neal Schaffer

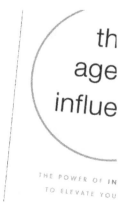

th
age
influe

THE POWER OF IN
TO ELEVATE YOU

Here are a few additional tactics for collaborating with influencers:

- **Host a giveaway or contest**. Partner with an influencer to host a giveaway or contest on their social media channels, where they promote your brand or product as the prize.
- **Invite them to be a podcast or webinar guest** to discuss their work and share their insights with your audience.
- **Collaborate on a joint project**, like a co-branded eBook or video series.
- **Offer a special deal or discount** by partnering with an influencer to provide their followers a special deal or discount on your products or services.
- **Invite them to an event or conference** hosted by your company and provide them with a VIP experience.

> For advertisers, partnering with creators who already have a large community gathered around them is a great way to borrow influence and increase relevance.
>
> Video Marketing Like a PRO
> Clo Willaerts

To maximise the potential of your content, consider partnering with influencers with a large yet engaged following. This can help you reach a new audience and achieve your marketing goals. When selecting influencers to work with:

- Consider influencers with a following **like your target market**, such as a fashion blogger, if you are a clothing brand.
- Set **specific goals** for the collaboration, such as increasing brand awareness or driving website traffic.
- Make sure to **clearly communicate** any guidelines or requirements to the influencer before the collaboration begins.
- In return for their promotion, you could offer an influencer a **fee** or **free product** or give them access to **exclusive content or events**.

USER GENERATED CONTENT

> User generated content (UGC)
> is any content - text, videos,
> images, reviews, etc. - created
> by people, rather than brands.

Video Marketing Like a PRO
Clo Willaerts

User-generated content (UGC) refers to any content created and shared by users of a brand's products or services rather than the brand itself. This can include things like

- reviews, ratings and testimonials
- social media posts, photos and videos

Benefits of User-Generated Content (UGC):

- **Trustworthy and authentic**, as it comes directly from real customers with first-hand experience with the brand's products or services.
- Builds **trust** and **credibility** with potential customers, influencing their purchasing decisions.
- Increases brand **reach and engagement** on social media, generating buzz and visibility.
- Serves as a source of **business intelligence**, allowing companies to gather customer insights and feedback.
- A **cost-effective** way to refresh a brand's content, requiring less money, time and resources than original content.
- Provides a **new perspective** on the brand, as it is created by customers rather than the business itself.

To effectively incorporate UGC into a content marketing strategy, businesses should:

- make it easy for users to create and share content. This could mean providing tools and resources, such as hashtags and branded templates, to help users create and share content about the brand.
- regularly monitor and curate UGC and engage with users sharing content about the brand.

The role of UGC in a content marketing context is significant and growing. By leveraging the trustworthiness and authenticity of UGC, businesses can increase their reach and engagement on social media and ultimately drive more sales and customer loyalty.

CASE IN POINT: GOPRO

GoPro is a company that makes action cameras and is known for its user-generated content campaign. This campaign encourages GoPro users to create and share videos and photos taken with their cameras. The company then showcases this user-generated content on its website and social media channels, which helps to build brand awareness and promote its products.

This type of campaign is an excellent example of content marketing because it showcases the capabilities of GoPro's cameras and allows the company to connect with its customers and create a sense of community among users.

Using user-generated content as part of its content marketing strategy, GoPro has engaged and connected with its target audience in a meaningful and authentic way. The company's user-generated content campaign has helped to build brand loyalty and trust among its customers, showing real people using and enjoying the company's products.

In addition to its user-generated content campaign, GoPro also produces its own branded content, such as product demonstrations and sponsored events, which helps to showcase the company's products and values. By combining user-generated content with its branded content, GoPro has created a comprehensive and effective content marketing strategy that resonates with its audience and helps drive business growth.

CONTENT CO-CREATION

In addition to collaborating with influencers, businesses can **partner with other companies or organisations** to promote their brand on social media. For example, a clothing brand might partner with a lifestyle magazine to co-create content and cross-promote each other's products. This can help expand both parties' reach and create a win-win situation for both companies.

> Collabs are a great way to help get your content in front of established audiences who may be unfamiliar with your YouTube presence. •Choose wisely: The most popular creator may not be the best choice; focus on audience reach and content style.
>
> Video Marketing Like a PRO
> Clo Willaerts

Content collaborations, also known as content co-creation, are strategic partnerships between two or more brands or individuals who create and share content together. This can help expand both parties' reach and bring their content to established audiences they may not have been able to reach on their own.

Content collabs can take many forms, such as:

- guest blogging;
- sponsored posts; or
- cross-promotion on social media.

Businesses can increase their visibility and engagement on social media by partnering with other brands or individuals with a similar target audience. This can drive more traffic to their website, generate leads and ultimately drive more sales and customer loyalty.

In addition to increasing reach and engagement, content collaborations can provide fresh and unique content for your audience. By working with other brands or individuals, you can tap into their expertise and unique perspectives to create interesting and engaging content for your audience. This helps keep your content fresh and relevant and helps build trust and credibility with your audience.

PROMOTING YOUR CONTENT

Promoting your content through news outlets and social media networks can be a powerful way to reach a wider audience and amplify your message. In the current media landscape, both channels can effectively drive traffic and engagement to your content.

WAYS TO PROMOTE YOUR CONTENT

You can reach a wider audience and build relationships with your customers and clients by promoting your content in various ways. Choose the best tactics for your business and audience and mix up your approach to keep things interesting and engaging.

Some tactics for promoting your content include:

- Share your content on **social media platforms** to reach a wider audience and build relationships with your followers. You can also use social media to engage with your audience and to get feedback on your content.
- Use **email marketing** to promote your content to your subscribers. This can be a great way to keep your audience informed and engaged with your content and to drive traffic back to your website.
- Partner with **influencers** or industry experts to promote your content. This can be a great way to reach a new audience and build relationships with others in your industry.
- Use **paid advertising**, such as Google AdWords or Facebook Ads, to promote your content to a targeted audience. This can be a great way to reach a specific audience and drive traffic to your website.

By using a variety of tactics to promote your content, you can reach a wider audience and build relationships with your customers and clients. Choose the tactics that work best for your business and audience and be sure to mix things up to keep things interesting and engaging.

GETTING PICKED UP ON SOCIAL MEDIA

In today's digital landscape, social media platforms such as Facebook, TikTok and Reddit are crucial channels for promoting your content and reaching a wider audience.

Understanding the strengths and characteristics of each platform can help you craft the most effective content strategy and increase the chances of your content being shared and reaching a wider audience.

- **Facebook** is more geared towards longer-form content and has a more diverse user base, making it a good platform for more in-depth articles and case studies. On Facebook, content likely to be shared easily includes personal stories, emotional or heart-warming content, funny or entertaining videos or memes and content that promotes causes or social issues. This is because Facebook is a platform where people connect with friends and family and share their personal experiences and thoughts.
- **Reddit** is known for its community-driven nature and is a great platform for discussions and Q&A sessions. On Reddit, content likely to be shared easily includes informative articles or discussions, exciting or unusual stories and content that relates to specific communities or interests. This is because Reddit is a platform where people connect with like-minded individuals and share content within communities or forums.
- **Twitter** is known for its fast-paced and concise nature, which makes it well-suited for quick updates and news bites. On Twitter, content likely to be shared easily includes news articles, industry insights, quotes or statistics and content that sparks debate or conversation. This is because Twitter is a platform where people follow influential figures and organizations and share timely or relevant information.

The key to encourage sharing on social media is to consider **what the reader wants to express** through sharing and whether they can **easily summarise and share** the content.

> People only share what makes them look smart, likeable, or attractive. Strong emotions like anger or surprise can also drive a lot more clicks than happy emotions.

Digital Marketing Like a PRO
Clo Willaerts

Encourage content sharing by creating content that:

- evokes **strong emotions**;
- aligns with the reader's **sense of identity**;
- provides **valuable insights or information** they want to share with their followers; and
- can be easily summarised and shared in a sentence or two to make it more cognitively accessible for readers.

To make sure your content gets picked up on social media, there are several key strategies to consider:

1. **Visual content** such as graphics and infographics is more likely to be shared on social media than text-based content. Ensure your content includes high-quality images and other visual elements that are eye-catching and engaging.
2. **Headlines** are the first thing people see when they come across your content on social media. Make sure your headlines are attention-grabbing and accurately reflect the content of your article or post.
3. To make sure your content gets picked up on social media, it is important to create **engaging and informative content**. This may involve addressing a specific problem or need your target audience is facing or providing valuable insights or information that they will find helpful.
4. Consider reaching out to **influencers** in your industry or related fields and asking them to share your content with their followers.

Here are some ideas for **shareable images** on social media:

- quotes from a famous person, yourself, or a fan or customer
- this or that?
- questions
- FAQs and Q&As
- facts or helpful tips
- reminders
- shortlists
- headlines of e.g. blog posts or web articles you wrote
- teasers
- an idea / try this
- behind the scenes
- where you get your inspiration
- customer photos of your product

Here are some tips for creating engagement on your social media posts:

- Saying **thank you** to your followers can be a great way to show appreciation and encourage more engagement from your audience.
- **Mentioning an influencer** in your post can be a great way to reach a wider audience and build relationships with others in your industry.
- **Mentioning a local business** in your post can be a great way to support your community and build relationships with local businesses.
- **Mentioning your most engaged fan** can be a great way to show appreciation and encourage more engagement from your audience.
- **Sharing a post from a fan** can be a great way to show appreciation and encourage more engagement from your audience.
- Sharing your thoughts on **a brand you love** can be a great way to connect with your audience and share your interests outside your brand.

By following these strategies, you can increase the chances that your content will be picked up and shared on social media and reach a wider audience.

SOCIAL MEDIA POST: ECO-FRIENDLY SKATE SHOES FROM MOONLIT APPAREL

Here is an example for a social media post on Moonlit Apparel's latest collection.

Are you a skateboarder who is always on the lookout for the perfect pair of shoes? In that case, you'll want to check out Moonlit Apparel's new collection. Here are five reasons why these shoes are perfect for you:

1. *Durability: These shoes are made from high-quality materials built to last. You do not have to worry about falling apart after a few sessions at the skatepark.*
2. *Performance: These shoes' design focuses on providing the best performance possible for skateboarders. They feature a sturdy sole and a supportive fit that will help you easily land your tricks.*
3. *Eco-friendly: These sneakers are made from recycled materials from skateboards, making them an eco-friendly choice for skateboarders who want to reduce their environmental impact.*
4. *Style: In addition to their performance and durability, these shoes have a sleek and stylish look that will turn heads on the streets and in the skatepark.*
5. *Designed by MC Grind: These shoes are created by the famous rap artist MC Grind, known for his love of skateboarding and streetwear fashion. With his input, you can be sure that these sneakers are the perfect combination of style and performance.*

These sneakers are worth considering if you are looking for a shoe that reflects your unique style and interests.

Moonlit Apparel's new collection of sneakers. Find your personal style.

The perfect social media format for this content could be a series of Instagram posts featuring photos of the sneakers in action, along with captions highlighting the key features of the shoes and how they cater to skateboarders.

These posts could be accompanied by a link to a landing page on the Moonlit Apparel website where users can learn more about the collection and purchase the shoes.

Additionally, incorporating hashtags related to skateboarding and streetwear fashion, such as #skateboarding #streetwear #skateshoes, can help increase the posts' reach and visibility. Alternatively, this content could be shared on Facebook or TikTok in a similar format, with the option of including a video showcasing the features and benefits of the shoes.

GETTING PICKED UP BY NEWS OUTLETS

To get your content picked up by **news outlets**, it is essential to use public relations tactics to build relationships with journalists and pitch your content in a relevant and exciting way to their audience. This may involve using press releases, press conferences, or other tactics to get the attention of reporters and editors.

Getting picked up by news outlets can be a powerful way to reach a wider audience and amplify your message. However, getting the attention of journalists and editors can be challenging, as they receive a large volume of pitches and press releases daily.

PUBLIC RELATIONSHIP TACTICS

To increase your chances of getting picked up by news outlets, it is essential to use public relations tactics to build relationships with journalists and editors. This may involve identifying the right journalists and editors to target based on their interests and coverage areas and reaching out to them directly through email or social media.

To effectively email journalists and promote your content, follow these tips:

- **Research your target journalists** Make a list of journalists or media outlets relevant to your industry or topic and have a track record of covering similar content. This will help ensure that your pitch is relevant and has a higher chance of acceptance.
- **Personalise your emails** Avoid sending generic or mass emails to journalists. Instead, take the time to customise your pitch for each individual journalist by addressing them by name and referencing their previous work or interests. This shows that you have taken the time to research them and are genuinely interested in getting their attention.

- **Keep it brief** Journalists are often busy and receive a lot of pitches, so keep your email brief and to the point. Use a clear and concise subject line. Provide a brief overview of your content and its relevance to the journalist's audience.
- **Make a compelling pitch** Explain why your content is exciting and valuable to the journalist's audience. Highlight any unique or noteworthy aspects of your content and provide relevant data or research to support your claims.
- **Follow-up** If you are still waiting to hear back from a journalist after your initial email, consider following up once or twice. This can be done through a brief email or a quick phone call to check in and see if they are interested in learning more about your content.

Remember, emailing journalists aims to pique their interest and get them to click on your content. By following these tips, you can increase your chances of success and get your content in front of a wider audience.

WRITING COMPELLING PITCHES

In addition to building relationships, it is also important to craft compelling pitches that grab the attention of journalists and editors. This may involve highlighting your content's unique angle or value and providing relevant background information or sources to support your story.

Here is an example of a pitch by streetwear clothing brand Moonlit Apparel to the editors of a skateboarding magazine.

> [Subject] Introducing the Eco-Friendly Skateboarding Sneakers Designed by MC Grind – A Must-Have for Skateboarders and Streetwear Fans

> Dear [Name of editor],

> We are excited to introduce the new collection of sneakers from Moonlit Apparel. This streetwear clothing company is rapidly gaining popularity among teenagers interested in skateboarding and streetwear fashion.

> Our new collection of sneakers from Moonlit Apparel is genuinely one-of-a-kind. It sets itself apart from other skateboarding shoes in several ways. Firstly,

the shoes feature a unique design that combines elements of streetwear fashion with the durability and performance that skaters demand. They are made from high-quality materials built to last and feature a sleek and stylish look that will turn heads on the streets and in the skatepark.

But that's not all – these sneakers are also made from recycled materials, making them an eco-friendly choice for skateboarders who want to reduce their environmental impact. And if that wasn't enough, the shoes were also designed by the famous rap artist MC Grind, known for his love of skateboarding and streetwear fashion. With such an impressive combination of style, performance and sustainability, it is no wonder these sneakers are quickly becoming a must-have for skateboarders and streetwear enthusiasts.

Moonlit Apparel has already established itself as a thought leader in the industry, with partnerships and sponsorships from top skateboarders and streetwear brands. Our new collection of sneakers is a perfect fit for skateboarding and streetwear fashion magazines, and we would be happy to provide you with high-quality images and other materials to support your coverage.

Thank you for considering our new collection of sneakers. We look forward to discussing this opportunity further with you.

Sincerely, [Your Name]

Another critical element of getting picked up by news outlets is timing. It is essential to understand the news cycle and pitch your content at a time when it is most likely relevant and exciting to journalists and their audiences.

Ultimately, getting picked up by news outlets requires a combination of solid relationships, compelling pitches and a strategic approach to timing. Following these best practices can increase your chances of getting your content picked up by news outlets and reaching a wider audience.

USING PAID MEDIA TO PROMOTE YOUR CONTENT

Advertising is an effective way to promote your content and reach a wider audience. Several types of paid media can be used to distribute your content, including PPC, social media ads, display ads, paid influencers and sponsored content.

Table 18. Paid Media

PAID MEDIA	TYPES OF CONTENT TO DISTRIBUTE	TARGET KPIS	METRICS TO CHECK
PPC	Search ads, Shopping ads, Remarketing ads	Traffic, conversions, ROI, Lead Generation	Click-through rate (CTR), conversion rate, cost per acquisition (CPA)
Social Media Ads	Sponsored posts, sponsored stories, promoted accounts	Engagement, reach, conversions	Impressions, click-throughs, engagement rate, conversion rate
Display Ads	Banners, display ads, native ads	Brand awareness, traffic, conversions	Impressions, click-throughs, conversion rate, cost per thousand impressions (CPM)
Paid Influencers	Influencer marketing campaigns: blog posts, reviews, collabs	Engagement, reach, conversions	Impressions, click-throughs, engagement rate, conversion rate
Sponsored Content	Sponsored articles, sponsored videos, sponsored podcasts	Reach, engagement, conversions	Impressions, click-throughs, engagement rate, conversion rate

- **PPC** or pay-per-click, is a form of advertising where you only pay when someone clicks on your ad. This advertising helps drive traffic to your website and increase conversions. In addition, PPC ads can target specific keywords, demographics and interests, which can help ensure that your content is seen by the right people.

- **Social media ads** are another effective way to promote your content. These ads can target specific demographics and interests and increase engagement, reach and conversions. Sponsored posts, sponsored stories and promoted accounts are different social media ads that can be used to promote your content.
- **Display ads** are a form of banner advertising that can increase brand awareness and drive traffic to your website. These ads can be placed on websites, blogs and other online platforms. In addition, they can be targeted to specific demographics and interests.
- **Paid influencers** and **sponsored content** can also be used to promote your content. These methods involve working with influencers and publishers to create and distribute content that promotes your brand. Influencer marketing can help increase reach and engagement, while sponsored content can help increase conversions.

When deciding whether to use advertising to promote your content, consider your target audience, your budget and your goals. Advertising can be a powerful tool for reaching a wider audience, increasing engagement and driving conversions. Still, make sure you are targeting the right people and using the right metrics to measure the success of your campaign.

PART 3
OPTIMIZE

MEASURING AND ADAPTING

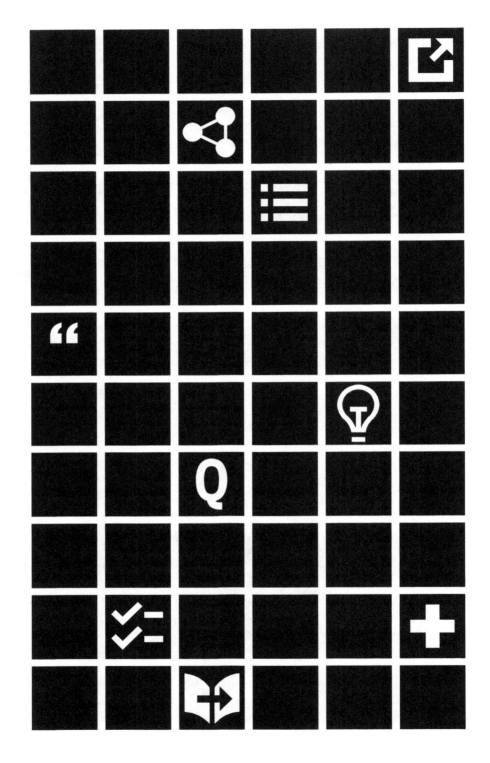

Marketing is an iterative process that involves regularly evaluating and refining your strategy to ensure that your digital content marketing efforts are as effective as possible and deliver the desired results.

Marketing is an iterative process.

Digital Marketing Like a PRO
Clo Willaerts

This is especially true in the digital age, where the landscape is constantly changing and evolving. By continuously reviewing and refining your marketing strategy, you can make sure that your efforts are aligned with your goals and target audience and that you are effectively reaching and engaging your audience. This process of iterative testing and adjusting your marketing efforts helps to ensure that your marketing is as effective as possible and that you can achieve the desired results for your business.

Ø 5

OPTIMISING FOR SEARCH AND SOCIAL

Content discovery can occur in two ways: searching for it or sharing it on social media. Occasionally, a piece of content can achieve both by ranking for relevant keywords and being shared by users.

To ensure your content is easily discoverable, it must be optimised for search engines and social media algorithms. This includes using relevant keywords and phrases and incorporating metadata, descriptions, titles and hashtags.

Optimisation should begin during the content creation process and focus on creating content that appeals to readers rather than solely catering to search engines or social media algorithms. **Create for people, not for robots or algorithms!**

In the following chapters, we'll dive into search engine optimisation (SEO) and social media optimisation (SMO). We'll cover best practices for optimising your content on each platform and strategies for maximising its visibility and reach.

CONTENT SEO (SEARCH ENGINE OPTIMISATION)

Regarding **search engine optimisation** (SEO), the goal is to make your content more visible and easier to find on **search engine results pages** (SERPs).

This is important because the higher your content ranks in the SERPs, the more likely users will see and click on it.

Search engine optimization (SEO) is a collection of strategies and techniques to ensure that the pages of a website are perfectly indexed and rank in the Search Engine Results Pages (SERPs). And not just any SERP, but the first one ideally, as this classic SEO joke illustrates: The best place to hide a dead body is on page 2 of the Google Search results.

Digital marketing like a PRO
Clo Willaerts

DO NOT CREATE GREY CONTENT

Grey content refers to material that is not original or unique but is not necessarily plagiarised or illegal. Examples of grey content include:

- Content that is scraped or copied from other websites without permission.
- Content that is created by spinning or rewriting existing articles.
- Content that is made for the sole purpose of including keywords for search engine optimisation (SEO).
- Content that is created by using automated tools, such as article generators.

Additionally, it can be considered content that may not align with the brand values and messaging but is created to drive traffic to a website and doesn't add any real value to the user.

While it may not be considered plagiarised or illegal, grey content is generally regarded as low quality and is not favoured by search engines or users. It can also be considered a form of black hat SEO, a technique that goes against the guidelines of search engines and can result in penalties or bans.

Here are some **best practices** for creating search-engine-optimised content:

- research and use relevant keywords
- create unique and valuable content
- use descriptive titles and meta descriptions
- optimise images and videos
- use header tags

RESEARCH AND USE RELEVANT KEYWORDS

Identifying the **keywords your target audience searches for** is essential in creating search-engine-optimised content. These keywords should be related to the topic of your content. In addition, they should be the words and phrases your audience uses to search for information online.

To find the right keywords, you can use a keyword research tool like Google's Keyword Planner or Ahrefs. These tools allow you to enter a seed keyword and see a list of related keywords, along with data on their search volume and difficulty.

Once you have a list of keywords, it is important to incorporate them into your content naturally. This means using them in a way that flows seamlessly with the rest of your content and doesn't feel forced or unnatural.

For example, suppose you are writing an article on meal planning for a meal planning app. In that case, you might include keywords like 'meal prep,' 'meal planning' and 'healthy recipes.'
However, you should avoid simply stuffing these keywords into your content as many times as possible, as this can come across as spammy and may harm your ranking in the SERPs. Instead, focus on incorporating these keywords into your content naturally in a way that flows seamlessly with the rest of your content and doesn't feel forced or unnatural.

By doing this, you'll be able to help search engines understand what your content is about and improve its ranking in the SERPs, increasing the visibility of your content and making it more likely to be found by your target audience.

CREATE UNIQUE AND VALUABLE CONTENT

Search engines prioritise high-quality content that is unique and provides value to users. Ensure your content is well-researched, well-written and addresses a specific need or question.

> Google and other search engines have made it clear that they'll love up the good stuff more than the regurgitated pabulum. Now let's focus on creating relevant, quality content experiences that our customers and prospects can trust.
>
> Everybody Writes
> Ann Handley

One of the most critical factors in creating search-engine-optimised content is ensuring that it is high quality and provides value to users. This means that your content should be **well-researched** and **well-written** and address a specific need or question your target audience has.

> YouTube videos are also an SEO shortcut: if a how-to YouTube video is the best answer to someone's Google query, it will rank very high in search results. YouTube videos are beneficial for SEO and help a product or brand to start ranking higher for search terms relative to the product or industry.
>
> Video Marketing like a PRO
> Clo Willaerts

The following tips help you create unique and valuable content that will be appreciated by your target audience and will be more likely to rank well on search engine results pages.

- Identify the needs and interests of your target audience. What are they looking for when they visit your site or app? What questions do they have?
- Research and gather as much information as possible on your topic.
- Write your content using clear and concise language. Consider breaking it up into sections or using bullet points to make it more visually appealing and easier to digest.

HOW TO CREATE SKYSCRAPER CONTENT

As the volume of online content continues to grow, standing out and making your content visible to your target audience has become increasingly challenging. One tactic that can help you achieve this is skyscraper content.

Skyscraper content is a comprehensive and informative resource that establishes your website as the authority on a given topic. It provides value to readers by being easy to read and engaging while also serving as a valuable resource for other bloggers and publishers. The goal of skyscraper content is to generate backlinks and attract traffic to your website.

To create skyscraper content, you will need to follow these three steps:

1. Identify a relevant topic or keyword cluster that is an effective linkable asset.

   Begin by analysing your competitors' top-performing pages to identify potential topics. Next, find the top 10 most linked pages from your top 10 competitors using an SEO suite. Keep in mind to only focus on pages with informational intent and remove pages with similar topics from your list.

2. Create a better piece of content.

   Conduct a Google search for your chosen topic and create a table of the top-ranking articles with informational intent. Analyse the strengths and weaknesses of each article and use that information to create more comprehensive and higher-word count content than your competitors. Consider including original research or reliable secondary sources to set your content apart.

3. Promote your content.

    Promoting your skyscraper content is essential to increase visibility and generate backlinks. Reach out to influencers and industry leaders and use social media platforms. Once you have created your skyscraper content, the next step is to promote it. The more people know about your content, the more likely it is to generate backlinks and attract traffic.

Here are some ways to promote your skyscraper content:

-   Reach out to influencers and industry leaders in your niche and ask them to share your content with their audience.
-   Use social media platforms like Twitter, LinkedIn and Facebook to promote your content and engage with your followers.
-   Submit your content to relevant online communities and forums, such as Reddit and Quora, where you can answer questions and provide value.
-   Email marketing campaigns can be a great way to promote your content to your subscribers and drive traffic back to your website.
-   Leverage your existing relationships with other bloggers and website owners and ask them to link to your content.

> Persistent, consistent, and frequent stories, delivered to an aligned audience, will earn attention, trust, and action.

This Is Marketing
Seth Godin

The key to promoting your skyscraper content is to be consistent and persistent. It can take time for your content to gain traction. Still, if you continue to promote it and build relationships with other industry leaders, eventually, it will.

STRUCTURE YOUR CONTENT

When publishing your content in your content management system (CMS), it is important to pay attention to the structure and formatting of your content. By structuring your content in a clear and organised way, you can make it easier for users to read and understand and improve its visibility in search results.

Here are some tips for structuring your content:

- **Use descriptive titles and meta descriptions**: Your content's title and meta description are essential for SEO because they give users a sneak peek of what your content is about and encourage them to click through to your site. Make sure your titles and meta descriptions are descriptive and include relevant keywords.
- **Optimise images and videos**: Search engines cannot see images and videos the same way humans can, so it is important to include alt text and captions to help them understand what is in your media files.
- **Use header tags**: Header tags (H1, H2, etc.) help break up your content into sections and give search engines an idea of the hierarchy of your content. Use them to highlight important points and organise your content.

By following these tips, you can structure your content in a way that is easy to read and understand and helps improve its visibility in search results.

GOOGLE'S FEATURED SNIPPETS

Featured snippets are short extractions of text from a website that appear in various parts of the search engine results page (SERP). Featured snippets can include paragraphs, images and other elements.

They can occur in:

- a standalone snippet,
- a dropdown,
- the People Also Ask section,
- voice queries,
- Google Lens searches,
- 'From sources around the web' accordions and
- knowledge panel dropdowns.

These snippets are constantly evolving, so it is worth optimising your content for them to increase organic reach and visibility. To do this, consider formatting your headers and list formats, including summary sentences and using structured data to help Google understand your content. It is also essential to understand what users are looking for and to provide clear, concise and accurate answers to their questions. Finally, track your progress and optimise your content to increase your chances of being featured in a snippet.

TOOL: SEMRUSH

SEMrush.com is a tool that helps content marketers improve their search engine optimisation (SEO), increase website traffic and track their performance. It offers keyword research, website audit, traffic analytics and brand monitoring.

SEMrush is one of several similar tools, including:

- Ahrefs.com is a powerful all-in-one SEO tool that helps content marketers to research keywords, analyse their website's SEO, track their traffic and rankings and research their competitors. It offers a range of features and tools like SEMrush.
- Moz.com is a popular SEO tool that helps content marketers to research keywords, analyse their website's SEO, track their traffic and rankings and research their competitors. It offers a range of features and tools like SEMrush. It is particularly well-known for its link analysis and keyword tracking capabilities.
- Google Keyword Planner (ads.google.com/aw/keywordplanner/)is a free tool provided by Google that helps content marketers to research keywords and see how much traffic they are getting. It is particularly useful for

identifying high-volume, high-competition keywords that might be worth targeting in your content.

These tools can help content marketers research keywords, analyse their website's SEO, track traffic and rankings and research competitors.

CONTENT SMO (SOCIAL MEDIA OPTIMISATION)

Optimising your content for social media is an integral part of any content marketing strategy, as it can help increase the visibility and reach of your content on these platforms.

Optimising your content for social media is crucial for increasing reach, engagement and conversions. Here are some tips on how to optimise your content for social media:

> Audiences on social media platforms communicate what they like through actions such as watch time, engagement, and clicks. The algorithm picks up on these social signals, improving the chances that your video gets recommended to more viewers.

Video Marketing Like a PRO
Clo Willaerts

SOCIAL SIGNALS AND THE GOLDEN HOUR

Social signals, such as likes, shares and comments, play a significant role in determining the reach and visibility of a social media post. These signals signal to the social media platform's algorithm that the post is valuable and relevant, leading to increased visibility in users' feeds and greater potential for organic reach.

Additionally, social signals from influencers or high-authority accounts can boost a post's visibility, as their endorsement adds credibility and weight to the content. By understanding the impact of social signals and utilising them effectively, content marketers can increase the potential reach of their social media posts and improve their overall performance on the platform.

Fuelling the feed on social media is crucial for increasing reach, engagement and conversions. One way to do this is by creating interesting, engaging and shareable content. Social media algorithms are constantly evolving, but one best practice remains the same: the more engagement your content receives in the first hour after posting, the more likely it will be shown to a wider audience. This is known as the '**Golden Hour**,' and taking advantage of this time window is crucial to boost engagement and reach.

To do this, you can organise your fellow employees in a messaging group and ask them to like, share and comment on your content immediately after you post it. This will help boost your content engagement and increase the chances of it being shown to a wider audience. Additionally, consider using paid promotion to boost your content's reach and engagement during the Golden Hour.

FEATURES AND FORMATS

Another tip for optimising your content for social media is to stay current with the latest features offered by the platform. Many social media platforms are constantly updating their offerings and adding new features. For example, Instagram has recently added the ability to reply to comments with a video in stories. This allows you to add a personal touch and increase engagement with your audience. By using the latest social media platform features, you can increase the chances of your content being seen by a wider audience and increase engagement. Keep an eye out for new features and test them out to see how they can be used to optimise your content.

It is also important to consider the type of content that works best for each platform. For example, Instagram and TikTok are great for short-form video content. At the same time, LinkedIn is better for long-form text-based content.

Knowing the best type of content for each platform will help you to optimise your content for maximum engagement.

Most social media platforms depend on advertiser revenue. This is why they want users to come back often and stay long on the platform. As a content creator, it is important to understand this and create content that will keep users engaged and on the platform longer.

1. **Live video** is a great way to increase engagement and reach on social media platforms. The algorithms favour live video content and are more likely to be shown to a larger audience.
2. **Native video** is a close second to live video in terms of engagement and reach. It is essential to upload videos directly to the platform rather than linking to an external video.
3. **Images** are a great way to capture attention and increase engagement on social media platforms. Use high-quality images, infographics and other graphics to make your content more shareable.
4. **Text-based content** is still important, but it is important to remember that images and videos get more engagement. So, make sure to include text but keep it short and to the point.
5. **Links** can be beneficial, but they can also be detrimental. Social media algorithms favour native content, so if you are going to include a link, make sure it is to a page or post on your own website.

By following these tips, you can create optimised content for social media and increase your reach, engagement and conversions. Remember to track your results and adapt your strategy as the algorithm changes.

Here are some tips for optimising your content for social media across the most well-known social media platforms:

Table 19. Social Media Platforms

PLATFORM	TIPS
Facebook	Use relevant hashtags, use eye-catching visuals, use descriptive titles and captions
Instagram	Use relevant hashtags, use high-quality visuals, use captions and tags
TikTok	Use relevant hashtags, use catchy music and sound effects, use engaging visuals and transitions

YouTube	Use relevant keywords in the title and description, include closed captions and transcripts, use visually appealing thumbnails
LinkedIn	Use descriptive titles and captions, include relevant hashtags and keywords, use high-quality visuals
Twitter	Use relevant hashtags, use eye-catching visuals, keep tweets concise and to the point

RELEVANT HASHTAGS

A **hashtag** is a word or phrase preceded by a pound symbol (#) used to identify and categorise content on social media. Hashtags are used to help users find and follow topics or themes that they are interested in. They can also create a sense of community or engagement around a particular topic or event.

Hashtags are primarily used on social media platforms such as Twitter, Instagram and Facebook. However, they are also used on other platforms such as TikTok, LinkedIn and Pinterest. On these platforms, users can search for or click on a hashtag to see a feed of all the content that has been tagged with that hashtag. This can help users discover new content and connect with others interested in the same topics.

Using relevant hashtags is an important aspect of optimising your content for social media, as it can help increase the visibility and reach of your content on these platforms. A hashtag is a word or phrase preceded by a pound symbol (#) used to identify and categorise content on social media. Using relevant hashtags in your content can make it more discoverable and increase its visibility to users searching for or following those hashtags.

Here are some tips for using relevant hashtags in your content:

- Use a tool like Hashtagify.me or the Hashtag Genius app to research **popular hashtags** in your industry or niche. This will help you identify hashtags that are likely to be used by your target audience and have a high traffic volume.
- Make sure the hashtags you use in your content are **relevant to the topic or theme** of your content. Using unrelated hashtags can confuse or mislead your audience and may even hurt your credibility.

- Use a **mix of popular and niche** hashtags: While it is important to use popular hashtags to increase the visibility of your content, you should also consider using more niche or specific hashtags to reach a more targeted audience.
- While using hashtags can be helpful, it is important **not to overdo it**. Using too many hashtags can make your content look spammy and decrease its visibility on social media platforms. Aim for a balance and use only the most relevant hashtags in your content.
- Follow hashtags in your industry or niche and pay attention to **trends** and events that are relevant to your audience. This can help you stay current and timely with your content and hashtags.

THUMB-STOPPING VISUALS

Eye-catching visuals can make a social media user stop scrolling through their feed and pay attention to your content. This way, they can help increase the engagement and reach of your content on these platforms. Social media platforms are highly visual, and users are more likely to engage with content that includes visually appealing images or videos.

Here are some tips for using eye-catching visuals in your social media content:

- Make sure the visuals you use in your social media content are **high-quality** and free of blurriness, pixelation, or other issues. This will help ensure that your content looks professional and appealing to users.
- There are many types of visuals you can use in your social media content, including photos, graphics, infographics and videos. **Experiment with visuals** to see what works best for your audience and message.
- The colours and design elements you use in your visuals can also play a role in their appeal to users. Use eye-catching **colours and design elements** consistent with your brand and stand out on social media platforms.

CATCHY MUSIC AND SOUND EFFECTS

Using catchy music and sound effects is essential to your content for TikTok and other video-based social media platforms. TikTok is about creating short, catchy videos set to music or sound effects. Using the right audio can make a big difference in the success of your content on the platform.

Here are some tips for using catchy music and sound effects in your TikTok content:

- The music you use in your TikTok videos should be catchy and relevant to the **theme** or **mood** of your content. You can use various music sources, such as licensed music tracks or royalty-free music, to find the right audio for your videos.
- **Sound effects** can add an extra layer of interest and engagement to your TikTok videos. Experiment with different sound effects and use them creatively to enhance the overall experience of your content.
- TikTok videos are limited to 15 seconds, so choosing music and sound effects that fit within that time frame is important. Make sure your audio is the right **length** and **tempo** for your content.

CAPTIONS AND THUMBNAILS

Optimising your content for YouTube involves more than just creating high-quality videos. Several technical and metadata factors can influence the visibility and success of your content on the platform.

> If your video title needs a hook to convince them to click, the thumbnail is often what sells it. If you can make your audience look at the thumbnail and wonder, "What's going on here?" you've successfully created a curiosity gap. You have their attention.

Video Marketing like a PRO
Clo Willaerts

A Practical Guide to
Publishing Videos T

Clo Willaerts

Here are some tips for optimising your YouTube content:

- The title and description of your YouTube videos are important for SEO, as they help search engines understand what your content is about and how to rank it in the search results. Include **relevant keywords in your title and description** to improve the visibility of your content.
- **Closed captions** and **transcripts** can make your content more accessible to a broader audience, including users who are deaf or hard of hearing or speak a different language. They can also improve the SEO of your content, as they provide additional context and keywords for search engines to index.
- The **thumbnail image** for your YouTube videos is essential in attracting clicks and views. Make sure to use visually appealing and eye-catching thumbnails that accurately represent the content of your videos.

06

WEB CONTENT
ACCESSIBILITY

Making web content more **accessible to people with disabilities** is essential for several reasons.

1. First and foremost, it is a matter of **fairness** and **equality.** People with disabilities have the same right to access and use web content as those without disabilities. Making content more accessible ensures that everyone can benefit from online information and resources.

2. In addition to ethical considerations, there are also practical and business-related reasons for making web content more accessible. For example, people with disabilities often rely on **assistive technologies** like screen readers to access web content. However, suppose a website's content is not designed with accessibility. In that case, these technologies may need to be improved to effectively parse and present the information to users. This can create frustration and discourage people with disabilities from using the site, potentially leading to lost traffic and revenue.

3. Furthermore, making web content more accessible can also benefit businesses and organisations. For example, **a website accessible to people with disabilities will likely be more user-friendly and intuitive for all users, leading to increased engagement and loyalty**. Additionally, making web content more accessible can help businesses and organisations demonstrate their commitment to diversity and inclusivity, which can attract a wide range of customers and stakeholders.

In the context of content marketing, it is particularly important to consider accessibility because the goal is to create content that is engaging, informative and valuable to a broad audience. By making content more accessible, businesses and organisations can make sure that their message effectively reaches as many people as possible, regardless of any disabilities they may have.

WEB CONTENT ACCESSIBILITY GUIDELINES (WCAG)

The **Web Content Accessibility Guidelines** (WCAG) are a set of internationally recognised standards that provide guidelines for making web content more accessible to people with disabilities. WCAG is developed and maintained by the World Wide Web Consortium (W3C). This international organisation sets standards for the World Wide Web.

WCAG consists of four principles that define the general goals of web accessibility: perceivable, operable, understandable and robust. Each principle is further broken down into specific guidelines that provide more detailed guidance on making web content more accessible.

Here are some key points to consider when optimising your content to follow the WCAG guidelines:

1. **Perceivable** Make sure that the content is presented in a way that is easy for users to perceive, whether through sight, hearing, touch, or any other sensory modality. This includes providing alternatives for audio and video content, such as closed captions or transcriptions and using clear and concise language.
2. **Operable** Ensure that the content is easy to use and navigate, especially for users who may be using assistive technologies or have mobility impairments. This includes providing clear and intuitive navigation, using meaningful link text and using headings and other formatting elements to structure the content.
3. **Understandable** Make sure the content is easy to understand, especially for users with cognitive or learning disabilities. This includes using clear and concise language, avoiding jargon and technical terms and providing context and explanations for complex or unfamiliar concepts.
4. **Robust** Ensure that the content is compatible with a wide range of devices and assistive technologies so that it can be accessed by as many people as possible. This includes using HTML and other web standards and providing fallbacks or alternatives for non-standard content or functionality.

To optimise your content to follow the WCAG guidelines, carefully review the guidelines and consider how you can apply them to your content.

You may also consider using tools, such as automated accessibility checkers, to help identify and fix any issues with your content.

CHECKING ACCESSIBILITY

Accessibility is an important aspect of content marketing that should not be overlooked. By taking the time to experience your content as someone who is blind, deaf, or has vision or hearing impairment, you can identify and address potential issues that could impede their ability to consume and engage with your content.

Here are some tips for ensuring your content marketing is accessible:

- Provide **alt text** for all images to ensure that visually impaired people can understand the image's content.
- Use **Pascal case** for hashtags (#ContentMarketing, not #contentmarketing) to make them more easily readable for those using screen readers.
- Provide **captions** for all videos so that people who are deaf or hard of hearing can still understand the content of the commonly used acronyms, terms, or phrases that do not translate well to the ear.
- Use **speech-to-text software** like Google Speech-to-Text, Amazon Transcribe, or Microsoft Azure Speech Services to ensure that spoken words are easily translatable into text and that no terms are used with multiple spellings that may cause confusion.

It is worth mentioning that these are just a few examples of the software that exists out there; there are many other options available depending on your needs and budget. Test a few before making a final decision.

Automated accessibility checkers can help identify potential issues with web content that may make it difficult for people with disabilities to access and use. These tools use algorithms to scan web pages and identify elements of the page that may not be compliant with accessibility standards, such as the Web Content Accessibility Guidelines (WCAG).

Some common issues that automated accessibility checkers can identify include the following:

- Missing or incomplete **alt text for images**. Add alt text to all images on the website. Alt text is a short description of an image used by assistive technologies, such as screen readers, to describe the image to users. Alt text should be concise and accurately describe the content and purpose of the image.
- Lack of proper **headings** or structure. Use headings and other formatting elements, such as lists and tables, to structure the website's content. This helps users understand the content's hierarchy and organisation and makes it easier for assistive technologies to parse and present the information to users.
- Poor **colour contrast**. make sure that the text and background colours used on the website have sufficient contrast. This helps users with visual impairments or low vision to read the text more easily.
- Missing or incomplete **labels for form fields**. Labels help users understand what information is being requested in each field and help assistive technologies identify and understand the purpose of the field.
- Inaccessible **links or buttons**. To fix this issue, the webmaster should ensure that all links and buttons on the website are correctly coded and can be activated by keyboard or touch. This helps users with mobility impairments or using assistive technologies navigate and interact with the website.

There are several automated accessibility checkers available that can help identify potential issues with web content. Here are a few examples:

- WAVE is a free web accessibility evaluation tool developed by WebAIM. This non-profit organisation provides resources and training on web accessibility. WAVE provides a visual representation of web pages, highlighting elements that may not comply with accessibility standards.
- aXe is an open-source accessibility testing tool developed by Deque Systems. It is available as a browser extension or a standalone tool that can scan web pages and identify potential issues with accessibility.
- Lighthouse is an open-source tool developed by Google that can audit the performance, accessibility and other aspects of web pages. It is available as a browser extension or as part of the Google Chrome DevTools.

- Siteimprove is a commercial web accessibility and website optimisation platform that provides tools and services for testing and improving the accessibility of web content.

Use the checker as a starting point for identifying potential issues and follow up with manual testing to make sure that your content is genuinely accessible. Remember, accessibility ensures everyone can access and engage with your content, regardless of their abilities. By reviewing your content through an accessibility lens, you can make sure that your content is inclusive and accessible to all.

07

MEASURING THE SUCCESS OF YOUR DIGITAL CONTENT MARKETING

Measuring the success of your digital content marketing is crucial to understanding whether your efforts are paying off and what areas need improvement.

There are several key metrics that you should track to gauge the success of your content marketing strategy.

- **Views or impressions** your content receives. This will give you a sense of how many people see your content and whether it is reaching your target audience.
- **Engagement metrics** such as the number of likes, comments and shares your content receives on social media. This will give you a sense of how well your content resonates with your audience and how likely they are to engage with it.
- Number of **clicks** your content receives and the amount of time users spend on your website. This will give you a sense of how effectively your content is driving traffic to your site and keeping visitors engaged.
- Number of **conversions** your content generates. This could be anything from email newsletter sign-ups to your product or service sales. This will give you a sense of how well your content is helping to achieve your business goals.

You will need to use various tools such as Google Analytics, social media analytics and email marketing software to track these metrics.

By regularly monitoring these metrics, you can gain valuable insights into the effectiveness of your content marketing strategy and adjust as needed to improve its success.

KEY PERFORMANCE INDICATORS

Key performance indicators (KPIs) are metrics that are used to measure the success of a content marketing strategy. These metrics can help you understand whether your content is resonating with your audience, driving traffic to your website and achieving your business goals.

> KPI is short for key performance indicator, a quantifiable measure used to evaluate the success of, in this context, your digital marketing efforts.
>
> Digital marketing like a PRO
> Clo Willaerts

Some common KPIs for content marketing include:

1. **Engagement Rate** that measures how well your content resonates with your audience. It can include metrics such as the number of likes, comments and shares your content receives on social media.
2. **Click-through rate** (CTR) that measures the number of clicks your content receives divided by the number of impressions it receives. It can give you a sense of how effectively your content drives traffic to your website.

3. **Time on page** that measures the amount of time users spend on your website after clicking on your content. It can give you a sense of how engaging and relevant your content is to your audience.
4. **Conversion rate** that measures the number of conversions (such as email sign-ups or sales) your content generates divided by the number of impressions it receives. It can give you a sense of how well your content is helping to achieve your business goals.

By regularly monitoring these KPIs, you can gain valuable insights into the effectiveness of your content marketing strategy and adjust as needed to improve its success.

TOOL: GOOGLE ANALYTICS

Google Analytics is a powerful tool that can help you measure the success of your content and keep track of your content marketing key performance indicators (KPIs). With Google Analytics, you can track various metrics, such as views or impressions, engagement, CTR, time on site and conversion rate, to get a comprehensive view of your content's performance.

To use Google Analytics to measure the success of your content, follow these steps:

1. Sign up for a Google Analytics account and add the tracking code to your website. This will allow you to track various metrics, such as page views, time on site and bounce rate.
2. Set up goals in Google Analytics. Goals are specific actions you want users to take on your website, such as making a purchase or signing up for a newsletter. By setting up goals, you can track how well your content drives conversions and achieves your business objectives.
3. Analyse your data. Google Analytics provides a range of reports and metrics that you can use to understand how your content is performing. For example, you can use the 'Acquisition' report to see how your content drives traffic to your website and the 'Behaviour' report to see how users interact with your content.
4. Use Google Analytics to identify opportunities for improvement. By analysing brand to build relationships your data, you can identify areas where your content is performing well and where it may need improvement.

For example, certain types of content drive more engagement or conversions than others. You can then use this information to optimise your content strategy and improve the performance of your content marketing efforts.

In conclusion, Google Analytics is a valuable tool for measuring the success of your content and keeping track of your content marketing KPIs. By tracking and analysing various metrics, you can get a comprehensive view of how your content is performing and identify opportunities for improvement.

ENGAGEMENT RATE

Audience engagement is an important aspect of content marketing, as it helps to measure the success of a brand's content and its ability to resonate with its target audience. Engagement is a key performance indicator (KPI) that can provide insight into how well a brand's content is being received and how it contributes to the overall marketing goals.

Several customer engagement signals can indicate how engaged a brand's audience is. Check this by:

- visiting their website;
- signing up for their emails;
- watching their videos;
- following them on social media;
- engaging with them on social media platforms such as Facebook or Instagram;
- reading their blog; and
- joining a brand's community or forum.

Tracking audience engagement can help a brand understand how its content is performing and make necessary adjustments to improve its effectiveness. It can also help a with its audience and foster a sense of community around the brand. By focusing on engagement, a brand can create more relevant and valuable content for its target audience, ultimately leading to better results and a more successful content marketing strategy.

There are a few different ways to track engagement. One way is through social media platforms like Facebook, Instagram and TikTok. Each platform has its own analytics tools that allow you to see how many likes, comments and shares your content is receiving. These metrics can help you understand how well your content is performing and identify opportunities for improvement.

In addition to tracking engagement on social media, consider other metrics, such as website engagement. This can include metrics such as time on site, pages per visit and bounce rate. These metrics can give you an idea of how well your content is holding your audience's attention and whether they are taking desired actions on your website.

Note that engagement is just one metric to consider when evaluating the effectiveness of your content marketing efforts. You can also track metrics such as views or impressions, conversions and sales to get a complete picture of your content's performance. By monitoring a combination of engagement and other metrics, you can better understand the impact of your content marketing efforts.

There are various ways to track engagement, such as through social media platforms, website analytics tools, or surveys and polls.

To calculate engagement, you must determine which metrics you want to track and gather the necessary data. Some common engagement metrics include likes, comments, shares and time spent on the page. You can then use the following formula to calculate engagement:

Engagement = (Total number of engagement metrics / Number of impressions) x 100

For example, let's say that your content receives 500 likes, 200 comments and 100 shares and receives 10,000 impressions. To calculate the engagement rate, you would add the total number of engagement metrics (500 + 200 + 100), divide it by 10,000 and then multiply by 100 to get an engagement rate of 8%.

It is important to note that engagement can vary depending on the type of content and the audience. Therefore, it is also important to track engagement over time to see how it changes and identify trends or patterns. By tracking and analysing engagement, you can better understand the effectiveness of your content marketing efforts and identify opportunities for improvement.

Here are a few additional strategies you can use to improve the engagement rate of your content:

- Create **visually appealing content** using images, videos and other visual elements to make your content more engaging and attractive. This can include using high-quality graphics and images, creating infographics and using video to convey information.
- Encourage your audience to share their own content, **user-generated content,** related to your brand or industry. This can include hosting contests, creating hashtags, or asking for user submissions.
- Write **compelling headlines**. Headlines are often the first thing users see when they come across your content. By writing compelling headlines that grab attention and clearly communicate the value of your content, you can increase the chances that users will click through and engage with your content.
- **Storytelling** can be a powerful way to engage your audience and create an emotional connection with your content. Consider using storytelling techniques, such as anecdotes, creating characters and a narrative structure, to make your content more engaging and memorable.
- **Interactive content**, such as quizzes, polls and surveys, can be a great way to engage your audience and encourage them to participate in your content. By creating interactive content, you can make a more immersive and engaging experience for your users.
- By creating a **sense of community** around your content, you can encourage your audience to engage with your content and each other. This can include joining social media groups, hosting webinars or live events, or offering exclusive content to your most engaged followers.
- By including **calls to action** in your content, you can encourage your audience to take specific actions, such as liking, commenting, or sharing your content. Calls to action can be as simple as asking your audience to share their thoughts or opinions in the comments or to share your content with their network.

In conclusion, engagement is an important metric to track in content marketing. By understanding how well your content resonates with your audience, you can identify opportunities for improvement and make sure that your content meets your target audience's needs.

CLICK-THROUGH RATE (CTR)

Click-through rate (CTR) is a key performance indicator (KPI) that measures the effectiveness of your content in driving traffic to your website. It is calculated by dividing the number of clicks your content receives by the number of impressions it receives. This metric can show you how well your content resonates with your audience and how effectively it drives desired actions.

There are a few different ways to track CTR. One way is through website analytics tools, such as Google Analytics. These tools can help you see how many people click on your content and how it drives traffic to your website. You can also track CTR on social media platforms like Facebook, Instagram and TikTok. Each platform has its own analytics tools that allow you to see how many clicks your content receives and how it performs.

In addition to tracking CTR, it is also essential to consider other metrics. For example, you may want to track engagement metrics like likes, comments and shares to see how well your content is resonating with your audience. You may also want to track conversion metrics, such as leads and sales, to see how well your content drives desired actions from your audience. By tracking a combination of CTR and other metrics, you can get a complete picture of the effectiveness of your content marketing efforts.

It is calculated by dividing the number of clicks your content receives by the number of impressions it receives. This metric can show you how well your content resonates with your audience and how effectively it drives desired actions.

Here is the formula for calculating CTR:

CTR = (Number of clicks / Number of impressions) x 100

For example, let's say that your content receives 500 clicks and receives 10,000 impressions. To calculate the CTR, you would divide 500 by 10,000 and then multiply by 100 to get a CTR of 5%.

It is important to note that CTR can vary depending on the type of content and the desired action you are trying to drive. For example, the CTR for an e-commerce website may differ from that for a B2B website. Therefore, it is also essential to track CTR over time to see how it changes and identify any trends or patterns. By tracking and analysing CTR, you can better understand the effectiveness of your content marketing efforts and identify opportunities for improvement.

In conclusion, CTR is an important metric to track in content marketing. By understanding how effectively your content is driving traffic to your website, you can identify opportunities for improvement and make sure that your content meets your target audience's needs.

TIME ON PAGE

Time on page is a key performance indicator (KPI) that measures the time users spend on your website after clicking on your content. This metric can give you a sense of how engaging and relevant your content is to your audience. It is an important metric to track because it can help you understand the effectiveness of your content marketing efforts and identify opportunities for improvement.

There are a few different ways to track time on a page. One way is through website analytics tools, such as Google Analytics. These tools can help you see how much time users spend on your website and how it performs in terms of engagement. You can also track time on the page on social media platforms, such as Facebook, Instagram and TikTok. Each platform has its own analytics tools that allow you to see how much time users spend on your content and how it performs.

In addition to tracking time on the page, it is also essential to consider other metrics. For example, you may want to track engagement metrics like likes, comments and shares to see how well your content is resonating with your audience. You may also want to track conversion metrics, such as leads and sales, to see how well your content drives desired actions from your audience. By tracking a combination of time on the page and other metrics, you can get a complete picture of the effectiveness of your content marketing efforts.

To calculate the time on site KPI, you will need to know the total amount of time users spend on your website and the number of users who visit your website.

Here is the formula for calculating time on site:

Time on site = (Total time spent on website / Number of users)

For example, let's say that your website receives 1,000 visitors in each month, and they spend a total of 50,000 minutes on it. To calculate the time on site, you would divide 50,000 by 1,000 to get an average time on site of 50 minutes.

It is important to note that time on site can vary depending on the content type and the visit is purpose. For example, a user researching a product may spend more time on your website than a user simply browsing. Therefore, it is also important to track time on site over time to see how it changes and identify any trends or patterns. By tracking and analysing time on site, you can better understand the effectiveness of your content marketing efforts and identify opportunities for improvement.

There are a few strategies you can use to increase the amount of time users spend on your website:

- Create **high-quality, relevant content.** By providing valuable, informative and engaging content, you can encourage users to spend more time on your website. Consider using a variety of content formats, such as blog posts, articles, videos and infographics, to keep users interested and engaged.
- A user-friendly website that is **easy to navigate** can encourage users to spend more time on your website. This can include using a clear and intuitive menu structure, descriptive and relevant page titles and descriptions and providing clear calls to action.
- By using **internal linking**, you can encourage users to explore more of your website and spend more time on your website. Internal linking refers to linking to other pages within your website.
- Use **related content widgets**. These boxes display links to other related content on your website. Using related content widgets, you can encourage users to explore more of your website and spend more time on your site.
- **Share your content on social media** platforms, such as Facebook, TikTok and Instagram and use hashtags and targeted ads to increase its reach. You can also use social media to interact with your audience and gather feedback on your content.

In conclusion, time on page is an important metric to track in content marketing. By understanding how long users are spending on your website after clicking on your content, you can identify opportunities for improvement and make sure that your content meets your target audience's needs.

CONVERSION RATE

Conversion rate is a key performance indicator (KPI) that measures the effectiveness of your content in driving desired actions, such as email sign-ups or sales. It is calculated by dividing the number of conversions your content generates by the number of impressions it receives. This metric can show you how well your content contributes to your business goals and how effectively it is driving conversions.

There are a few different ways to track conversion rates. One way is through website analytics tools, such as Google Analytics. These tools can help you see how many conversions your content generates and how it drives desired actions. You can also track conversion rates on social media platforms like Facebook, Instagram and TikTok. Each platform has its own analytics tools that allow you to see how many conversions your content generates and how it performs.

In addition to tracking conversion rate, it is also essential to consider other metrics. For example, you may want to track engagement metrics like likes, comments and shares to see how well your content is resonating with your audience. You can also track CTR, or the number of clicks your content receives, to see how well your content drives traffic to your website. By tracking a combination of conversion rate and other metrics, you can get a complete picture of the effectiveness of your content marketing efforts.

To calculate the conversion rate, you will need to know the number of conversions your content generates and the number of impressions it receives.

Here is the formula for calculating the conversion rate:

Conversion rate = (Number of conversions / Number of impressions) x 100

For example, let's say that your content generates 50 conversions and receives 1,000 impressions. To calculate the conversion rate, you would divide 50 by 1,000 and then multiply by 100 to get a conversion rate of 5%.

It is important to note that the conversion rate can vary depending on the type of content and the desired action you are trying to drive. For example, the conversion rate for an e-commerce website may be different than that for a B2B website. Therefore, tracking the conversion rate over time is essential to see how it changes and identify any trends or patterns. In addition, by tracking and analysing conversion rates, you can better understand the effectiveness of your content marketing efforts and identify opportunities for improvement.

In conclusion, the conversion rate is an important metric to track in content marketing. By understanding how well your content is driving desired actions, such as email sign-ups or sales, you can identify opportunities for improvement and make sure that your content is meeting the needs of your target audience and contributing to your business goals.

GATHERING FEEDBACK FROM CUSTOMERS AND STAKEHOLDERS

By **gathering feedback**, you can gain valuable insights into what is and isn't working with your content and adjust as needed to improve its effectiveness.

> Listen to customer service inquiries. Watch how customers behave. See what problems they have. "Look for patterns.

Everybody Writes
Ann Handley

There are several ways to gather feedback from customers and stakeholders.

- Conduct **surveys or polls** on your website or social media channels. These surveys can ask questions about the quality and relevance of your content. In addition, they can help you understand what your audience is looking for.

- **Engage directly** with your audience on social media. By responding to comments and questions on your social media channels, you can gain valuable insights into your audience's likes and dislikes about your content.
- Conduct **focus groups or in-person interviews** with customers and stakeholders. These sessions can provide more detailed and in-depth feedback on your content. In addition, they can help you understand the thoughts and opinions of your audience.

SURVEYS AND POLLS

Conducting surveys and polls is a helpful way to gather insights and feedback from your audience about the quality and relevance of your content. Surveys and polls can be conducted on your website or on social media channels like Facebook and Twitter.

There are a few key benefits to conducting surveys and polls:

- **Understand your audience's needs and preferences**. Surveys and polls can help you understand what your audience is looking for in terms of content. By asking questions about the topics and formats that interest them, you can create more relevant and valuable content for your audience.
- **Identify areas for improvement**. Surveys and polls can help you identify areas where your content may fall short and where you can improve. For example, suppose you receive a lot of feedback about specific topics or formats that your audience would like to see more of. In that case, you can adjust your content strategy accordingly.
- **Build relationships with your audience**. Surveys and polls can be a great way to engage and build relationships with your audience. By asking for their input and taking their feedback into account, you can show your audience that you value their opinions and are committed to meeting their needs.

There are a few key considerations to keep in mind when conducting surveys and polls:

- Surveys and polls should be **short and focused**, with clear and concise questions. This will make them more likely to be completed and help you gather more meaningful data.

- Make them **visually appealing**: Use images, graphics and other visual elements to make your surveys and polls more engaging and appealing. This will make them more likely to be completed and help you gather more accurate data.
- **Analyse and act on the results**: After conducting a survey or poll, analyse the results and use them to inform your content strategy. This can help you create more relevant and valuable content.

Keep an open mind when gathering feedback and to be willing to make changes based on the feedback you receive. By regularly collecting and acting on feedback from customers and stakeholders, you can improve the effectiveness of your content marketing strategy's effectiveness and better serve your audience's needs.

LEARNING FROM YOUR FOLLOWERS

Engaging directly with your followers on social media can be a valuable way to gather insights and feedback about your content. By responding to comments and questions on your social media channels, you can better understand what your audience likes and dislikes about your content and what they would like to see more of.

Here are a few tips for learning from your followers on social media:

- Make sure to **check your social media channels** regularly and respond to comments and questions promptly. This will help you stay engaged and build relationships with your audience.
- **Social listening tools** can help you track and analyse conversations about your brand and industry on social media. By using these tools, you can identify trends and patterns in the feedback you receive from your followers.
- Be bold and **ask your followers for feedback** on your content. You can do this by posing questions or polls on your social media channels or sending out surveys to your followers.
- **Use the feedback you receive**: Once you have gathered feedback from your followers, analyse it and use it to inform your content strategy. This can help you create more relevant and valuable content for your audience.

By following these tips, you can learn from your followers and use their feedback to improve the performance of your content marketing efforts.

TOOL: HOOTSUITE

Hootsuite.com is a social media management platform that offers a range of tools and features for tracking and analysing conversations about your brand and industry on social media. Using Hootsuite as a social listening and monitoring tool, you can gain valuable insights into your audience's thoughts and opinions about your content and use this information to improve the performance of your content marketing efforts.

Here are a few steps to follow when using Hootsuite as a social listening and monitoring tool:

1. To use Hootsuite as a social listening and monitoring tool, you will need to **connect your social media accounts** to the platform. This will allow you to track and analyse conversations about your brand and industry across multiple social media channels.
2. In Hootsuite, streams track and organise conversations about specific topics or hashtags. You can **set up streams** for your brand, competitors, industry keywords and more.
3. **Monitor your streams**. As conversations about your brand and industry are posted to social media, they appear in your Hootsuite streams. You can use the platform's filtering and search tools to find specific conversations and analyse their content.
4. Hootsuite offers a range of **analytics and reporting tools** that can help you track and analyse the performance of your social media campaigns. You can use these tools to understand how your content is performing and identify areas for improvement.
5. Hootsuite also allows you to **interact with your audience** by responding to comments, messages and reviews. Engaging with your audience can build relationships and gather valuable insights into their thoughts and opinions about your content.

Several alternatives to Hootsuite offer similar social media management and analytics tools. Here are a few examples:

- Sproutsocial.com is a social media management platform that offers features such as social listening, analytics and team collaboration.
- Buffer.com is a social media management platform that offers scheduling, analytics and team collaboration tools.

- SocialFlow.com is a social media management platform that uses artificial intelligence to optimise the performance of your social media campaigns.
- Agorapulse.com is a social media management platform that offers features such as social listening, analytics and team collaboration.
- Sendible.com is a social media management platform that offers tools for scheduling, analytics and team collaboration.

Considering these and other alternatives, you can find a social media management platform that best meets your needs and budget.

FOCUS GROUPS

Conducting **focus groups** or **in-person interviews** are a useful way to gather in-depth and detailed feedback on your content. These sessions can provide valuable insights into your customers' and stakeholders' thoughts and opinions. In addition, they can help you understand what they are looking for in terms of content.

There are a few key steps to conducting focus groups or in-person interviews:

1. **Identify your target audience**: Before planning your focus group or interview, you must identify who you want to include in the session. This can consist of customers, stakeholders, or a combination of both.
2. **Determine the format and length of the session**. Focus groups and in-person interviews can be conducted in various formats, including online, in-person, or over the phone. Decide on the format best suited to your needs and the needs of your audience.
3. **Prepare a list of questions** before the focus group or interview. These questions should be focused and relevant and help you gather the information you need to understand your audience's thoughts and opinions.
4. Once you have prepared your questions, it is time to **conduct the focus group or interview**. Create a welcoming and comfortable environment and encourage participants to freely share their thoughts and opinions.
5. After the focus group or interview, **analyse the results** and use them to inform your content strategy. This can help you create more relevant and valuable content for your audience.

Here is a list of model questions that you might consider asking during a focus group or in-person interview:

1. What do you like or dislike about our current content?
2. What topics or formats would you like to see more of in our content?
3. How does our content compare to that of our competitors?
4. How do you typically discover and consume our content?
5. How does our content add value to your life or business?
6. What would you like to see more of in our content?
7. What do you find most engaging about our content?
8. How can we improve the quality of our content?
9. What are your favourite and least favourite types of content that we produce?
10. How does our content influence your purchasing decisions or loyalty to our brand?

By asking these questions, you can better understand your audience's thoughts and opinions about your content and use their feedback to inform your content strategy.

By conducting focus groups or in-person interviews, you can gather detailed and in-depth feedback on your content and use it to improve the performance of your content marketing efforts.

CONTINUOUSLY IMPROVING

One approach that can be helpful in continuously improving your content marketing strategy is the Japanese concept of kaizen. **Kaizen** is a philosophy of **continuous improvement**, focusing on small, incremental changes that can lead to significant improvements over time.

In content marketing, kaizen could involve making small, regular changes to your strategy based on data and feedback.

Some examples:

- Regularly **review your analytics** to see which types of content are performing best and adjust your strategy accordingly.
- Regularly **update your content calendar**. This could involve adding new content topics, changing your content frequency, or shifting your content's focus to better align with the needs and interests of your audience.
- Ask for **feedback from your audience** to see what they like and what they would like to see more of.

By consistently making small changes and tracking the results, you can gradually improve the effectiveness of your content marketing efforts.

> Get comfortable with failure. Not every piece of content you produce will be a winner. Learn from the experience and move on quickly.

The Stripped-Down Guide to Content ...
John Egan

Another way to apply the principle of kaizen to content marketing is through **continuous learning**. This could involve:

- Experiment with **different formats and tones for your content.** For example, you could use more visual content, such as videos and infographics, or experiment with a more conversational tone in your writing.
- Experiment with **new tactics and channels for distributing your content.** This could involve using new social media platforms, guest posting on other websites, or partnering with influencers to reach a larger audience.
- Learning from the successes and failures of others.
- Staying up to date on content marketing industry trends.

To stay up to date on content marketing industry trends, there are a few key strategies you can follow:

- Subscribe to **industry publications and blogs**. Some examples of content marketing industry publications include the Content Marketing Institute's blog and newsletter (contentmarketinginstitute.com/blog/), HubSpot's Marketing Blog (blog.hubspot.com/marketing) and Copyblogger.com. By subscribing to these resources, you can receive regular updates on the latest trends and best practices in the field.
- There are many **conferences and events**, both in-person and virtual, that focus on content marketing. Examples include the Content Marketing World conference and the Digital Marketing Innovation Summit. Attending these events can allow you to learn from experts and network with other professionals.
- Join **industry groups and communities**. Many online groups and communities focus on content marketing, such as the Content Marketing Association and the Inbound Marketing Association. Joining these groups can allow you to connect with other professionals, ask questions and share insights and resources.
- Many **content marketing experts and thought leaders** share their insights and observations on social media platforms such as Twitter and LinkedIn. Following these influencers can be a great way to stay informed about industry trends and learn from their experiences.

Here are some content marketing thought leaders and how to follow them on social media:

- **Joe Pulizzi** (@JoePulizzi) – Founder of the Content Marketing Institute and author of several books on content marketing. Follow him on Twitter for insights and updates on the industry.
- **Ann Handley** (@annhandley) – Chief content officer at MarketingProfs and author of 'Everybody Writes.' Follow her on Twitter for tips on content creation and marketing.
- **Neil Patel** (@neilpatel) – Founder of Crazy Egg and Kissmetrics and a renowned digital marketing expert. Follow him on Twitter for SEO, content marketing and social media updates.
- **Rand Fishkin** (@randfish) – Founder of Moz and author of 'Lost and Founder.' Follow him on Twitter for insights on SEO, content marketing and entrepreneurship.

By following these thought leaders on social media, you can stay up to date on the latest trends and best practices in the content marketing industry and learn from their experiences.

In summary, the key to continuously improving your content marketing strategy is to be open to change and willing to experiment.

Furthermore, regularly reviewing and adapting your strategy based on data and feedback ensures that your content resonates with your audience and effectively achieves your business goals.

08

CONCLUSION

RECAP OF THE KEY POINTS

Digital content marketing is a valuable strategy that involves creating and sharing online content to attract and engage customers. By providing helpful and relevant information, businesses can build trust and credibility with their audience and establish themselves as leaders in their industry.

Here are the key steps to implementing a successful digital content marketing strategy:

1. Define your **business goals** and translate them into **content marketing objectives**. Start by identifying what you want to achieve with your content marketing efforts and how it aligns with your overall business goals. This will help you create a clear plan for your content marketing strategy.
2. Use the information you gather about your target audience to create detailed profiles of your ideal customers, known as **buyer personas**. These personas will help you understand their needs, preferences and behaviours, informing the content channels, formats and tactics you use to reach them.
3. Based on the information you have gathered about your target audience, determine the **content channels, formats and tactics** that will be most effective in reaching them. This might include social media, email marketing, podcasting, or video marketing.

4. Plan and schedule the creation and distribution of your content using a **content calendar**. This will help you consistently create and share valuable content that resonates with your audience.

5. **Create and distribute digital content**. Use the information you have gathered about your target audience and the content channels, formats and tactics you have identified to create compelling digital content that meets the needs and interests of your audience.

6. Continually **review and analyse** the effectiveness of your content marketing efforts to identify any areas for improvement. Use metrics and analysis to track the success of your content and make any necessary adjustments to your strategy.

In conclusion, content marketing is a powerful tool for driving traffic, engagement and conversions for your business. By carefully planning and executing your strategy, you can build relationships with your audience, establish your brand as an authority in your industry and ultimately achieve your business goals.

THE FUTURE OF DIGITAL CONTENT MARKETING

Content Marketer: I'm really worried about the future of digital content marketing. I feel like AI is going to take over and there won't be any room for human writers like me.

AI Language Model: There is no need to worry. While it is true that AI is revolutionising the way we create and consume digital content, it doesn't have to be a threat to human writers. In fact, AI can enhance content marketing efforts in several ways.

Content Marketer: Like what?

AI Language Model: Well, one significant advantage of AI-generated content is its ability to be produced quickly and at a large scale. While human writers may take longer to produce a larger volume of content, AI algorithms can quickly generate a large amount of content. This means that businesses and organisations can create more content quickly without the need to hire additional staff.

Content Marketer: That does sound useful. But what about personalisation? Can AI really create content that speaks to individual users?

AI Language Model: Yes, another advantage of AI-generated content is its ability to be personalised to individual users. AI algorithms can analyse user data and create content specifically designed to appeal to users' unique interests and preferences. This level of personalisation is not possible with traditional content marketing methods and it has the potential to significantly improve the user experience.

Content Marketer: Okay, that makes sense. But what about distribution? How can AI help with that?

AI Language Model: AI can also optimise the distribution of content. For example, machine learning algorithms can analyse consumer behaviour data to identify the most effective channels and times to share content. This can help businesses to maximise their reach and engagement with their target audience.

Content Marketer: Hmm, that's definitely helpful. But I'm still not convinced that AI is going to be a good thing for content marketers like me.

AI Language Model: It is important to remember that AI is not meant to replace human writers, but rather to assist and enhance their efforts. There are several ways in which AI can assist enterprise marketing teams in creating better content, such as brainstorming topics, suggesting more engaging headlines, refreshing existing content and optimising content for search engine visibility. AI can also automate repetitive and time-consuming content marketing tasks, such as AI can also automate repetitive and time-consuming content marketing tasks, such as distributing content across social media platforms, launching blogs and gathering data and reports. Some examples of AI-powered tools that can help with these tasks include Articoolo, Wordsmith, Persado, Grammarly and Jasper.

Content marketer: I'm worried about the potential for AI to replace human writers and marketers.

AI language model: It is true that AI has the potential to automate some tasks that were previously done by humans. However, it is important to keep in mind that AI is not a replacement for human creativity and strategy. While AI can assist with tasks such as generating content and optimising its distribution, it is still important for human content marketers to be involved in the process.

Content marketer: So, what does the future hold for human content marketers?

AI language model: While it is hard to predict exactly what the future will hold, it is likely that content marketing will continue to evolve as technology advances. It is important for content marketers to stay up to date on industry trends and to be open to incorporating new technologies, such as AI, into their strategies. By being adaptable and constantly learning and improving, human content marketers can remain relevant and valuable in the digital age.

(Text written by ChatGPT (chat.openai.com/chat) on 30 December 2022, using the prompt: Rewrite the final chapter, *The Future of Digital Content Marketing*, in the form of a Socratic dialogue between a very worried content marketer and an AI driven language model like you.)

ADDITIONAL RESOURCES FOR FURTHER LEARNING

- Bailey, Cassandra M. and Dana M. Schmidt. Pay Attention!: How to Get, Keep and Use Attention to Grow Your Business. 2022.
- Bovee, Courtland L. and John V. Thill. Business Communication Today. 14th edition. New York: Pearson, 2018.
- Brunskill, Ian and Times Books. The Times Style Guide: A Practical Guide to English Usage. London: Times Books, 2022.
- Chapman, C. C. and Ann Handley. Content Rules: How to Create Killer Blogs, Podcasts, Videos, Ebooks, Webinars (and More) That Engage Customers and Ignite Your Business. Hoboken, NJ: John Wiley & Sons, 2012.
- Deziel, Melanie. The Content Fuel Framework: How to Generate Unlimited Story Ideas. 2020.
- Daugherty, Scott. On Writing: A Memoir of the Craft. New York: Scribner, 2000.
- Egan, John. The Stripped-Down Guide to Content Marketing: Success Secrets for Beginners. 2022.
- Godin, Seth. This is Marketing: You Cannot Be Seen Until You Learn To See. Penguin UK, 2018
- Kane, Brendan. Hook Point: How to Stand Out in a 3-Second World. 2020.
- Merriam-Webster. Merriam-Webster's Collegiate Dictionary. 11th edition. Kindle version. Springfield, MA: Merriam-Webster, 2009.
- Miller, Donald: Building a StoryBrand: Clarify Your Message So Customers Will Listen. HarperCollins Publishers, 2017
- Opresnik, Marc Oliver, Philip Kotler and Svend Hollensen. Social Media Marketing: A Practitioner Guide. New York: Springer Nature, 2020.
- Provost, Gary. 100 Ways To Improve Your Writing. Berkeley; Reissue edition, 1985.
- Pulizzi, Joe. Content Inc.: How Entrepreneurs Use Content to Build Massive Audiences and Create Radically Successful Businesses. Hoboken, NJ: John Wiley & Sons, 2015.
- Schaffer, Neal. The Age of Influence: The Power of Influencers to Elevate Your Brand. Hoboken, NJ: John Wiley & Sons, 2020.
- Strunk Jr., William and E.B. White. The Elements of Style. 4th edition. New York: Allyn and Bacon, 1999.
- The University of Chicago Press Editorial Staff. The Chicago Manual of Style. 17th edition. Chicago: The University of Chicago Press, 2017.

- Willaerts, Clo. Video Marketing Like a PRO: A Practical Guide to Creating and Publishing Videos That Convert. Leuven: LannooCampus, 2022.
- Willaerts, Clo. Digital Marketing Like a PRO: Prepare. Run. Optimize (completely revised edition). Leuven: LannooCampus, 2022.
- Zissner, William. On Writing Well: The Classic Guide to Writing Nonfiction. 30th anniversary edition. New York: HarperCollins Publishers, 2006.